# Going Agile

## Project Management Practices

## Third Edition

Gloria J. Miller
Quiz by Thomas Göttsche

maxmetrics
Atlanta • Heidelberg

Going Agile: Project Management Practices Third Edition



Published by Maxmetrics LLC, Atlanta, Georgia. www.maxmetrics.com.



The publisher offers discounts on this book when ordered in quantity for bulk purchases or special orders. Special orders can include customized covers and company-specific examples. For more information, please contact publish.us@maxmetrics.com.



Library Congress Control Number: 2020905806

International Standard Book Number:

978-0-9983484-2-1 Paperback United States

978-0-9983484-3-8 Paperback Europe

978-0-9983484-4-5 Kindle

Cover images: Victoria Vaca Núñez

First Edition January 2013

Second Edition January 2016

Third Edition April 2020

# Testimonials

"If you want to understand why adopting an agile framework like Scrum sounds simple enough at first, but becomes a complex affair in change at a variety of levels, Going Agile is the book for you.

—**Dave Moran**, Sr Product Manager, blogger/writer on agile topics

"This book, like any other agile book, is packed with information a Project Manager needs to embark on an Agile journey. What it also does well is having the insight and tips from seasoned professionals to get you the desired result."

—**Winson Choo**, PMP CMQ/OE CSM CSP

"If you don't know where to get started, start with 'Going Agile.'"

**Nick Argall**, Australian Software Development Manager

"The focus of this book is very clear: much has been written about agile methodologies and techniques, but little about how to succeed in transforming organizations through value-driven and self-empowered teams."

—**David de Francisco Marcos** MSc, MBA, PMP, PMI-ACP

"This is a wonderful book providing the insight on various practices followed in Agile and is a wonderful summary of all Agile methodologies."

—**Anees Haidary**:PMP, CSM, ITILv3, ISO9K LA, ISO14K LA

"Case studies and guest posts by other long-time project management experts round up the book very nicely."

—**Frank Leistner**

"Short articles and easy to read."

—**Wong Hong Jone**

# About the Author

Gloria J. Miller has more than 20 years of experience providing management consulting, program and project management, and Information Technology (IT) consulting to Fortune 500 and government organizations. She is the founder of and Managing Consultant at maxmetrics, an International Management and Information Technology Consulting firm. www.maxmetrics.com (Twitter @maxmetrics)

Previously, Gloria has held senior management and leadership positions in such organizations as SAS Institute, Oracle, CDSI, Ultra Tech, and MCI Telecommunications. During her time at SAS, Gloria was responsible for starting and building SAS Institute's International professional services operations to provide implementation services for business intelligence, analytics and data warehousing. In addition, as the Executive Director for SAS Research and Development India, she led the development and product launch of the SAS Industry Intelligence Solutions, a family of solutions for various industries, including banking, telecommunications, retail, manufacturing and insurance.

Gloria has co-authored several methodologies and books on implementing software and modernizing organizations to use information more effectively, including *Business Intelligence Competency Centers: A Team Approach to Maximizing Competitive Advantage* and the *Information Revolution*, published in the Wiley and SAS Business and Information Series.

Throughout her career, she has worked in or had oversight of hundreds of projects. She gained her experience as a hands-on manager or consultant. Her focus is on delivering results in all types of projects, but she excels when there is some type of complexity. Some examples of complexity from her experience include:

- Short timeframes—a multi-national, enterprise systems introduction in 3 months,
- Large teams—43 external consultants, 120 internal business and IT people, 10 companies, and 13 countries,
- Important procurements—54 Enterprise Software License, System integrators, and hardware agreements in 1 year
- Geographically distributed—40 country product design, implementation and roll-out
- Outsource, out-task, and offshore—Switzerland, United States, Canada, France, Germany; India; Poland; China; Philippines
- Strategically important—120 million euro new product launch; Executive Balanced Scorecard for 40 countries

- Multiple workstreams—36 parallel projects from IT infrastructure to Human Resource consolidation

- Innovation projects—open-ended questions within a fixed timeline and budget, i.e. what can we do with big data, visual analytics, high-performance analytic computing

Gloria has also been in her share of not-so-successful projects including a failed agile project, a product launch with lack-luster sales, a solution implementation with poor performance, a project or two that ran over budget or delivered later than planned, a technology solution delivered on-time, on-budget but too complex for the users to accept, and a business solution delivered with missing capabilities.

Based on her collection of experiences, Gloria is a big believer in agility. Agility is about people, quick feedback, and transparency. If you bring bright people together, give them a clear goal and good support, they can achieve anything. For a profitable business, you have to maintain flexibility and adaptability; establishing processes that offer quick feedback is critical to this flexibility. Transparency is a great management tool. The more you know and see, the quicker you can respond should things go in the wrong direction.

Gloria has a doctorate and master's degrees business and undergraduate degrees in computer science and electronic technology. Her doctorate degree specialized in project and program management. She is a Certified ScrumMaster, and a Project Management Institute Agile Certified Practitioner and Project Management Professional.

# About the Contributors

The author would like to thank the following individuals for contributing their personal experience and case studies. They added valuable real-world considerations. The table below details the chapter where you can find their article.

| | Article | Contributor |
|---|---|---|
| Chapter 2 | Scrum to evolve the system and improve the business process | Winson Choo |
| Chapter 3 | My personal journey to agility | Nick Argall |
| Chapter 8 | Release Prioritization: Silence is Golden | David Moran |
| Chapter 10 | Teamwork to a reasonable comprise | Edward Krzeminski |
| Chapter 11 | The Testing Mindset | Adrian Stokes |
| Chapter 12 | Traditional Management or the Death of Empowerment | Dr. Thomas Juli |
| Chapter 16 | Project Revitalization | Augusto Evangelisti |
| Chapter 17 | Customizing the methodology | David de Francisco |
| Chapter 18 | Recommendations based on an enterprise transition | Irene Michlin |
| | Recommendations from a ScrumMaster | Winson Choo |
| | Recommendations from an agile team member | Nicky Hewgill |
| Chapter 20 | Business Case on agile implementation at Betfair: Quantifying costs, benefits, and risks of implementing | Johannes Ritter |
| | Company transition to Agile | Winson Choo |
| | How to kill Taylorism using bottom-up intelligence | Ralf Tauscher |
| | Agile practices in traditional project management | Gloria J Miller |

**Adrian Stokes (Ady)** has over 2 decades of experience in Software Testing; Quality Assurance; Risk Management and Business Intelligence. Ady is a member of many mailing lists; Agile Yorkshire and is more than happy to discuss any aspect of testing, quality assurance, how 'Agile' applies or any related subject. (Twitter @CricketRulz; email adystokes@sky.com)

**Augusto Evangelisti** is a software development professional, blogger, foosball player with great interest in software quality, agile practices, and people. He enjoys cooking; eating, learning and helping agile teams exceed customer expectations while having fun.

**Dave Moran** has 30 years of industry experience as a developer, development manager, and product manager. Dave has found agile development to be THE WAY he wants to work and manage. Dave is an active blogger on the subject of agile leadership and it is his sincere hope that organizations embrace agile for everything, not just software development. http://www.softwareresults.us/

**David de Francisco Marcos** is a recognized IT professional with experience as a consultant, developer and leader in research and exploitation initiatives within European Union-funded projects. He is interested in business and product development roles in IT environments, working in stimulating cross-disciplined teams in international projects. He holds qualifications in business (MBA executive), research (MSc and research merits), and management (certifications and training in both agile and traditional methodologies).

**Edward Krzeminski** is a mechanical and automation engineer with a strong scientific background. He has 25 years of experience gained in the automotive industry as a manager in direct supplier for auto manufacturers like General Motors, FIAT, SCANIA, as well as in the reengineering and automation of industrial processes as a consultant and designer. Edward participated in more than 100 major complex engineering projects using the synergy of engineering knowledge in the area of mechanics, electrical engineering, computer science and modern management. He also has more than 15 years of lecturing, training and coaching experience. Edward has university degrees in mechanical technology, automation and robotics, as well as business

**Irene Michlin** has a degree in Computer Science from Tel-Aviv University (1995). She worked as a software developer across a wide range of technologies. She has CSM and CSP certifications. Currently she works at NCC Group as Managing Consultant. One of her main professional interests is establishing secure development practices in an agile environment

**Johannes Ritter** is Partner at Solution Matrix since 2003. Solution Matrix is a consulting firm that specializes in Business Cases that evaluate complex and large-scale projects. With more than 12 years of Business Case experience, Johannes has established himself as a leading Business Case authority in Europe. He is the author of various journal articles, a frequent speaker at international conferences, Business Case coach, and co-author of "Getting Your Budget Approved," a book on business case methodology. After his studies of Economics at Passau, Helsinki, and Harvard, Ritter was a consultant at IBM's former European Headquarter in Paris for five years. IT-projects have therefore been a focus over his entire career. http://www.solutionmatrix.de

**Nick Argall** is an Australian software development consultant. He has a broad range of experiences from within and outside the IT department that gives him a capacity to build bridges between the technology and the business need and the various stakeholders on both sides.

**Nicky Hewgill** is a marketing professional with a specialization in IT and technology marketing. She has proven experience of using new technology for marketing; she is a technology leader and innovator in online, multimedia and v-mail marketing, marketing automation, social networking and augmented reality. She has most enjoyed roles that exploit her passion for innovation in marketing ideas and techniques. She participated in agile projects while working for Nokia Corp. to develop and launch a strategic mobile application.

**Ralf Tauscher** is a graduate in Business Information Systems. He facilitates agile at Haufe Group for seven years as Scrum Master and later Agile Coach in various projects from desktop to web. Besides that, he is a "Mozillian" and a fellow of the Free Software Foundation Europe.

**Dr. Thomas Jull** is an experienced, enthusiastic and results-driven manager and leadership expert. He is offering more than 18 years of progressive leadership and management experience. He leads a strategic organizational development program at a global automotive supplier and has worked as as an independent consultant.

**Winson Choo** is Software Test Director at MNC responsible for the testing team, quality direction, product and services for the Asia Pacific region. He has over 12 years' experience in software deployments and setting up technical partnerships. Winson is a strong believer in agile methodology and has Scrum Master experience for major development projects. He is a Certified Scrum Master & Professional, Project Management Professional (PMP), and Six Sigma green belt. Winson provided a case study and his personal experience to this book. http://www.winsonchoo.com.

The following people reviewed advanced copies of the book: Anees Haidary, Augusto Evangelisti, Axel Aldenhoven, Sivaram Athmakuri, Bijoy BG, Dave Moran, David de Francisco, Dov Tsalsela, Elaissa Hardy, Frank Murphy, Gail Jones, Irene Michlin, Nick Argall, Raymond Miller, Ruth Ray, Srivalli Veeravalli, Stephan Tobler, Swaminathan Kothandaraman, Thomas Goettsche, and Winson Choo.

# Contents

## 2 AGILE & PROJECT MANAGEMENT

# QUIZ



# APPENDICES

# Figures

# Tables

# Preface

I started in the information, communications and technology (ICT) field after graduating from college with an electronic technology and a computer science degree in the 1980s. Since then, I've led or managed projects, in the U.S. and 25 countries, in government and most industries. I've seen almost every type of IT project from infrastructure to enterprise resource planning, to business intelligence, as well as many different types of organizational change programs.

Since 1986, my consistent experience has been that projects must be both iterative and incremental. In the late '90s, I started with timeboxing my projects and following frameworks based on the agile principles: it's very comforting for clients to know they'll get the results in, say, 90 to 120 days. In 2000, I had my first extreme programming (XP) experience; it wasn't very successful. We didn't have the right team space — pair programming was impossible because of physical separation. We weren't able to get a good product backlog; the market was demanding things the product owner couldn't reconcile. We had 'real users,' but we avoided them like the plague. I remember having to sit in a meeting and tell the client's executive board that we wouldn't be able to deliver. Since then, I've learned to use agile practices in many different types of projects, including projects that didn't follow a specific agile methodology.

In 2012, I prepared for the Project Management Institute — Agile Certified Practitioner (PMI-ACP)® exam. In doing so, I found several terms that were unfamiliar to me (e.g. osmotic communications). There were many ideas I was practicing already, but there were also some new ones (e.g. acceptance test-driven development) that I wished I had known about for prior projects. I thought I would just jot my learnings down so that other people on the journey from traditional to agile would have the information handy. Since I wanted to be sure I was giving valid advice, I had to research each topic. I soon realized there were more than a few experts and gurus that could provide input: many field consultants and agile coaches have done it all before! They each have valuable insights to share. Well, one thing led to another and this work is the result.

The book is an extensive review of the literature with the content selected and influenced by my 20+ years of experience. Agile and project management field consultants helped to review and form its structure and content. They also added their expertise in the form of case studies and personal experiences. At a high level, the book is organized to introduce agile as a concept along with its benefits, practices and methodologies; to explain my understanding of the agile coach's role; to describe how agile practices fit into the project management practices; and to give some considerations for going agile.

Gloria J. Miller

## How to use this book

This book was written with executives, managers, project managers and team leaders in mind. It assumes you understand the relevant project management practices. Maybe you've heard about agile but can't believe it's so different from what you've been doing in the past. Nevertheless, you now need to consider 'going agile' and adapting your practices.

Agile projects have been around since the first XP project in 1997. Many books provide details on managing and running agile projects, but this one aims to provide just enough background to describe the topic and get you started. There's a reference list at the end should you want to deep-dive into any topic.

It's not specific to any one agile practice, and it doesn't cover every agile methodology out there. The book makes general statements about agile projects; thus, the terminology is generalized. In certain cases, examples from different methodologies are given. The following are terms from specific agile methodologies along with how they're used here.

| **Book Term** | **Methodology specific terminology** |
|---|---|
| Product owner | Product owner, customer—the person from the customer or business responsible for defining the product requirements |
| User | Real user, customer, user proxy—the person who is intended to use the system |
| Customer | Product owner, user, purchaser, or client—the person with a direct interest in the product from a consumer point of view |
| Iteration | Sprint, timebox—a fixed-length time increment |
| Event | Meeting, event, ceremony |
| Artifact | Artifact, deliverable, work product |
| Developer | Developer, consultant, programmer (unless 'programmer' is specifically meant) |
| Agile coach | Scrum master, coach—the person responsible for coaching the team on agile practices |

A glossary of terms can be found at the back as a reference.

## What to read

The book is designed as an introduction to different agile themes and as a reference when details are needed on the application of agile practices. Therefore, you should be able to jump around to different sections as needed. For people...

- ... interested in an overview of agile definition, benefits, and a comparison thereof, Part 1 is sufficient.
- ... who must lead agile projects, Part 2 provides the details on applying agile project management practices.
- ... who want to introduce agile practices at their organization, go to Part 3.

**Part 1: Introduction to agile**

Part 1 is an overview of agile software development methodologies. It starts at the high-level with the definition of agile, describes agile practices and the role of the agile coach, and it provides a comparison of selected agile methodologies.

- **Chapter 1: Agile is an Innovation.** Provides some justification for considering the agile practices, including an introduction to the state of the agile movement and the benefits of agile methodologies.
- **Chapter 2: The Rationale for Agility.** Introduces the agile manifesto and its applicability. It discusses the kind of projects that are suitable for agile practices and the benefits — and potential pitfalls — of going agile.
- **Chapter 3: Methodology Comparison.** Provides an overview and comparison of selected software development methodologies, including plan-driven and agile methodologies.
- **Chapter 4: Agile Practices.** Describes some of the roles, practices, and principles that the different agile methodologies have in common.
- **Chapter 5: The Agile Coach.** Explains the characteristics of an agile coach, some of the skills that should be part of the agile coach's knowledge, and some ideas about building the agile team.
- **Chapter 6: The Role of the Project Manager.** List of project management tasks that are typically performed by a project manager or the project sponsor.

**Part 2: Agile & Project Management**

Part 2 describes applying agile practices in project management. The chapters and agile practices are organized by the knowledge areas from the *Project Management Body of Knowledge (PMBOK®) Guide*. The *PMBOK® Guide* is a standard that describes the norms, methods, processes and practices for the project management profession. Part 2 doesn't assume any knowledge of the *PMBOK® Guide*, nor does it suggest that you must organize your project according to it. The *PMBOK® Guide* was used as a framework to ensure that important project management topics were covered.

- **Chapter 7: Integration.** Describes the processes and activities needed to unify and coordinate the project and the other knowledge areas. This chapter covers the agile practices for chartering the project, building a business case, and conducting a retrospective. It also includes a summary of the agile practices for planning and monitoring the project.

- **Chapter 8: Scope.** Includes the activities needed to ensure that the project includes the work needed to deliver a working solution. This chapter introduces the agile practices for writing and prioritizing user stories, compiling the backlog, and establishing the scope baseline.

- **Chapter 9: Schedule.** Introduces the activities needed to ensure the timely delivery of the project. It covers the agile practices for task boards, Kanban boards, project work estimation, and establishing the schedule baseline.

- **Chapter 10: Cost.** Covers the activities needed to ensure the project establishes a budget and cost baseline.

- **Chapter 11: Quality.** Introduces the activities needed to ensure the delivered product is of sufficient quality to meet the needs that spawned its undertaking. This chapter covers agile engineering practices for testing.

- **Chapter 12: Resources.** Describes the process from designing the team through staffing and managing the team. It describes the characteristics of an agile team.

- **Chapter 13: Communications.** Covers the process for the flow of information from collection through disposition. It introduces the concept of osmotic communications and team space.

- **Chapter 14: Risks.** Describes the processes for decreasing the impacts of risks and increasing the impacts of opportunities. This chapter covers the team's role in the identification, quantification and management of risks.

- **Chapter 15: Procurement.** Covers the processes for acquiring and managing products and services from a third party for the project. It covers the setup of agile contracts.

- **Chapter 16: Stakeholders.** Includes the process for identifying and engaging the stakeholders in the project. This chapter identifies the typical stakeholders and their interests, and it describes how they're engaged in agile projects.

**Part 3: Agile Adoption**
Part 3 provides the considerations for getting started with agile practices, including selecting a methodology, transitioning to agile, and managing large agile projects.

- **Chapter 17: Selecting an Agile Project Approach.** Covers the options for selecting an agile project approach.

- **Chapter 18: Going Agile.** Describes introducing change, difficulties in going agile, and selecting a pilot project.

- **Chapter 19: Scaling Agile.** Outlines the considerations to scale agile from a single agile team to a large project. It covers a collection of practices for managing the people, the product, the project and the process in large agile projects.

- **Chapter 20: Experience from the Field** Includes stories from some project managers and agile coaches have implemented agile practices in their projects.

- **'Afterwords'.** Some closing thoughts.

**Part 4: Quiz**
This section includes quiz questions and answers for each chapter of the book.

**Appendices:**
The Appendices include references to the source material that was used to create this book.

- **Software Development Methodologies.** Provides an overview of the waterfall, spiral, and six agile methodologies.

- **Roles and Tasks.** Provides a list of tasks for scrum roles and the agile tester.

- **Bibliography.** A list of the reference material used in the book

- **Glossary.** Glossary of terms used throughout the book.

- **Index.** Book index.

# Acknowledgments

The author would like to thank everyone who provided invaluable case studies, personal experiences, and reviews. The contributors wrote articles and reviewed chapters that were focused on their area of expertise. They offered insights into what happens in different situations and willingly shared their knowledge and experience.

The reviewers spent hours offering input, guidance, rewrites and their professional opinion. They helped to shape the book and, in so doing, increased the value of the content.

In the production of this book, we've referenced works from other authors of books, articles, conference proceedings, and blogs as well as source materials from organizations. We thank all who have contributed to the agile, management, and project management body of knowledge and experience. It has been our sincere intention to quote and reference their materials accurately.

The author would also like to thank many colleagues for their creativity, contribution, and assistance: Katja Pétillon, Victoria Vaca Núñez, Jeremy Collins, and Mary Beth Robinson. Without their contribution, this book would not have been possible.

## About maxmetrics

Maxmetrics is an International Management and IT consulting firm, offering services in implementing complex projects and programs and in optimizing management and decision taking. Their portfolio encompasses consulting engagements, seminars, workshops and assistance. MaxMetrics has offices in Atlanta, Georgia and Wiesloch and Heidelberg, Germany.

# 1 Agile

# Chapter 1 Agile is an innovation

The agile movement is a sort of evolution in project management practices for software development, but at the same time, it is a revolution in project leadership.

For years, there has been improvement after improvement in defining the process for delivering software projects: from 1970 with the introduction of waterfall methodology, to 1988 with the spiral methodology, to now with agile. Each of those practices defined a process to manage and control software projects so that they delivered on-time, to-budget, with the right quality. The agile movement has gone a step further than just making improvements to the software development life cycle. The movement focuses very strongly on the people aspects of software development. It focuses on the relationship of the team to the customer, of the team to the stakeholders, and of the leaders to the team. This focus on relationships aims to enhance team collaboration. This clear focus on the people side of the software development process is an innovation. The agile movement aligns all people around delivering the highest value possible.

Agile methodologies are not just another set of methodologies. They are something new and different and require a completely new leadership style. They require leadership from the bottom of the organization and trust from the top of the organization. They require partnerships and strong collaboration between the business and technical teams. They require a different division of work between the business and the technical functions than has ever seen before. They require shared metrics to reach the project goals. Agile approaches and methodologies do not represent a small adjustment to processes and practices that already exist. They require a complete change in mindset to be successful.

Going for an agile methodology is not something that can be considered by a single team or group within an organization, it must be carefully considered and a conscious agreement made to go agile.

## State of agile

In his book *Crossing the Chasm,* Geoffrey Moore (1991), describes the process a product goes through from its market entry, to early market where a few visionary customers use it, to a mainstream market where a large block of customers with a pragmatic orientation use it. The chasm is a location between having a few visionary customers and having many pragmatic customers. Many products fail to make the transition across the chasm. The agile methodologies have crossed the chasm; they are mainstream with many organizations using them.

The Project Management Institute (PMI) recognized that the marketplace was demanding versatile project professionals for managing successful projects. They noted that agile was a topic with growing importance and there as a need for project managers with an understanding of applying agile tools and techniques. Consequently, in January 2012, PMI launched an agile certification, the PMI-Agile Certified Professional (PMI-ACP®). The PMI-ACP covers multiple agile methodologies and practices and is PMI's fastest-growing certification. As of January 2020, 32,471[1] people have been certified.

Since 2012, the research on agile methodologies and practices has increased in the academic community. A 2019 literature review of peer-reviewed journal articles and conference proceedings — using the keywords agile and project management or project manager — found 178 articles. The number of articles by year and theme is depicted in Figure 1-1. The majority (66%) of the articles were published since 2014, and cover agile and hybrid (mixed agile and non-agile) methodologies from different perspectives; they describe agile methods, practices, and tools (43%), report on experiences, use cases and challenges (40%), success factors and indicators (5%), and various other topics (13%). The trend reflects the growing importance of agile methodologies to project management. Furthermore, project management research suggests that agile and iterative methodologies are wide-spread, with more than half of the project's surveyed having some agile or iterative components (Miller, 2019; Serrador & Pinto, 2015).

## The agile decision

Agile methodologies have an iterative and incremental development or a continuous flow philosophy, promote self-organizing teams, and the requirements and architecture evolve during the project. They are perfectly suited for projects where the product details cannot be specified in advance or agreed with any degree of accuracy. On the other hand, traditional methodologies (such as waterfall) are well suited for projects where it is possible to collect a complete set of requirements up front. Therefore, the project type should inform the decision to go agile.

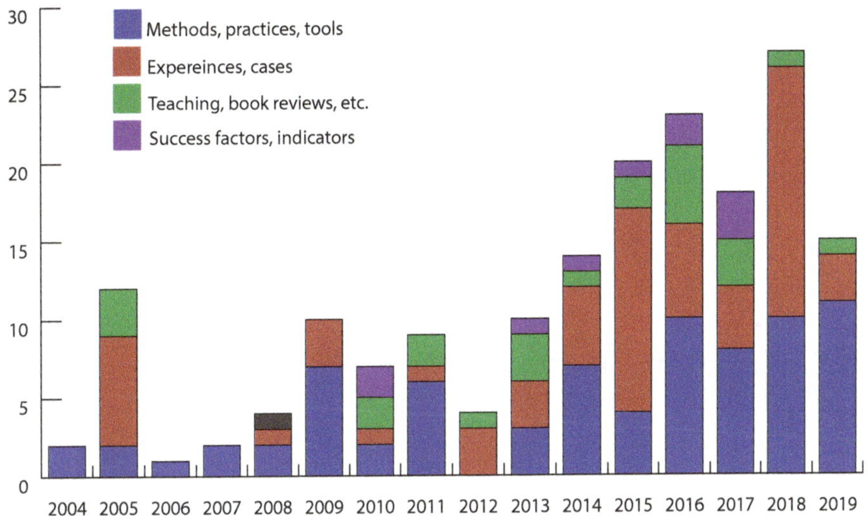


Figure 1-1 Agile project management articles by year and theme

The Standish Group is an Information Technology organization that assesses risk, cost, return, and value of software projects. Since 1994, they have published the CHAOS report that studies software failures and successes. The CHAOS report 2015 recommends agile processes as one of the ten project success factors.

The agile benefits have been proven over hundreds of agile projects. Organizations that have used agile practices report the following benefits.

- **Time and cost performance.** A higher than average number of projects are delivered on time and on budget
- **Low risk.** Risks caused by lack of user input and incomplete or changing requirements and specifications are reduced.
- **Productivity.** Teams have improved focus through better prioritization, improved communications and coordination, and reasonable processes.
- **Quality**. Sustainable work patterns and improved engineering practices produce higher-quality work (e.g. fewer bugs).
- **Ability to respond to change.** Flexibility of the design and an adaptive process mean teams are better able to manage changing priorities.
- **Employee engagement and job satisfaction.** Better collaboration and sustainable work patterns result in improved morale.

- **Fast time-to-market.** Short iterations and small releases mean agile teams are able to release their product more quickly than non-agile teams

- **High benefits-to-cost ratio**. Reasonably high benefits to cost ratio have been reported (i.e. 7:1 and 32:1).

- **Predictable Return-on-Investment (ROI).** Collaboration between project leader and management is cited as the reason for achieving business objectives and predicted ROI. ROIs ranging from the hundreds to thousands have been reported (580 percent to 3,108 percent).

- **Stakeholder satisfaction.** Alignment between IT and business objectives for project visibility results in stakeholder satisfaction.

Agile failures have been reported when management is not properly informed or engaged in implementing agile practices.

## Summary

- Agile is very powerful for projects that have some degree of uncertainty, blurred scope, knowledge intensive, or need to adapt to many changes (e.g. regulations, business markets). By using agile practices such projects benefit from high project performance and increased productivity and stakeholder benefit.

- The agile methodologies are mature. They have been around since the '90s. There are thousands of organizations using them. They provide numerous benefits, including a high return on investment. If a specific agile methodology is not outright adopted, the individual agile practice should be adopted until the desired level of agility is reached.

- Agile projects focus heavily on organizing and motivating people to execute projects in a highly collaborative environment. They require organizational and project leaders to create a working environment for teams, to trust them, and to facilitate that they learn from their experience.

## Endnotes

[1] PMI Today (January 2020)

# Chapter 2 The Rational for Agility

To decide on going agile, one must first understand what it is, where it fits and what the benefits or pitfalls of going agile are. This chapter covers the following topics:

- The Agile Manifesto
- What changes when you use agile practices
- Applicability of agile practices
- Agile performance

## The Agile Manifesto

Software development is a complex task. Over time, numerous development lifecycles and methodologies have emerged for structuring projects to meet user requirements and manage project risks. In reality, though, users don't have requirements: they have needs. Business environments and user needs change more frequently than desired, and the risks to on-time, on-budget delivery vary greatly from project to project.

Published in 2001, the *Manifesto for Agile Software Development* (www.agilemanifesto.org) (Beck et al., 2001) represented a seminal point at which the software community acknowledged that requirements evolve and cannot be fully pre-defined. Today, there are several software development methodologies, frameworks, and processes that embody the Agile Manifesto's values and principles, for example scrum, lean software development, Kanban, feature-driven development (FDD), extreme programming (XP), the Crystal method, and dynamic systems development methodology (DSDM).

At a high level, the Agile Manifesto describes a framework for software development. It was published after several agile methodologies were already in use: the first XP project was carried out in 1997 and DSDM was published in 1994. The original signatories of the Agile Manifesto were among the authors and creators of the early agile methodologies.

## Manifesto for Agile Software Development

We are uncovering better ways of developing software by doing it and helping others do it. Through this work we have come to value:

**Individuals and interactions** over processes and tools

**Working software** over comprehensive documentation

**Customer collaboration** over contract negotiation

**Responding to change** over following a plan

That is, while there is value in the items on the right, we value the items on the left more.

## Principles behind the Agile Manifesto

Our highest priority is to satisfy the customer through early and continuous delivery of valuable software.

Welcome changing requirements, even late in development. Agile processes harness change for the customer's competitive advantage.

Deliver working software frequently, from a couple of weeks to a couple of months, with a preference for the shorter timescale.

Business people and developers work together daily throughout the project.

Build projects around motivated individuals. Give them the environment and support they need, and trust them to get the job done.

The most efficient and effective method of conveying information to and within a development team is face-to-face conversation.

Working software is the primary measure of progress.

Agile processes promote sustainable development. The sponsors, developers, and users should be able to maintain a constant pace indefinitely.

Continuous attention to technical excellence and good design enhances agility.

Simplicity—the art of maximizing the amount of work not done—is essential.

The best architectures, requirements, and designs emerge from self-organizing teams.

At regular intervals, the team reflects on how to become more effective, then tunes and adjusts its behavior accordingly.

## What changes when agile practices are used

The following are a few of the things that change when agile methodologies, frameworks, and processes are used.

- **User engagement**—the way that the user is included in the project operations and software development
- **Project organization**—the way that the team is composed, organized and managed, and how the team collaborates
- **Feedback**—the frequency of reviews by the customer and the project team, in order to incorporate new knowledge into the product or project process
- **Project scope**—the way that the scope is established and prioritized for development
- **Estimation**—the way that the effort is estimated and tasks are managed
- **Development and release cycles**—the way the software is developed and released
- **Cycle times**—the length of time between development releases
- **Quality assurance**—test cases, acceptance criteria and testing practices
- **Reporting**—the techniques used for monitoring and reporting the project status
- **Documentation**—the types of documentation and the responsibilities for documentation

Specific agile practices are discussed in detail in chapter 4.

The requirement for agility — or having the ability to adapt quickly and easily — doesn't apply exclusively to software development. In its 2017 *Pulse of the Profession In-depth Report— Achieving Greater Agility*[1], the Project Management Institute (PMI) found that organizations with diverse skill sets and process capabilities had higher agility than those without. The report also found that the average percentage of projects meeting their original goals and business intent is greater in organizations claiming high agility than in those declaring low agility. Furthermore, agile methods have been applied to such projects as service management, business startup decision making, and engineering energy media flow. While agile practices are widely applicable, this book primarily focuses on software development projects.

## Boundary for work

As a form of temporary organization, projects are "a set of organizational actors working together on a complex task over a limited period of time" (Bakker, 2010). Both the PMI (2017c) and the Association of Project Management (APM) (2012) define a project to be an undertaking with a limited lifespan, for producing something unique and for delivering a defined output. The project encompasses the features and functions of the output to be delivered, namely the 'product scope,' and the work required to deliver the product features or function, or the 'project scope' (PMI, 2017c).

There are at least three containers for work (i.e. boundaries) in an agile project: product, project and iteration. A life cycle for new product development consists of conceptual activities, development, and production, and then market growth, maturation, decline, and withdrawal (Pons, 2008). The typical life cycle phases of a project are initiation, execution, control, and closing. An iteration is a timeboxed unit, where the goals of the work and the team remain constant. An agile methodology can be applied by a team without the existence of a project, and a product can exist without a project. This book focuses on the application of agile methodologies within the boundaries of a project. Figure 2-1 demonstrates the time relationship between the product, iteration and project boundaries.

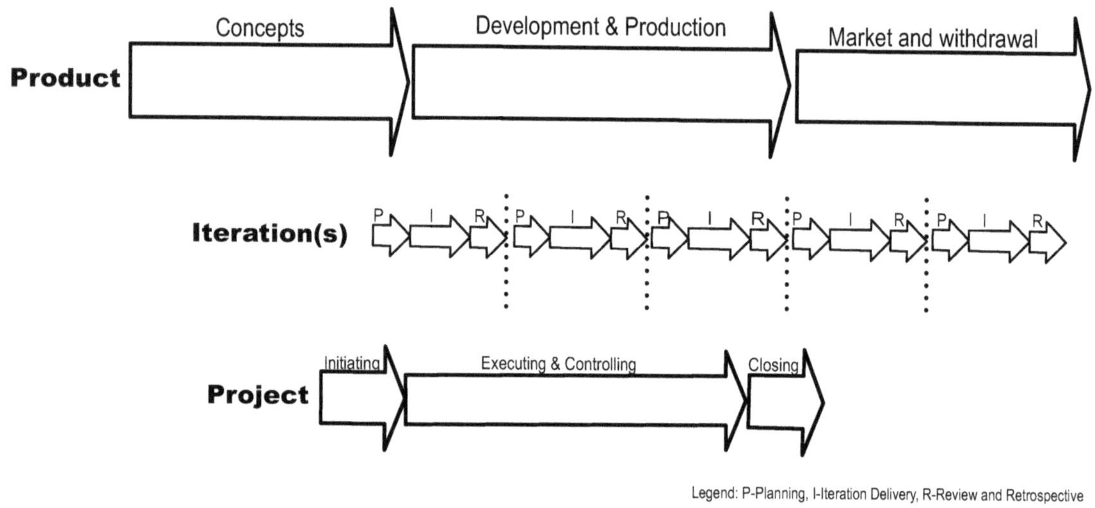


Figure 2-1 Time relationship and work boundaries

## Applicability of agile

Ralph Stacey (2011) developed a model to help managers and leaders choose between the different decision-making and management approaches to use in various situations.

### The Stacey Matrix

The eponymous Stacey Matrix is a two-dimensional model (see Figure 2-2) based on the degree of certainty and the level of agreement. It helps clarify where the agile methodologies are especially applicable.

On the horizontal (x) axis, the degree of certainty relates to how sure or defined the linkage between cause and effect is. Issues are close to certainty when cause and effect linkages can be determined. In this case, you can use past experience to plan a course of future action and expect — with a good degree of certainty — a positive outcome. When issues or decisions are far from certain, the link between cause and effect is not clear, and the situation is new or unique.

On the vertical (y) axis, we have the level of agreement on an issue or decision within a community (e.g. group, team, organization).

At the one end of the spectrum, if there's a high degree of both certainty and agreement on the issue, decision-making is easy. In this area (known as the 'rational zone'), traditional methods and approaches are effective.

At the other end of the spectrum, there is no agreement on the issue and no certainty on causes and effects. In this region, plans are usually insufficient: it's an area where chaos or anarchy prevails. According to Stacey, "'chaos' here does not mean utter confusion but pattern that we are not used to noticing or thinking about" (p. 238). He's referring to "mathematical chaos," which he describes as "not a little bit of stability and a little bit of instability, but a completely different dynamic in which instability and stability are inextricably intertwined so that in every stability there is also instability and they cannot be separated out." (p. 238) The chaos area should be avoided!

Between these two extremes, there's a large area called the 'complexity zone.' Here, traditional approaches are not effective. Systems in the complexity zone are unpredictable. They "display a regular degree of irregularity so that within each space of stability there is always instability," according to Stacey (p. 231). In this zone, the systems must emerge organically. It is not possible to develop a blueprint and plan for the whole system. A diverse, self-organizing group with conflicting constraints and many interactions must produce solutions in this zone. Creativity, innovation, and conflict are needed.

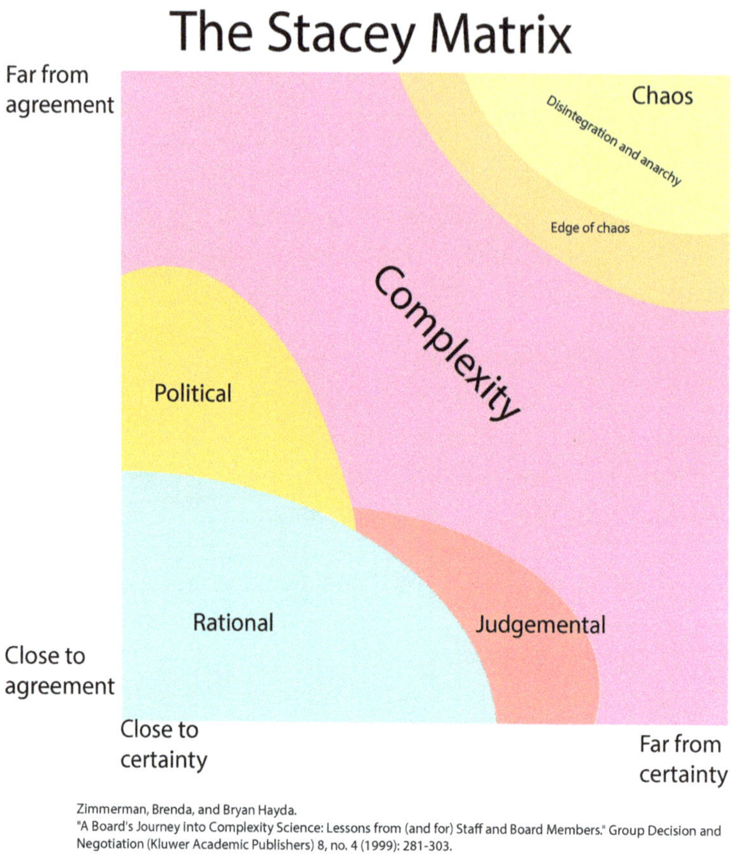


Figure 2-2 The Stacy matrix (Zimmerman & Hayday)

## Normative methodologies

In the rational zone, you can agree on requirements in advance and apply either a normative (plan-driven) methodology or a defined control process. Whereas normative methodologies are based on solutions or sequences of steps known to work for the discipline, a defined process control produces an output of acceptable quality when repeatedly executed. According to Lindvall et al. (2002), "plan-driven methods are those in which work begins with the elicitation and documentation of a "complete" set of requirements, followed by architectural and high level-design development and inspection" (Lindvall et al., 2002, p. 197). Waterfall and spiral methodologies are plan-driven methods (also referred to as traditional methodologies.)

## Agile methodologies

The complexity zone is an area in which you can neither specify the product details in advance nor agree upon these details with any degree of accuracy: exactly the conditions that require a collaborative environment between the user and the developer. Therefore, projects assessed to be in the complexity zone have the most to gain from an agile approach.

Agile methodologies are based on the philosophy of empirical process control, which is a continuous cycle of inspecting the process for correct output and operations and adapting the process as needed.

## Agile performance

According to Turner and Zolin in their research paper *Forecasting Success on Large Projects: Developing Reliable Scale to Predict Multiple Perspectives by Multiple Stakeholders Over Multiple Time Frames*, "project success is measured not just by completion of the scope of work to time, cost, and quality, but also by performance of the project's outputs, outcomes, and impacts, and thereby the achievement of the desired business objectives, as assessed by different stakeholders over different timescales" (2012, p. 87).

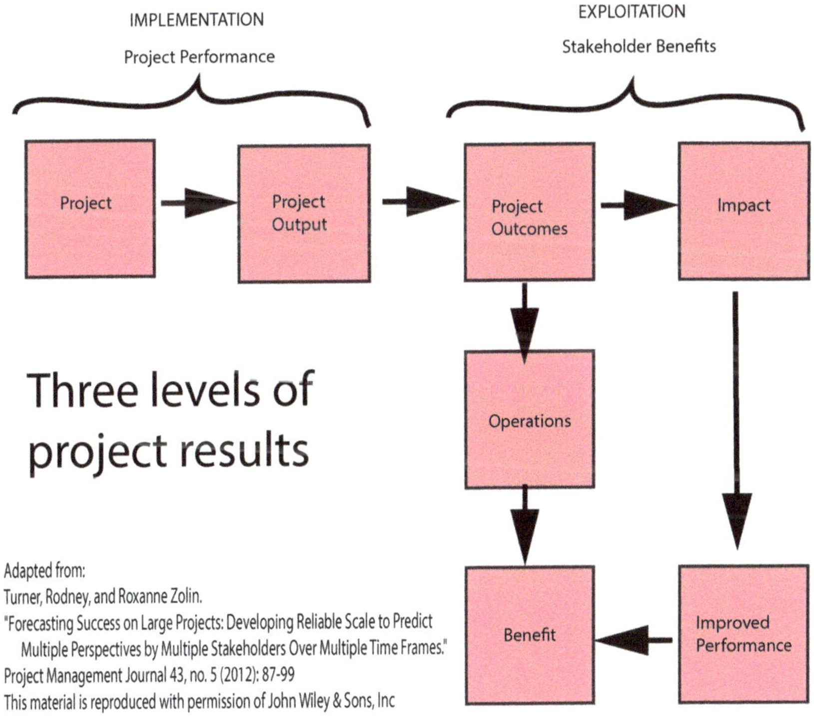


Figure 2-3 Three levels of project results (Turner & Zolin)

Figure 2-3 indicates that a project has three levels of results: the project output, the project outcome, and the project impacts. The 'project output' is the product produced during the project, and success can be evaluated at the end of the project. At that time, performance on time, cost and quality can be measured, as well as learnings, features, profit from the work (for suppliers), and client appreciation (for suppliers).

The 'project outcome' comprises the new capabilities that using the new product should provide to the sponsoring organization. Thus, the faster the product is put into operation, the sooner the organizational benefits and impacts can be realized. The higher the quality, the lower the organizational costs to resolve defects found during the operation. The more productive the team, the lower the project costs. These are benefits for the project sponsor, executives and investors alike.

The 'impacts' are the long-term results expected by the sponsoring organization that result from the new capabilities delivered through the project. They can be judged after several periods or years of operation. Higher returns on investment (ROI), shorter payback periods, and other business metrics (e.g. product sales) are measures of performance at this stage.

Agile projects directly benefit project performance, output, and outcomes and they indirectly benefit organizational impacts. To understand the consequences of going agile, this section reviews the performance of agile projects and the benefits to their stakeholders, as well as the problems and pitfalls of agile projects.

## Project performance

Several surveys and studies[2] have reported that agile teams perform better with regard to time and cost, are more productive, produce higher quality products, and show several other advantages over traditional projects. These findings are discussed in the following section.

### Better time and cost performance

While presenting mixed results, research leans towards agile projects performing better on time and cost than plan-driven methods. Serrador and Pinto[3] (2015) found that agile methodologies have a positive impact on project efficiency — time, cost, and quality — stakeholder satisfaction and the perception of overall project performance. Conversely, Miller (2019) found that agile and plan-driven methodologies performed at similar levels. Ambler (2011)[4] concluded that iterative and agile projects were better than ad hoc and staged methodologies at delivering on-time and on-schedule. The CHAOS Report 2015 concluded agile methods were better than waterfall.

Michael Mah from the Cutter Consortium (2008) benchmarked two agile projects with industry data from a worldwide database of 7,500 completed projects. One company used a scrum approach with a distributed team and the other an XP approach with a co-located team. Compared to the industry as a whole:

- The scrum project was able to achieve a nine-month time advantage at a lower cost (USD 300,000), and with fewer defects (11% less), although they did have a larger than average team size (92 vs. 40).

- The XP project achieved a schedule reduction of five months, produced half the defects, and — across six releases — saved USD 7.8 million. The team size was the same as the industry average (35 people).

### Reducing risk

According to the Standish Group, the primary reasons on which projects are challenged include lack of user input and incomplete or changing requirements and specifications. At the XP2002 conference, Jim Johnson from the Standish Group (2002) explained that 64% of product features are rarely or never used and that projects deliver only 30% of their intended value; the remaining 70% are project or user waste. Today, the Standish Group recommends using agile processes as one of the 10 project success factors (2015).

Furthermore, 62% of respondents to the VersionOne (2018) survey adopted agile practices as a measure to reduce risk and 50% indicated that reduced risk was one of the benefits of going agile.

### Improved productivity

In 2006, Microsoft[5] conducted research among its development teams and found that 59.6% of them used agile practices for both legacy (e.g. not first release) and new products. Some of the benefits reported by respondents included increased productivity, improved focus through better prioritization, improved communications and coordination, and more reasonable processes.

In 2007, salesforce.com completed an agile transformation of 200 people across 30 teams in three months. Implementing agile practices from the scrum, XP, and lean methodologies, they realized a variety of benefits including reduced software defects. According to an organizational survey, 80% of the technology staff felt the new practices made their teams more effective. Additional salesforce.com results are referenced in other sections of this book.

After evaluating over ten surveys on agile adoption, Dr. David F. Rico (2008) found that "the benefits of using agile methods range from 10% to 100% for increased cost-effectiveness, productivity, quality, cycle-time reduction, and customer satisfaction."

Surveys from VersionOne and Scott Ambler (2011) also show that agile teams are more productive than the industry average or traditional projects.

### Higher quality

These studies indicate improved or enhanced software quality as a result of 'going agile.' Agile teams that employ some of the agile testing methods such as test-driven development (TDD) and continuous integration produce higher-quality work because:

- Having fewer bugs to chase down allows them to move on sooner to new topics Salesforce.com reports that they were also able to eliminate 1,500 software defects by adopting an agile approach.
- Sustainable work patterns (that is, less overtime) prevent sloppiness.
- New engineering practices (pair programming, refactoring, early testing, and automated testing) provide additional improvements.

### Improved ability to respond to change

Microsoft reported that its teams were quicker at responding to change due to the flexibility of the design. VersionOne reported that the most often cited (69% of respondents) benefit of 'going agile' was an improved ability to manage changing priorities.

### Improved employee engagement and job satisfaction

Scott Ambler discovered that agile team members say they enjoy working at their company and would recommend agile to other teams. VersionOne and Microsoft reported improved morale.

### Faster time-to-market

In the VersionOne survey, respondents reported shorter times-to-market with their product. Correspondingly, Scott Ambler found that agile teams release their product more quickly than non-agile teams. Microsoft also reported quicker releases. Michael Mah's findings of five- and nine-month time advantages in the two companies he studied also attest to faster time-to-market.

### Improved stakeholder satisfaction

VersionOne reported improved stakeholder satisfaction due to better alignment between IT and business objectives and improved project visibility.

## Problems and failure

Scott Ambler's survey defines success as a solution being delivered and meeting its success criteria within the acceptable range defined by the organization, and it defines failure as the project never delivering a solution. Since projects of all types fail, the key question is: Do agile projects fail more or less frequently than others and what are the reasons for the failures?

According to the Ambler report:

- Agile and iterative methodologies have the same success and failure rates
- Agile projects are more successful than either traditional (those following a staged process) or ad hoc projects (those not following any formal process)
- Large projects are challenging for all methodologies

In 2011, Michael Sahota, an agile coach, performed an informal survey with eight agile coaches at the Play4Agile conference. His findings were:

- Agile works well for small projects or small teams
- For large projects lacking strong management support, a sense of urgency, and a no-failure disposition, the agile approach was challenging or unsuccessful.

VersionOne indicated that the top three reasons for agile project failure are:

- Inadequate experience with agile methods

- Little understanding of the broader organizational change required
- A company philosophy or culture at odds with agile values

The Microsoft study revealed the top three perceived problems with the agile approach to be not scaling to larger projects, too many meetings, and insufficient management buy-in.

**Scaling.** The highest-rated concern (reported by 10% of the respondents) was the perception that agile doesn't scale to large projects. However, most of the teams surveyed were in the same building or on the same floor, with average team size estimated at 30 people or fewer. This concern is related to teams with hundreds of people.

**Too many meetings.** This problem was expressed when the team size was more than eight to ten people or if the team was inexperienced with agile processes.

**Management buy-in.** This dilemma was due to upper management continually asking for progress reports and productivity metrics that were difficult to provide from an agile work environment.

**Other challenges.** The remaining concerns reported by Microsoft can be categorized as cultural clashes or challenges and perceived difficulties in adopting an agile approach.

In addition to the survey data, there are also highly visible cases of programs struggling to implement agile methodologies. The Universal Credit project in the United Kingdom was one such program.

Based on a report by the Comptroller and Auditor General of the National Audit Office, the UK government undertook a program to reform the welfare system. The program is expected to cost GBP 2.4 billion and deliver benefits of GBP 38 billion by 2023. At the time of the report, more than 70% of the GBP 425 million already spent went to contracts for designing and developing IT systems. For the initial pilot delivered by the program, the scope "is narrower than originally planned, covers only the simplest new claims and includes limited IT functionality" (*Universal Credit: early progress*, 2013, p. 6).

The organization chose to use an agile approach to implement the IT system and define policy and processes at the same time. According to the report, "the Department experienced problems incorporating the agile approach into existing contracts, governance and assurance structures" (*Universal Credit: early progress*, 2013, p. 8).

From selecting an agile approach in December 2010 to the time of the report in May 2013, there were at least three attempts to adapt the agile approach. Adjustments were made to integrate with other projects that were following a waterfall approach, to simplify processes, or to separate roles, among others. For example, one adjustment made "stopped developing systems for national roll-out and focused on short-term solutions" putting an end to incremental deliveries.

Some of the problems faced by Universal Credit can be attributed to inexperience, while others were based on not adapting organizational practices to the agile values and principles including not scaling agile practices to fit with the size of the project organization, some 1,000 people.

In summary, agile projects don't fail more frequently than other projects. And they succeed at the same rate as other iterative methodologies. Most problems and failures occur due to a perceived lack of management engagement or understanding of agile practices. Scaling agile practices to large projects is a specific concern and requires special attention.

### Stakeholder benefits

Scott Ambler reported that agile projects provide higher ROI and stakeholder value than projects conducted using other methodologies.

PMI reported that the average percentage of projects achieving business objectives and predicted ROI is significantly greater in organizations reporting high agility than those reporting low agility. Better collaboration between the project leader and management was cited as a critical success factor in achieving this performance.

Dr. David Rico reported that the agile methodologies had a benefits-to-cost ratio ranging between 7:1 and 32:1 across the 29 agile projects in his study. The ROIs ranged from 580% to 3,108%. However, some traditional methodologies produced even higher benefits-to-cost ratios.

### Agile benefits

The upshot of the studies and reports referenced here is that applying agile practices can result in better project performance and higher stakeholder benefit. Using agile processes and engineering practices, projects deliver sooner, are more flexible for change, and produce higher-quality software. The result is higher ROI and stakeholder value. The teams and stakeholders perceive greater satisfaction due to improved communications, smoother collaborations and increased flexibility.

## Case study: Enterprise implementation

In 2007, Chris Fry and Steven Greene presented a case study of the salesforce.com transition to agile practices. The following information is a summary of the case that they presented.

Salesforce.com offers a software-as-a-service customer relationship management solution and an on-demand application platform. At the time, they were processing over 85 million transactions per day and had 646,000 subscribers.

The group responsible for product development had doubled its staff every year since its inception (eight years). Over time, they went from delivering four major software releases a year to one. The research and development (R&D) teams were functionally organized (e.g. program management, user experience, product management, development, quality, and documentation). They used a waterfall-based process.

The agile transformation was designed to address issues they had with inaccurate estimates, lack of visibility in the development process, long and unpredictable release schedules, and gradually declining productivity.

The company founder and head of the R&D technology group took the organizational change in-hand. He developed a cross-functional team to address the issues that they were facing. The organization already had a business model that fit with agility (on-demand software), an automated testing system, and the majority of R&D was co-located. The team couched the change in terms of returning to its core values as a technology organization.

Feedback collected from 45 internal meetings with key people was incorporated into a working paper on the new process and the justifications for change. The team evaluated the rollout strategy and chose to go for a big-bang approach (all-at-once) to avoid organizational confusion and show decisive action.

Large groups of people were sent to 'Certified Scrum Master' training and a consolidated training presentation comprising scrum, XP and lean concepts was completed. They conducted two-hour training for every team and provided on-site schooling for 'Certified Scrum Product Owner' and 'Agile Estimation and Planning'. They built an internal information platform

The cross-functional rollout team used the scrum process for its own operation, creating a global schedule for the entire product, providing coaching and guidance, removing impediments, monitoring success, and promoting agile practices throughout the organization.

Thus, they were able to move 200 people in 30 teams to an agile methodology in a three-month window. Within six months, they had accomplished two major product releases. Now, they produce potentially releasable code every month, and their software bug count has been reduced by more than 1500.

Some elements of their implementation include a focus on team throughput (instead of individual productivity), a simple agile process, user stories, new estimation methods, defined roles (scrum master, product owner, team member), organization-wide daily tests, test automation, daily metrics, daily cross-functional team meetings, prioritized work for each team, weekly product-line 'scrum of scrums,' and monthly R&D-wide reviews and retrospectives.

Critical success factors in their transformation were:

Executive commitment: It is necessary to enforce agreed decisions, for example, sticking with the agreed timebox duration.

A dedicated cross-functional rollout team that included someone from each function. They gathered practices and input from other companies, industry experts, and success stories.

Focus on values and principles: They referred back to the agile principles and core values to analyze and correct situations when something was not working. They distributed a handout describing the agile values to the entire technology organization.

Automation: They used continuous integration, automated units, and functional testing. They focused on code health, reducing end-to-end testing times, and having a single code base.

Transparency: The cross-functional rollout team's daily stand-up and task boards were held in a public place. They published daily metrics with automation results, test results, budget counts, and deployment activities. They created a "daily metrics drumbeat."

Training: They trained a quarter of the R&D staff and hired consultants to support the scrum masters, product owners, and functional managers.

**Reference:**

Fry, Chris, and Steve Greene. "Large Scale Agile Transformation in an On-Demand World." AGILE 2007. Washington, DC, 2007.

## Case study: Scrum to evolve the system and improve the business process

**—Winson Choo, PMP CMQ/OE CSM CSP**

This five-year project is to design, develop, and deploy an online program management information system for a charitable non-profit organization. The system strives to give stakeholders visibility into long-running (5-10 years) programs and projects, as well as being a tool for improving business processes. Supporting a wide variety of users including project team members, funding approval personnel, and executive management, the system includes features for information input, project repository, information sharing, communication, reporting, and approval.

Because the project is huge, with requirements that continually change due to the newness of the initiative and the fast pace of technological advancement, Scrum is selected as the methodology. As a prototype in the charitable non-profit sector, this project simply had no benchmark to model after; therefore, the mandate was foremost to keep the project evolving so that the end result would address the organization's needs to track its programs effectively and efficiently.

The huge volume of feedback from various departments and countries further complicates things. User needs vary from region to region and approaches are not standardized. Changes in technology repeatedly send developers back to the drawing board, for example, when 'improved' browser versions render the project outdated before it is even rolled out.

The team of 10–12 developers engages in frequent team building and coaching activities such as sports, taking meals together, going on group outings and retreats, as well as conducting extensive discussions within the organization. The more interaction, the better the team works together.

While there's some strong internal support for the scrum methodology — and downright enthusiasm within the scrum team itself — people outside this circle don't understand or support the initiative. This makes the organizational ecosystem a tough environment for agility to flourish, or indeed, to be shared across functional areas.

The benefits and wins resulting from using scrum as the project approach include:

- Quick and rapid release (every 3 weeks),
- Fast response to stakeholders needs,
- Stronger bond for the software development, testers, and business analyst involved in this project, and
- Improved work efficiency

## Summary

- Agile is a set of values and principles, not a prescriptive process methodology. Organizations that have pursued an agile strategy are able to produce quality software in the shortest possible time and adapt to changing environments. These pioneers have openly shared their learnings, knowledge, and experience, contributing to our current understanding of agile practices.

- Agile practices are most applicable to projects and environments where uncertainty requires a collaborative working environment between users and developers. In addition, agile is an option for reducing project risks.

- Implementing agile approaches is an organizational change that affects management as well as individual team members. Problems and challenges will occur (and failure may result) if management is not adequately involved.

- Agile projects don't fail more frequently than other projects. Scaling agile to accommodate large projects requires that the practices be adapted for working with a large number of team members.

- The benefits of agile practices are better project performance and enhanced stakeholder value.

## Endnotes

[1] The study had 1,469 project management respondents.

[2] The several surveys referenced include surveys and studies from CHAOS Report (2015), VersionOne (2018), Scott Ambler (2011), Dr. Dobb's Journal (2011), PMI (2012), and Microsoft (2006), Michael Mah (2008), Dr. David F. Rico (2008).

[3]Serrador and Pinto had 1002 respondents, Miller 120 and Ambler 178.

[4] The survey asks about ad hoc, iterative, agile, traditional, and lean methodologies: ad-hoc is with no defined process; iterative is a timeboxed iteration; agile is a lightweight, collaborative, timeboxed iteration; traditional is a staged process; and lean is a value-focused mindset.

[5] Microsoft had 492 survey respondents.

# Chapter 3 Methodology Comparison

The following chapter provides an overview of selected plan-driven and agile methodologies. The purpose of this chapter is to give insights into the characteristics of the methodologies, along with their similarities and differences. This chapter covers the following topics:

- Plan-driven methodologies
- Agile methodologies
- Methodology comparison

## Plan-driven methodologies

Plan-driven methods (also referred to as traditional methodologies) start with collecting a complete set of requirements, and then sequentially performing the design, development, and testing of those requirements. The following section describes the waterfall and spiral plan-driven methodologies.

**Waterfall.** A sequential design process that progresses through a series of phases from conception through to the maintenance of the solution. As originally defined, the waterfall model consists of six development phases, five documents, and five risk mitigation strategies. Waterfall is characterized by a sequential process with sign-offs at the end of each process step, and documents being the main communication tool between the team members (Winston, 1987).

**Spiral.** An iterative and incremental methodology presented by Barry Boehm. In incremental projects, parts of the system are developed, integrated, and released at different times. In iterative development, parts of the system are developed, integrated, released and revised based on feedback from the users or new requirements.

The spiral method for software development suggests progressive elaboration of the software. Each iteration begins with a definition, a prototype, and a risk assessment, followed by the design, coding, testing, and implementation of the software; it finishes with creating a plan for the next phase and a review of the current phase. Thereafter, the next phase starts as a new iteration with the same activities (Boehm, 1985).

## Agile methodologies

Agile methodologies are based on an iterative and incremental development philosophy; they promote self-organizing teams, are emergent, and follow the 12 principles of the Agile Manifesto (Lindvall et al., 2002).

- Incremental development stands for the development, integration, and release of parts of the system at different times. With iterative development, parts of the system are developed, integrated, released and revised based on feedback from the users or new requirements.

- In self-organizing teams, the team members assign tasks amongst themselves, participate in decision-making, and resolve their own problems and conflicts.

- In emergent projects, the technology and requirements (i.e. scope) evolve and emerge through product development. They are adapted, expanded, or changed as needed. (Figure 3-1)

- Each agile process or lifecycle employs different roles, practices, and values in addressing the 12 Agile Manifesto principles. Nevertheless, they all are based on maintaining a flexible scope.

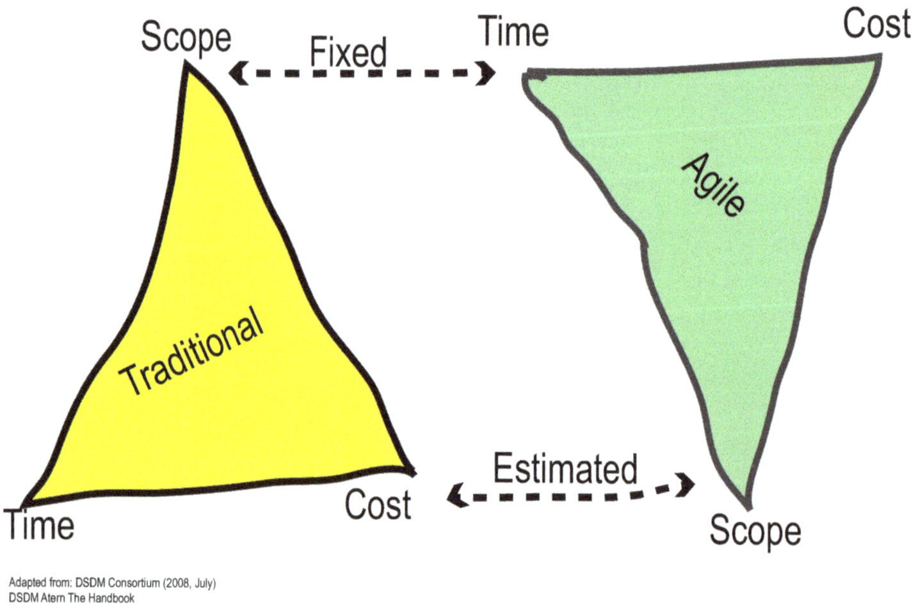


Figure 3-1 Agile and traditional triple constraints

The following section provides a high-level description of six of the agile methodologies.

**Lean.** Lean production practice is to eliminate any activity that absorbs resources but doesn't create value (in other words, waste). There are seven lean principles that can be applied to software development (Poppendieck & Poppendieck, 2003).

**Kanban.** A scheduling system concept related to lean and just-in-time (JIT) production that helps determine what to produce, when to produce it, and how much to produce. A Kanban process requires explicit limits to work-in-progress and a signal to pull the work through the system. Five Kanban processes create lean behaviors in software development activities (Anderson, 2010).

**Feature-driven development (FDD)**. Breaks a product down into features, plans and delivers the product features in an iterative and incremental method, and provides standardized progress reports. FDD consists of five processes across two phases, nine practices and six key roles (Palmer & Felsing 2002).

**Scrum.** An interactive, incremental methodology that has a highly flexible development phase that empowers the team to act as needed to meet the customer requirement and be productive. Scrum has five events (called ceremonies), three deliverables (called artifacts), three roles, and a set of rules that govern the relationship and interaction between the different components (Schwaber & Sutherland, 2017).

**Extreme programming (XP)** An iterative, incremental development methodology with values that emphasize simplicity, communication, testing and aggressiveness. XP has four values that are realized through the execution of 13 practices. There are five key roles required for executing XP (Jeffries, 2001).

---

## Personal Experience: My personal journey to agility

### —Nick Argall, Australian software development consultant

When I started out, I had no methodology, and I suffered greatly as a result. Then I was trained in several waterfall and staged planning methodologies that focus on change control, risk management, and configuration management. They solved the problem of trying to hold too much in my head, which caused an inability to complete large projects and difficulties in maintaining my code. Nevertheless, it turned out that there were problems with speed and responsiveness that I still couldn't solve using those methods.

As agile methodologies started coming out, I began adding individual techniques to what I was already doing and conducting experiments of my own. I experimented with the Personal Software Process and PRoxy Based OBject Estimation (PROBE). I regard it as the best way to predict programming work; unfortunately, it's extremely difficult to implement. (Botched attempts to implement statistical control have given it a bad name.)

Design Patterns was a big influence on my technical work, as was working with (and coming to understand) the Delphi object framework. Delphi was the framework that Anders Hejlsberg did before moving on to design .NET; it remains one of the cleanest examples of applied design patterns ever made. Scrum was interesting when it came out. The idea of formalizing sprint length was attractive. I was already doing daily team meetings by that point and having the team participate in planning.

I read very widely and often, making sure that I read at least two authors on any major topic. It isn't enough to know how to code if you're going to lead software development. I'm proud to have read and applied most of the authors and works cited by "Going Agile."

I now study what the masters themselves have studied: William Deming, Christopher Alexander, Toyota, HP, and IBM. When you study Toyota, IBM, and HP, multiple histories can be compared against each other. We can clearly say what policies of Toyota, HP, and IBM contributed to their success. Microsoft has been the dominant software company for 30 years. It's quite clear that they got something right. At this time, we don't really know what that is, although Bill Gates' marketing vision and his ability to recruit the best and brightest undoubtedly played a part. By 2050, there should be multiple histories and we'll be able to assess what Microsoft was doing in 2000, and what outcomes it led to.

I think my progression is a reasonable model for others. When you're just starting out, just get started! When you encounter your first methodology, use it to solve the problems that it solves. Once you're confident with one recipe for success, you can learn another. Once you're confident with four or five recipes, you can study how the ingredients interact with each other. Eventually, you might want to investigate how the ingredients are made.

In the beginning, a methodology is a great way to train yourself in new skills and habits that may be uncomfortable at first. Once you've mastered those skills and habits, you can afford to be more flexible about when and how you use them.

In the end, agility doesn't come from a methodology; it comes from paying attention to people, to what those people are doing, and why they're doing it. You don't have to be perfect — no one is.

## Methodology comparison

Table 3-1 Comparing methodologies provides some insights into the characteristics of selected methodologies. The cell is blank when the methodology is silent on the topic or doesn't prescribe a practice. Chapter 4 describes the agile practices.

| | | Agile | | | |
|---|---|---|---|---|---|
| Characteristic | Waterfall | FDD | Scrum | Lean-Kanban | XP |
| Emphasis | Build a plan upfront and follow-the plan | Model the business and deliver by feature | Prioritize and deliver value through empowered teams | Eliminate waste and visualize, monitor and improve the workflow | Software engineering focus on small, high-quality, user-centric delivery |
| Product acceptance | At the end of the project | By feature | Each iteration | Continuous | Each iteration |
| Final product scope is set / definition of planning | Details are fixed during requirements & design | Details are set once during the phases: develop an overall model, build a features list, plan by features phases | Set multiple times during project by product backlog | Details set when agreed prioritize when needed | Set multiple times during the project by release and iteration planning |
| Scope change | Controlled during project | 10% change can be absorbed without schedule slippage | Encouraged during review changes locked out of the sprint | Allocate time to change requests based on demand Resist change during a workflow state | Continuous |
| Dev iterations | One as planned | Multiple by feature | Multiple by timebox | Continuous at regular pace | Multiple by timebox |
| Completion date | Determined during planning | Determined during planning | Set during project possible each iteration | Continuous limit coordination, prioritization costs | Set during project possible each iteration |
| Delivery frequency | Determined during planning | By feature in 2-week increments | 2 - 4 week cycles | At a regular pace timeboxes not used | Small releases 2-week iterations |

Continued

| | | Agile | | | |
|---|---|---|---|---|---|
| Characteristic | Waterfall | FDD | Scrum | Lean-Kanban | XP |
| Project costs | Determined during planning | Set during project estimation | Set during project early stop possible | Set during project resource leveling | Set during project early stop possible |
| Testing frequency | Determined during planning | By feature | Per iteration | Continuous | Daily |
| Team size | Determined during planning | Roles prescribed | 7 ± 2 individuals prescribed roles | Based on demand and WIP Limits | Pair-wise programming recommended prescribed roles |
| Team flexibility (for making decisions) | Limited after planning | Limited after planning | Unlimited during an iteration | Limit work-in-progress otherwise unlimited | Follow standards otherwise unlimited |
| Engineering practices | | Domain object modeling, unified modeling language, config. mgmt | | | Pair programming, test-driven development, continuous integration, coding standards |
| Business and IT Collaboration | Determined during planning | Frequent progress reporting | Prescribed roles daily meetings review meeting | Review meetings | Onsite customer daily working |

Table 3-1 Methodology comparison

## Summary

Each agile method defines its own processes or techniques for realizing the core principles for agile methods. Scrum, FDD, and XP advocate iterative development and incremental release of software development. Lean and Kanban are continuous processes.

# Chapter 4 Agile Practices

This chapter describes some of the roles, practices, and principles that the agile methodologies have in common. It should impart an understanding of software development practices and provide some guidance on choosing practices for implementation. The following topics are included in this chapter:

- Process or lifecycle
- The agile coach
- Project organization
- Requirements
- Planning
- Monitoring
- Engineering practices
- Practices in use

## Process or life cycle

The systems development life cycle (SDLC) for developing software usually consists of collecting requirements, analyzing the requirements, creating a design, programming or customizing the solution, testing it, and documenting it. These activities are still required, but for agile projects the approach for executing them is not a sequential one. Many process steps are performed in parallel. Any unnecessary or counterproductive activity that wastes resources is eliminated or minimized. The following are some of the process characteristics the agile methodologies have in common.

**Timebox or continuous flow iterations.** Using a fixed-length time window for each project iteration with each iteration having the same length. The project team agrees with the product owner on what features to deliver within each timebox. The complete SDLC is executed within the timebox. Kanban doesn't fix a timebox, but rather uses a continuous flow. The workflow is visualized on a board, and cards that represent the work are pulled through the workflow as team members are available to perform the work.

**Short iterations.** Delivering product increments in one- to four-week iterations. The length of the timebox is determined by the needs of the project. The more dynamic the requirements are or the more innovative the solution, the shorter the timebox. This gives more opportunities for feedback from the customer. However, timeboxes should be long enough to produce a meaningful product.

**Face-to-face interactions**. Short timeboxes with a review at the end of each iteration and an on-site customer ensure frequent interactions between the project team and the customer. Co-located team space and daily stand-ups are two methods for effecting frequent interactions between team members.

**Daily stand-up**. The 'stand-up' involves all team members and discusses progress, next steps, and identifies any issues that may be impeding progress.

**Frequent feedback.** Demonstrations, prototypes, wireframes, or working software are presented as needed to gain feedback on the capabilities being proposed or delivered. Frequent feedback allows the direction to be adjusted at the earliest possible stage.

**Limiting the number of intermediate documents.** Through face-to-face conversations and regular interactions, information should flow within the development team and from the development team to the customer, thus, eliminating the need to create large intermediate document deliverables. By minimizing the documenting, reviewing and updating of intermediate documents, the project reduces the costs associated with producing these documents, and the team can spend that time and effort on producing working software.

**Documentation (such as user manuals, help manuals)**. The product owner determines the extent to which end-user or maintenance documentation should be produced; this is prioritized into the backlog. This method of addressing documentation focuses the team on understanding its utility and importance in terms of the overall product delivery. It also makes the cost of the documentation visible.

**Low ceremony.** 'Ceremony' indicates the amount of formality and controls imposed on the process, for example, stage gates, approvals, reviews, or sign-offs. Agile projects recommend that the ceremony should be kept as low as possible to suit the type of project. The higher the system's criticality, the more process ceremony required. The system criticality is defined by the impact or consequence of undetected defects being used in production.

**Emergent design.** Decisions about the product's architectural design are made only at the last possible moment. This facilitates making just-in-time decisions, which is especially valuable when the customer's requirements emerge or change. The feature-driven development methodology makes use of a high-level object model as a basis for evolving the design through the iterations.

**Small releases.** Splitting the product requirements into small components (e.g. user stories or features) and delivering in small increments. By releasing small increments into production, users can derive value by using the product, as well as providing feedback.

**Allowing for change.** 'Process events' are defined to prioritize and incorporate changing requirements into the project activities. That is: the timebox duration, review meetings, small releases, frequent releases, emergent design, and backlog priorities are all constructed to solicit the customer's changing views on the product as frequently as needed, and those views are incorporated into the product in a managed way.

High visibility. 'Visibility' is how much a project outsider can determine whether the methodology is being followed. High visibility indicates that it's transparent to outsiders that the process being followed, while low visibility indicates it's difficult for outsiders to judge this. Through the use of 'big visible' charts and defined project events, the agile methodologies go for a high level of visibility.

**Inspecting and adapting.** Frequently reviewing the process and adapting it as necessary for better performance. 'Retrospectives' and 'refactoring' are two agile practices for reflecting on past work and seeking improvement opportunities: A retrospective is a meeting for just this purpose, while refactoring is an engineering practice to improve and restructure code without changing its behavior.

**Measuring performance.** Using metrics, such as process cycle efficiency, to tune and optimize performance. The 'lead time' is the time it takes to go from a user story or feature to a completed software. 'Cycle time' is the time it takes to complete a task once started. The 'process cycle efficiency' is the time in the process divided by the cycle time for the process.

**Definition of done.** Each iteration should focus on producing a shippable or production-ready product. This includes designing, coding, and testing the solution, as well as having the necessary documentation available to make the product usable. In some methodologies (e.g. scrum), the definition of done is agreed between the team and product owner. It defines how they'll know when the product is completed. In other methodologies (e.g. FDD), the methodology prescribes the definition of done.

**Optional scope contracts.** Use contract types that reflect the evolutionary nature of scope, encourage collaboration and commitment on delivering the scope, and fix the aspects of the project that are known at the start.

## The agile coach

Agile projects rely on self-directed teams, and they don't expect a single person to have command and control over the project. But there may be an agile coach that facilitates project success by coaching and mentoring the project team, supporting the customer, and managing the stakeholders. The agile coach must understand the principles and values of agility, as well as having a command of the agile practices and techniques from the different agile methodologies. Furthermore, an agile coach uses the following practices:

**Servant-leader.** The servant-leader meets the needs of the team by coaching and not controlling, by encouraging the team to make the maximum contribution, and by having the skills and foresight to stay out in front of the team and lead them to success.

**Coaching and mentoring.** Understanding and applying the agile values, goals, and methods in realizing the project. Building team cohesion and engaging the team in decision making, risk management, and other project responsibilities.

**Adaptive leadership**. Varying the style of coaching and leadership depending upon the project team's maturity with agile practices and the members' readiness to execute the new practices.

**Active listening.** Providing feedback to confirm what's been heard — and whether it's been understood correctly.

**Problem solving and conflict resolution.** Recognizing when conflicts occur — what kind, their depth, potential resolutions thereof — and then supporting the team in resolving the problem or conflicts.

## Project organization

Agile projects seek to optimize the information flow and project performance by collecting the people who need to perform the work into an optimal team structure. They encourage frequent and face-to-face communication between the project team and the customer or product owner, as well as amongst the team members. Agile projects are organized so that they have:

**Team space.** The team's physical working space, or an open work area that encourages collaboration and osmotic communications. Collaborative techniques and tools are used as part of the team space to manage distributed teams.

**Small teams.** Small team sizes, to allow for co-location of the team members in the team space, facilitating communications and coordination without the need for written documents.

**Generalist skills.** Team members who can perform a variety of activities and tasks within the team so people can contribute to multiple aspects of the project work. FDD places an emphasis on having strong domain knowledge.

**Experience.** Experienced team members maximize the productivity and throughput of the team's work. This includes experience with software development (most important) and agile practices.

**Dedicated customer.** A dedicated, knowledgeable, and authoritative customer or product owner responsible for maintaining feature priorities, writing acceptance criteria, and reviewing and accepting the product.

**Real user.** A real user or user proxy to clarify usage requirements and support the project team.

Team self-organization. The team members assign tasks among themselves, participate in making decisions, and resolve their own problems and conflicts. They collaborate to produce one collective product instead of each person considering only his or her personal tasks.

**Pairing.** XP has a concept of pairing two programmers at the same computer to create the production code; this increases both information flow and code quality. However, the pairing concept can be applied to other team roles, e.g. paring a tester with a programmer.

## Requirements

In agile projects, there no 'big requirements up-front' (BRUF) document before the development team is engaged. Instead, the requirements are collected in small increments and documented as individual user stories or features that are progressively elaborated through discussions with the developers, test cases, and examples. Agile projects typically use the following elements for requirements management:

**User story or product feature.** This is a requirement that should be implemented in the product. It's written from the user's or customer's point of view and contains a definition of the capability required, the user profile, the priority, and the tests that will be used to know when the story is complete. User stories are usually written on post-it notes.

**Agile prioritization.** User stories or product features are prioritized based on their business value. This prioritization guides the order in which work is scheduled as well as the level of detail in which each story is defined. Brainstorming techniques and innovation games are used to engage the stakeholders in prioritizing the stories.

**Progressive requirements.** A user story or feature become requirements specification based on a collection of information: the story card, the test for the story, discussions between the customer or product owner and team that adds understanding about the story, and examples that describe what the story means. This level of detail is collected as the project progresses. Thus, stories become requirements the closer they get to being scheduled for implementation.

**Backlog.** A prioritized list of user stories or features that the team should implement. The user stories are prioritized and organized in the product backlog based on their value to the business.

**Story map.** A two-dimensional view of the product backlog that organizes user stories to show the priority of stories and their relationships to one another.

## Planning

Agile methodologies include practices for progressive planning, which use the information that's known at the start of the project to create high-level plans; as more information and details are uncovered, the plans become more detailed. This allows the team to focus on creating plans for just the work to be done and not waste time and effort planning details that are likely to change. Agile plans have some or all of the following planning elements:

**Project charter.** Defines the vision for the project, why it's being undertaken and the business outcomes and impacts that are expected.

**Roadmap planning.** Details the long-range planning for the product, has a time horizon of a year or longer; it details, at a high-level, the upcoming releases.

**Release planning.** Has a time horizon of a quarter year and details the product scope across a number of iterations. Used to determine what user stories should be assigned to what release.

**Iteration planning.** Has a time horizon that equals the duration of the iterations (usually monthly to bi-weekly). The iteration plan details the user stories or features that are included in the iteration.

**Daily stand-up.** A short meeting for task planning with a time horizon of a day; details the tasks that occur during the next 24 hours.

**Agile estimation**. Different estimation techniques quickly gather estimates from the people who will perform the work. The level of detail corresponds to the purpose of the estimate, for example, story points, ideal days, or hours.

**Velocity.** A measure for the rate at which teams consistently deliver business value. It's a performance measure that's also used in estimating how many features can be addressed in an iteration.

## Monitoring

In agile projects, project progress is updated daily and at the end of an iteration to show how the project is proceeding in reaching its goal. This frequent updating of information allows the team and the stakeholders to maintain visibility over the project status. The status is displayed on charts that are visible in the team space and/or electronically. The charts are known as 'information radiators' or 'big visible' charts. The following may be used to manage the project progress:

**Task board.** A visible project board that uses cards to represent a task, story, or feature placed on a timeline that depicts the overall project workflow.

**Kanban board.** A type of task board that contains cards for the work that needs to be completed, showing the limits for the work-in-progress per step and signals for progressing the cards.

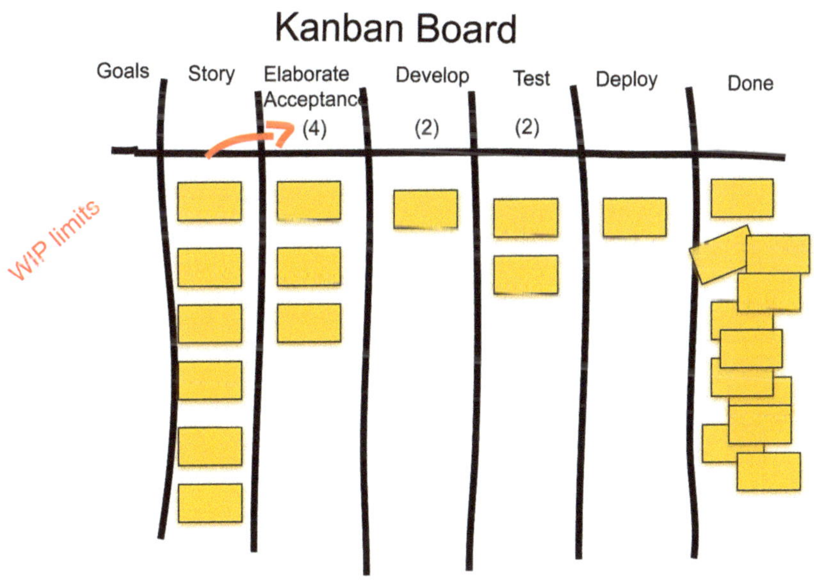


Figure 4-1 Kanban board

**Burndown chart.** A graph that shows planned and actual work remaining until the target end date. Each iteration has its own burndown chart.

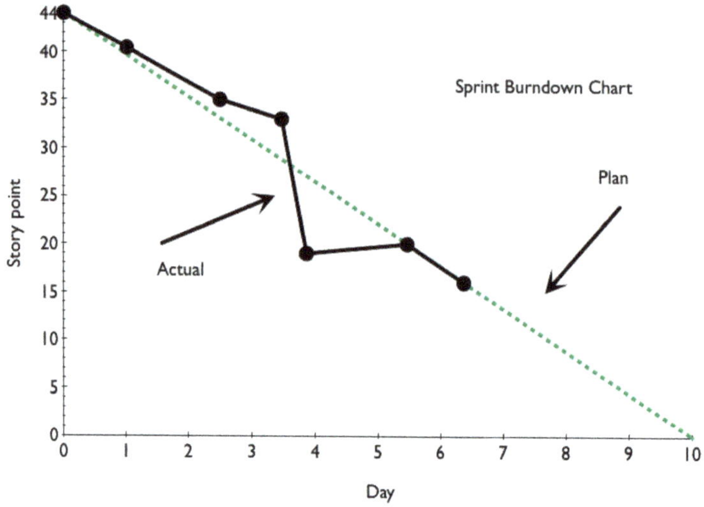


Figure 4-2 Iteration burndown chart

**Burnup chart.** A graph that shows how much work is included in the project and how much work is completed. Each release has its own burnup chart.

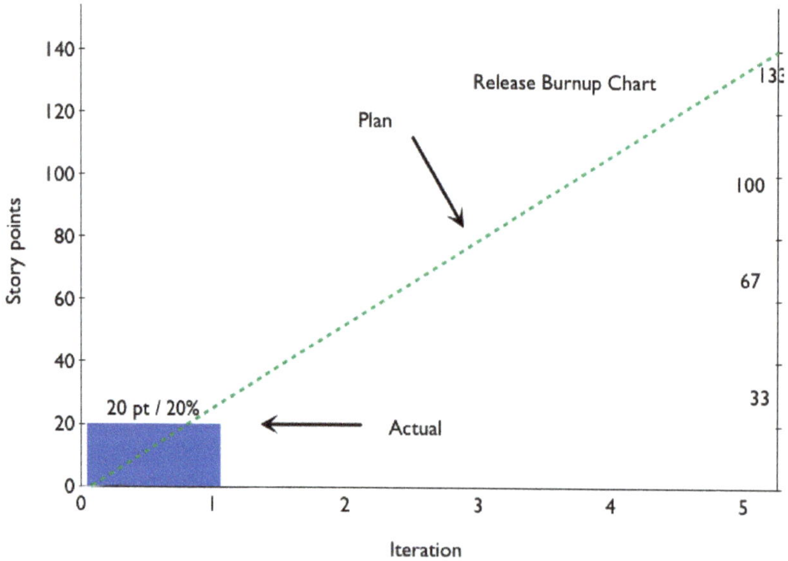


Figure 4-3 Release burnup chart

**Parking lot chart.** A visual, low maintenance way to report the progress of feature sets.

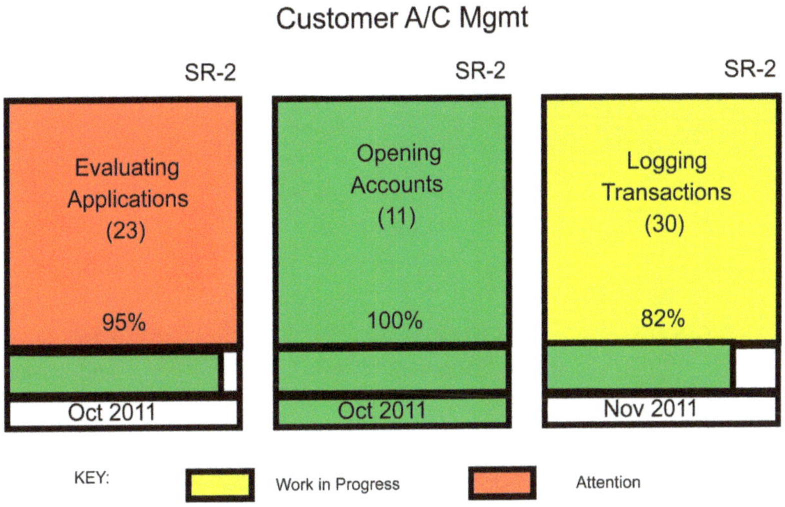


Figure 4-4 Parking lot chart

**Cumulative flow diagrams.** A graph of individual items accumulated with respect to the total for the item is used to track the changes in the impact, probability, and severity of over time. A cumulative flow diagram can be used to graph task flows, risks, or defects.

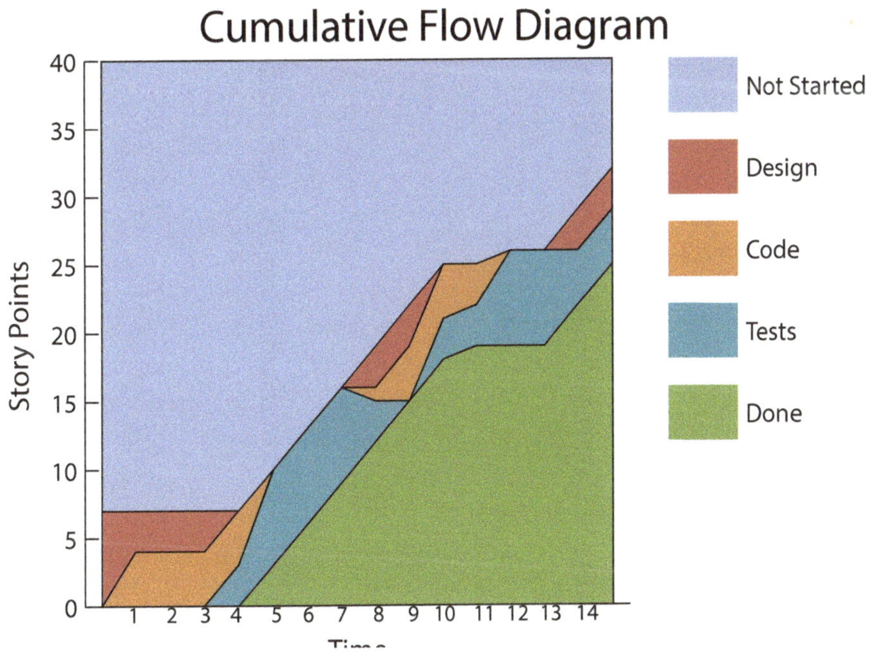


Figure 4-5 Cumulative flow diagram

## Engineering practices

The engineering-based methodologies (e.g. extreme programming) use technical practices to maintain a system that is always ready to go-live and easy to change as needed. The following are some of the engineering practices applied in agile projects:

**Configuration management.** With each iteration the product should be at a state where it's ready to go live. This means the team should always know the last good or safe software configuration by using configuration management practices.

**Refactoring**. A practice to improve and restructure programs without changing their behavior. Programmers can work on getting a functional concept completed and working as a first priority. Then, focus on improving the code for such things as readability, reducing complexity, or improving maintainability.

**Continuous integration**. A practice to combine the code from all programmers into the software baseline, integrate and build the baseline. Continuous integration can occur daily or multiple times a day. The goal is to identify integration problems as soon as possible so that they may be resolved.

**Coding standards.** A set of rules that the developers should use to create their code in a consistent way.

**Code ownership.** Focuses on who is responsible for changing the software code once it's created. XP suggests collective ownership so that any team member can update the code after it's created. FDD suggests that individual team members for code ownership.

**Test-driven development.** TDD, or test-driven design, is a programming concept that encourages simple designs. With TDD, one test is written, the test is run to make sure it fails, the programmer writes the minimum code necessary for the test to pass, the code is refactored, and the process begins again.

**Acceptance test-driven development.** ATDD is a concept to define, early on in the project, a set of unambiguous test cases that describe what the function or feature should receive as inputs and produce as outputs. These become acceptance tests. They can be used as requirements specifications and to create automated test scripts. Preferably, these acceptance tests are defined in advance of development, but they can be defined in parallel with development.

**Behavior-driven development.** BDD is a concept for writing stories that starts by identifying the expected business outcome, and then the feature set that will deliver that outcome. Each feature becomes a user story with its acceptance criteria or tests.

## Practices in use

Multiple studies[1] describe what agile practices are most applied by agile teams. The comparison between the studies indicates that there is no one right set of practices. For example, in one survey, daily stand-ups with the whole team are ranked at position one as being used by the majority of agile teams. In another survey, daily stand-ups are ranked at position three and in the third survey at position 11. Furthermore, there are variances in the practices from year-to-year. VersionOne conducts an annual agile survey. The ranking by the percentage of use based on the 2018 VersionOne study are provided in Figure 4-6.

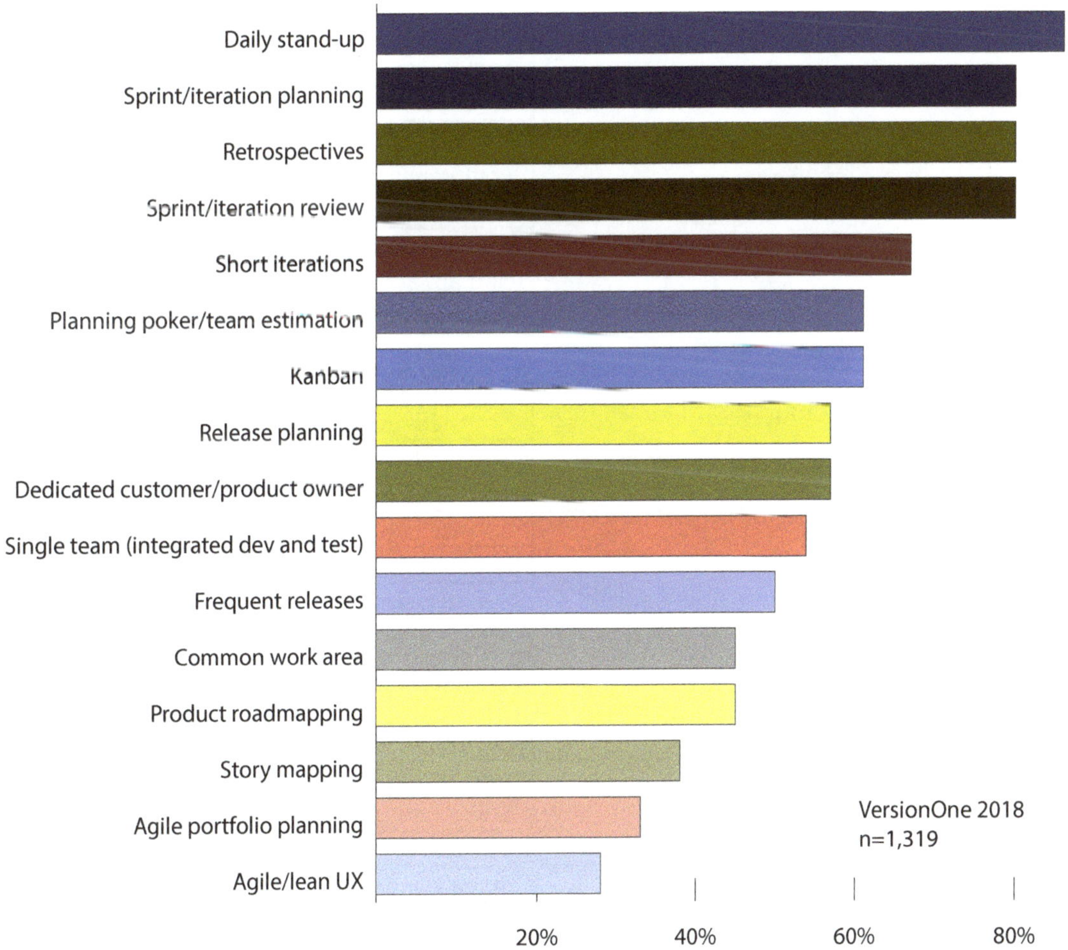


Table 4-1 VersionOne survey agile practices used

In 2013, Federico Bellani published research on the "Adoption and evolution of agile method practices." The research is an extensive literature review supported by survey results from 194 worldwide participants and extensive survey analysis. The research provides significant insights into how agile methodologies are implemented throughout the world.

The research identified nine of 35 practices that had a strong correlation with at least three other practices. The correlation identified sets of practices that are likely to be applied together by a certain team. The results show that some practices are often used when they are correlated with other practices. Thus, they can be seen as a group, meaning the use of a certain practice enhanced the use of other practices. Table 4-2 is a summary of the practices that were correlated together as a group.

| **Practice** | **Correlated Practices** |
|---|---|
| Coding standards | Refactoring |
| | Synchronized communication |
| | Test-driven development acceptance testing |
| | Test-driven development unit testing |
| Prioritized product backlog | Iteration reviews/demos |
| | Release planning |
| | Short iterations (30 days or less) |
| | Stand up/Scrum meetings |
| Release planning | Iteration reviews/demos |
| | Prioritized product backlog |
| | Stand up/Scrum meeting |
| Short iterations (30 days or less) | Prioritized product backlog |
| | Stand up/Scrum meeting |
| | Task board |
| Stand up/Scrum meeting | Prioritized product backlog |
| | Release planning |
| | Short iterations (30 days or less) |
| Refactoring | Coding standard |
| | Synchronous communication |
| | Test-driven development acceptance testing |
| | Test-driven development unit testing |
| Test-driven development acceptance testing | Automated unit testing |
| | Coding standard |
| | Refactoring |
| Test-driven development unit testing | Coding standard |
| | Test-driven development acceptance testing |
| | Timeboxing |
| | Abandoned practices |

Table 4-2 Correlated agile practices

VersionOne (2018) found daily stand-up, sprint/iteration planning, retrospectives, sprint/iteration review, and short iteration to be the most popular agile practices:

## Summary

- Agile frameworks and methodologies constitute a different way of setting up, managing, and collaborating in software projects. The project life cycle uses either iterative and incremental timeboxes or continuous flow.
- The self-organizing teams are coached and supported to deliver instead of managed through a command-and-control structure. The users are considered integral parts of the teams.
- The requirements and planning start at a high level; more detail is added as the project progresses. Big visible charts are used to monitor the project progress.
- Engineering practices maintain the current state of the software configuration, which is integrated and tested as often as possible.

## Endnotes

[1] VersionOne 6th Annual State of Agile (6,042 respondents) (2012), the Microsoft usage survey from Begel and Nagappan (2006) (492 respondents), Federico Bellani's (2013) research on the "Adoption and evolution of agile method practices" with 194 worldwide respondents, and VersionOne 13th annual State of Agile (1,219 respondents). The Microsoft survey respondents are from different Microsoft software development groups. The VersionOne survey respondents are from different industries.

# Chapter 5 The Agile Coach

The agile coach (called scrum master in the scrum methodology) has the responsibility to build the team into a self-organizing unit that can make its own decisions and resolve its own conflicts, as well as collaborate as a team to deliver the product. Thus, the agile coach must have an adaptive leadership style. The chapter covers the following topics:

- Building the team
- Problem solving and conflict resolution
- Leadership skills

## Building the team

The agile coach must understand what's required to take a group of individuals from being a working group to being a team. This involves forming the team and developing it through different stages, building collaboration among the team members, setting the framework for group decision-making, and facilitating conflict resolution.

The agile coach needs a target and a vision for how to help the team to its best performance. A high-performance agile team is able to achieve consistently high velocity.

## Team

The first act for an agile coach is to meld a team out of a newly formed group of individuals who happen to work together (a working group). Katzenbach and Smith (2017) define the differences between teams and working groups as follows in Table 5-1.

| | Team | Working Group |
|---|---|---|
| Leadership | Share the leadership role | A focused leader |
| Accountability | Individual and mutual | Individual |
| Mission | A common team purpose that it must deliver | Group's purpose is aligned under organizational mission |
| Work Product | Collective work product | Individual work products |
| Meetings | Open-ended discussions and active problem solving | Efficient meetings |
| Performance measures | Assessment of the collective work product | Indirectly measured through influence on others |
| Authority | Discuss, decide and work together | Discuss, decide, delegate |

Table 5-1 Teams vs working groups (from Katzenbach & Smith)

### Forming the team

Teams go through stages of development and they tend to reach their best performance after having been established for a while. Bruce W. Tuckman (1965) identified that, in terms of interpersonal relationships and task performance, teams evolve through four phases of development:

1. **Forming**—an orientation phase for testing interpersonal and task dependencies and boundaries with leaders, other group members, and preexisting standards.

2. **Storming**—a conflict and polarization phase during which there's resistance to group influence and task requirements.

3. **Norming**—a cohesiveness phase when new standards evolve, new roles are adopted, and opinions about tasks are expressed.

4. **Performing**—a structural phase in which roles become flexible and functional; group energy is channeled to the tasks, and the structure supports task performance.

To facilitate moving the team quickly through the forming stage, the agile coach should undertake steps to increase team cohesion. The following are examples of activities that could be undertaken.

- Co-locate the team members in the team space. For distributed teams, consider ways to ensure they are involved and engaged in the team environment. The act of moving and co-locating the team is a signal that they're a distinct entity that belongs together.

- Use a collaborative event (such as the chartering session) to ensure the team members are clear about the project's goals and objectives. During the session, make clear the interdependence the project has on each team member, and that there is a clear relationship between the project success and each individual's contribution.

- Have the team create a brand for the project, which could include a name, a logo, a song, a flag, etc. This step gives the team an identity.

- Have the team establish ground rules for cooperating and working together. The ground rules should establish acceptable and non-acceptable behavior, as well as regular routines (e.g. the start time for the daily stand-up). Have each individual team member buy into and agree to abide by the ground rules.

## Building collaboration

The agile coach's goal is to create an environment that allows the team to collaborate in the creation of the product. Collaboration is two or more people or organizations working together to realize shared goals. It requires that the team members cooperate and build on each other's ideas and sharing visions. According to Yaffee and Wondolleck (2000), the benefits of collaboration in teamwork include:

- Producing better decisions than adversarial processes do

- A better understanding of shared and individual concerns

- Promoting the sharing of information

- Better commitment from the participants

- Joint problem solving

- Complex decision making

Using meetings as collaborative events and participatory decision-making are two methods for encouraging collaboration.

## Collaborative events

In her book *Collaboration Explained*, Jean Tabaka suggests that the most successful meetings are those where productive results are derived through the engagement of the participants. That is, meetings with collaboration and decision-making opportunities. Consequently, Tabaka defines meetings as collaborative events that are methods for the team to communicate with itself and the stakeholders.

The agile coach needs to properly prepare, set the agenda, organize, and facilitate the meetings toward an outcome based on the category to which the meeting belongs.

Additional collaboration tools may be needed for distributed teams. These can include such tools as live video conferencing and speakerphone meetings as well as the use of chat tools to allow for interactive communications between team members.

During collaborative events, when a new idea is introduced and the team needs to make a decision about it, the team will go through different stages of thinking. First, team members will share their individual ideas, which may differ from one another (that is, diverges); then there will be a stage where no one is sure what is going on (that is a period of uncertainty); next the ideas will start to jell into a common cohesive direction until the decision is reached (that is, converge). Kaner (2007) refers to the period of uncertainty as the 'groan zone,' which is the stage of uncertainty when team members may feel like they may never reach a decision.

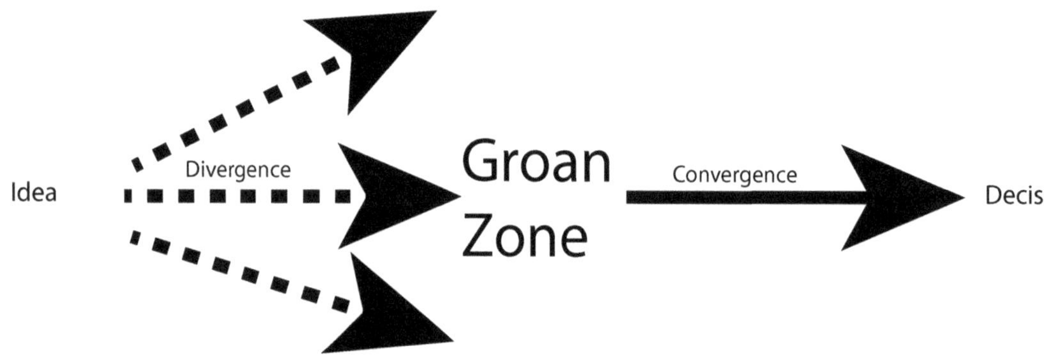


Figure 5-1 Decision-making convergence (adapted from Kaner)

It's important to acknowledge that the 'groan zone' exists — and not to attempt to drive decisions during that stage. The discussions and related efforts need to continue until the ideas start to come together. Decisions should be reached as soon as there's a convergence of ideas.

Consequently, it's useful to use multiple techniques for full engagement in collaborative events, including individual work, collaboration, and relative ranking. It's also important to gauge the degree of consensus or convergence of ideas to confirm the agreement.

**Individual work** is used to encourage the active participation of each individual and avoid groupthink. By performing individual work first, it gives people the opportunity to establish their own opinion on a topic and document it before group discussions begin. This method also keeps individuals from becoming spectators rather than actively contributing.

Writing ideas or responses on cards is a form of individual work.

**Collaboration** is when team members work together to realize shared goals. Collaboration promotes a common understanding, widens perspectives (by including different viewpoints), and generates commitment through team involvement in the decision making.

**Relative ranking** places items in an ordered list based on their closeness to other items. This makes it easier for team members to position items relative to another — as opposed to predicting the probability that something will occur or precisely estimating something. Furthermore, positioning items in specific locations triggers the loci memory technique, which helps to recall an item by mentally associating it with its relative position. The relative ranking is used for such activities as estimation or prioritization.

**Consensus**, or the degree of convergence of ideas, can be ascertained using a round-robin technique or the 'fist of five.' The round-robin technique gives each person the opportunity to be heard on an issue or topic as each individual is asked for his or her feedback, feelings or decision. Fist of five (Fletcher, 2002) is a group consensus technique where team members vote on a topic using their fingers. Once prompted by the facilitator, each team member shows a fist or number of fingers based on their opinion.

- A fist is a no vote and blocks consensus
- One finger: still need to discuss or wants changes
- Two fingers: have minor issues
- Three fingers: don't totally agree, but could live with it
- Four fingers: ok with the idea
- Five fingers: think it's a great idea

Anyone voting with three fingers or fewer should further discuss their concerns. The fist of five is continued until there's a consensus (a minimum of three fingers or more).

## Participatory decision making

Agile projects use a variety of rules to agree on when a decision is final. For example, in scrum, the product owner decides on the priority of the user story after a discussion with the team. In other cases, the team decides as a group. Nevertheless, in all cases, the decision rules should be clear for each type of meeting or situation. All the team members should be engaged in the decision making to ensure their commitment to the delivery.

Participatory decision making is based on a set of principles that produce stronger agreements within a group. The principles include the following:

**Full participation**—all members of the group must be able to share their views. The members become accustomed to raising difficult issues and they discover a diversity of opinions and backgrounds. Furthermore, they learn to share ideas that may be sketchy or incomplete.

**Mutual understanding**—members develop an opinion only after having listened to the viewpoints of others. This allows them to accept the values and legitimacy of the other participants, making the agreement sustainable over time.

**Inclusive solutions**—integrating the ideas from all members ensures the solutions have a range of realities (realism, truths). It doesn't restrict itself to only the opinions of a few individuals.

**Shared responsibility**—the members share responsibility for the efforts that went into making a good decision. They've given and received input and they've done due diligence before the decision was reached. Thus, they're more willing and able to implement or execute upon the final decision.

## Facilitating thinking

'Six thinking hats' is a way to divide thinking into six distinct modes; it offers a method for mapping out problems, supporting decision making, and facilitating discussions. The concept was created by Dr. Edward de Bono and published in his book *Six Thinking Hats* (1985). Based on the idea of 'putting on your thinking cap,' the idea is to look at something from several angles. Dr de Bono's concept suggests that there are six thinking modes; using the role-playing concept of putting on a hat, you can create a mind map to think through a topic.

The six thinking hats is a role-play that you can use:

- For yourself, as in — "let me put on my red thinking hat"
- To get a team member to see an issue in a different way, as in — "Joe, that's your black thinking hat; now put on your yellow one"
- To brainstorm an issue from all the different aspects.

Using role-play has the advantage of directing the discussion towards a specific theme, asking someone to switch gears in an easy way, and establishing rules that help clarify thinking. Figure 5-2 and the following section provide a summary of the six thinking hats technique.

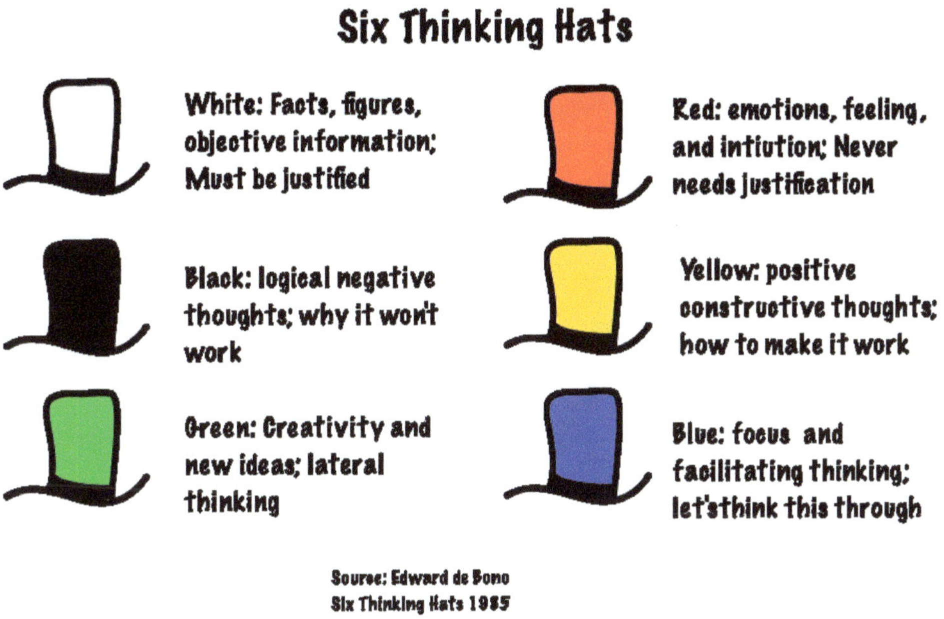


Figure 5-2 de Bono's six thinking hats

#### WHITE THINKING HAT

The white hat is for thinking about facts and figures. There's no interpretation or opinions. It's considered a neutral or objective role.

When asking questions using the white hat, focus on gathering information. There are two tiers of information: The first tier is proven facts that have been checked and verified, the second tier is facts that are not yet verified. The second-tier responses should be framed with a qualification to indicate the degree of certainty: 'most likely,' 'maybe,' 'sometimes.'

#### RED THINKING HAT

The red hat is for emotions and feelings (e.g. fear, anger, dislike), as well as intuition. Feelings don't have to be verified, justified or logical, and they should not be judged by others.

When asking questions using the red hat, focus on what the person thinks or believes. These are subtle feelings — likes, dislikes, and fears — and complex judgments such as intuitions or senses that aren't really explainable but rather a belief in something.

#### BLACK THINKING HAT

The black hat is for negative assessments: why something won't work, or is wrong, incorrect, or in error. It's an objective way to identify the negative elements of a situation.

When asking questions using the black hat, you seek the reasons why something will or did fail. If there are no objective facts backing up the responses, then it's really a red hat topic.

#### YELLOW THINKING HAT

The yellow hat is a positive assessment of the situation or topic: why it will work, what's good about it.

Yellow hat questions explore what we have to do to make something work or happen. The spectrum ranges from logical and practical to pipe dreams — it allows for speculation and opportunities.

#### GREEN THINKING HAT

The green hat is for creativity and innovative ideas and concepts. It's useful when searching for alternatives.

While 'wearing' the green hat, you ask provocative questions to prompt creative thinking.

#### BLUE THINKING HAT

The blue hat is for control and direction to organize the thinking in a structured way to move from point 'A' to point 'B.' It's thinking about the tasks that have to be completed and the best way to get there. It's a facilitation mode.

When asking questions with the blue hat on, you redirect the focus back towards a destination or goal. Blue hat thinking helps you identify the target and figure out how to reach it.

## Problem solving

Problems can arise with the process, the product quality and performance, or with team dynamics. One of the agile coach's daily activities is to monitor the project for (potential) problems.

Agile uses the metaphor of smells to talk about problems. A smell indicates that something is wrong or not going in the right direction. For example, if the team members are reporting to the agile coach instead of to one another in the daily stand-up, then it 'smells' like there's a command-and-control relationship between the team and the coach. If deadlines are consistently being missed, then it 'smells' like stories haven't been adequately estimated in the planning sessions.

The agile coach should take problems to the team for resolution. The following section covers some of the methods that may be used to identify and resolve problems and to identify and resolve conflict.

## Problem identification

The following techniques can be used to identify or detect problems.

### Surveys

- A health check, questionnaire or checklists can identify process-level problems
- Product critiques may identify problems with the product value or quality
- A team survey with open and closed questions to identify issues that are not openly discussed.

### Pain snake

A 'pain snake' is a technique to track issues using post-its on the wall. Created by Kevin E. Schlabach in 2008, the concept was first used to identify what kinds of activities were interrupting the team's work. As an interruption occurred, a team member would record that there was an interruption, including the amount of lost time, and post it on the wall at the end of the snake. The snake was monitored for repetitive patterns.

### Boundary authority role task analysis

A boundary authority role task (BART) analysis can identify problems with team dynamics. When agile coach Dan Mezick (2009) applied BART to scrum, he created an approach to identify boundary issues by using authority maps for the scrum roles. BART analysis evaluates four dimensions of team dynamics:

- **Boundary.** The container for group work. Task, time and territory are the boundaries that should be clearly defined, agreed upon, and adhered to.
- **Authority.** The right to do work. Formal or delegated authority should be clearly defined, taken up accordingly, and accompanied by tools to exercise it. Personal authority is how an individual executes formal authority.
- **Roles.** Occupied by people; they can be achieved, acquired or assigned. A formal role defines the responsibilities that must be executed to complete the task, in other words, a job description. Informal roles are executed by individuals to fill gaps in authority or to accomplish tasks that have otherwise been abandoned.
- **Tasks.** The activities that have to be completed. Tasks can refer to the company's mission or group dynamics. Tasks should be clear, and people should be able to differentiate between different kinds of tasks.

Figure 5-3 is a radar diagram with an example of the BART applied to the role of scrum product owner. For each responsibility, there's a rating for how well the product owner fulfills his or her role according to the team's assessment. This can be compared with the typical responsibilities for the role as defined by the scrum framework to identify gaps. Sample responsibilities for several agile roles are provided in the Appendix.

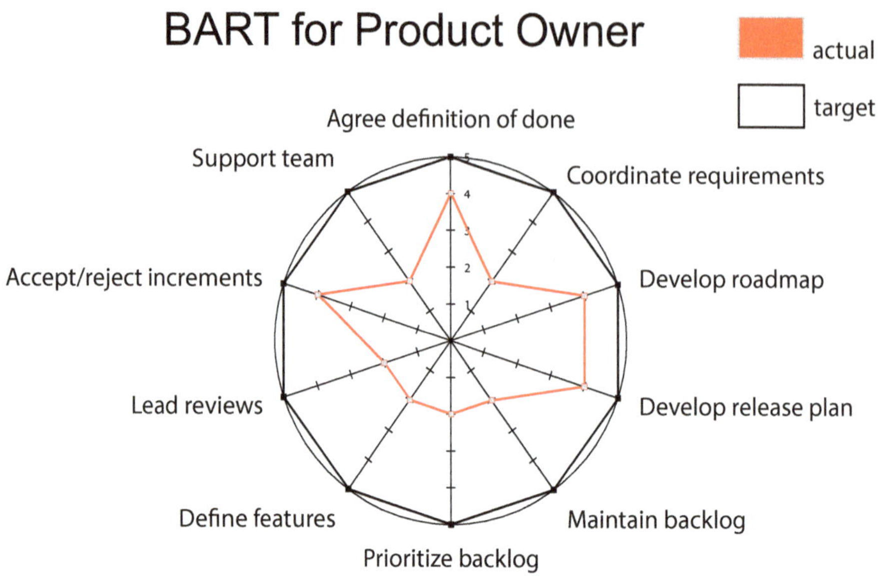


Figure 5-3 BART diagram for the product owner role

## Problem resolution

The following techniques can be used to take the problem to the team for resolution:

- **Address the problem directly.** State the symptoms you see and the hypothesis for why it's a problem, and ask the team what to do about it.
- **Reaffirm agile values and principles.** Reiterate the values and principles from the Agile Manifesto, as well as rules, events, and ceremonies of the agile method as a way of bringing up something that's not going well.
- **State the observation.** State what you observe and let the team discuss the topic until the team sees the issue and starts to seek a resolution.
- **Use the retrospective.** Design a retrospective that will likely raise the issues that you see.
- **Make the problem visible.** Add something to the team process for revealing the issue. (e.g. pain snake).

## Conflict resolution

First, agile projects need a diverse set of team members and they need a healthy conflict that supports innovation. Therefore, the agile coach should observe the team and understand when conflict is happening. However, he or she shouldn't just dive in and try to resolve all conflicts or keep the peace. The team has to solve its own conflicts.

The agile coach should take the following approach:

- Listen and observe the conflict
- Understand what level of conflict is occurring
- Get multiple viewpoints on the disagreement or issue
- Understand the degree of conflict
- Focus the team on finding a resolution.

Ultimately, the conflict has to be taken to the team for resolution. In the first step, the agile coach should see if the team can resolve it themselves; then analyze and respond. The response mode will vary depending upon the conflict level.

The agile coach should use the agile values, principles, roles, practices, events, etc. for navigating conflicts. That is, identify if and how the conflict is inconsistent with agile as a tool for understanding the conflict and deriving a path to resolution.

As a final step for the highest level of conflict, the agile coach may need to work with the team and the stakeholders for a resolution.

## Types of conflict

Speed B. Leas (1989) defined characteristics for various levels of conflict and suggested some methods for de-escalation. Lyssa Adkins (2010) applied Leas's work to agile projects. Table 5-2 lists the levels of conflict, the types of conflicts that occur, and some potential responses.

**CONFLICT LEVEL 1: PROBLEM TO SOLVE**

- **Issue:** Disagreement; conflicting goals, values, needs
- **Emotions:** Short-lived anger; parties uncomfortable around one another
- **Orientation:** Problem rather than person orientation
- **Sharing information:** Openly sharing information
- **Language:** Discussion is clear and specific
- **Each party's objective:** Solve the problem
- **Resolution techniques:** Collaboration

| Level | Issue | Resolution Techniques |
|---|---|---|
| Level 1: Problem to solve | Disagreement; conflicting goals, values, needs | Collaboration |
| Level 2: Disagreement | Disagreement: mix personalities and issues; problem cannot be clearly defined | Collaboration |
| Level 3: Contest | Begins the dynamics of win/lose; resistance to peace | Accommodate, negotiate |
| Level 4: Fight/fight | Shifts goal from winning to getting rid of the person | Negotiate |
| Level 5: Intractable | Personalities are the issue; situation is unmanageable | Whatever it takes; potentially removing someone from the team |

Table 5-2 From Speed B. Leas conflict resolution

### CONFLICT LEVEL 2: DISAGREEMENT

- **Issue:** Disagreement: mix personalities and issues; problem cannot be clearly defined
- **Emotions:** Distrust; caution
- **Orientation:** Begins to be about the person
- **Sharing information:** Selectively sharing information; some information is held back
- **Language:** Discussions is vague and general: "Some people . . . ," "They . . ."
- **Each party's objective:** Save face; come out looking good
- **Resolution techniques:** Collaboration

### CONFLICT LEVEL 3: CONTEST

- **Issue:** Begins the dynamics of win/lose; resistance to peace
- **Emotions:** Unable to be in the presence of the other person

- **Orientation:** Personal attacks; people take sides
- **Sharing information:** Information shared only with one's own group or faction; there is some distortion of the information.
- **Language**: Very broad generalizations: "You always . . ." "We never . . ."
- **Each party's objective:** Shifts from self-protection to winning
- **Resolution techniques:** Accommodate, negotiate

#### CONFLICT LEVEL 4: FIGHT/FIGHT

- **Issue:** Shifts from winning to getting rid of the person
- **Emotions:** Self-righteousness; doesn't speak to one another
- **Orientation:** People have taken sides of the issue
- **Sharing information:** Limited information is shared; doesn't accept or listen to information that is contrary to one's own views
- **Languages:** Principles are discussed not issues
- **Each party's objective:** Eliminate or hurt the other person
- **Resolution techniques:** Negotiate

#### CONFLICT LEVEL 5: INTRACTABLE

- **Issue:** Personalities are the issue; the situation is unmanageable
- **Emotions:** Accomplish the objective at all costs; no objective emotional control
- **Orientation:** Sees the person as dangerous to everyone
- **Sharing information:** Information is skewed
- **Language:** Discussions use destructive words
- **Each party's objective:** Destroy the other person forever
- **Resolution techniques:** Whatever it takes; potentially moving someone from the team

## Conflict responses

Kilmann and Thomas's (1975) model identifies five styles for how individuals respond to conflict based on assertiveness and cooperativeness dimensions. Assertiveness reflects the individual's attempt to satisfy his or her own concerns, and cooperativeness is the attempt to satisfy the concerns of the others. The five conflict styles are:

- **Avoiding**—ignore the conflict
- **Competing**—try to control and persuade the other to meet one's own needs
- **Accommodating**—defer to the needs of the other person and ignore one's own needs
- **Compromising**—attend to the concerns of both parties with a solution mid-way between both parties
- **Collaborating**—agree to a settlement that meets the needs of both parties.

The conflict response will vary from person-to-person (some people always avoid, other people are good a compromising, etc.) and situation-to-situation (see Table 5-2). The agile coach should recognize the different responses to conflict and support the team members in applying the best approach for the situation and person. Thus, understanding and using negotiation principles will be necessary in for conflict resolution.

## Principles for negotiating

Fisher, Ury and Patton, in their 1991 book *Getting to Yes*, advocate negotiating on the merits of an issue. Do not take a position and defend that position. For this type of principle negotiation, they recommend the following four steps:

1. **Separate the people from the problem.** Separate substantive issues from psychological problems. Psychological (that is, people) problems are based on inaccurate perception, high emotions, or misunderstandings. Educate to correct inaccurate perceptions; find ways to release pent-up emotions; work on communications to improve misunderstandings. Don't give in to substantive issues to solve psychological problems.

2. **Focus on interests, not positions.** A position is the thing on which a person has to decide. Desires, concerns, wishes, and fears are interests, and interests motivate people and cause them to decide. "A position is likely to be concrete and explicit; the interests underlying it may well be unexpressed, intangible, and perhaps inconsistent." (Fisher, Ury and Patton 1991, 44) Understand the opponent's issue as well as your own issues. Acknowledge their interests and negotiate for yours.

3 **Invent options for mutual gains.** Having an abundance of options to choose from in a negotiation may prevent failure to reach an agreement at all or failure to reach the best agreement. Broaden the options under discussion from having just a single option, separate the act of creating options from the act of judging the options, invent ways of making the opponent's decision easy, and search for mutual gains.

4 **Insist on using objective criteria.** Negotiate based on objective criteria such as standards of fairness, efficiency, or scientific merits as a basis to reach a fair agreement. Benefit from experience by referring to previous agreements, community practices, team polices or procedures, agile values and principles.

### Conflict resolution diagram

The conflict resolution diagram (CRD) (Figure 5-4), also known as an 'evaporating cloud,' is a tool that can be used to understand conflicts between two ideas, courses of action, or situations that seem mutually exclusive.

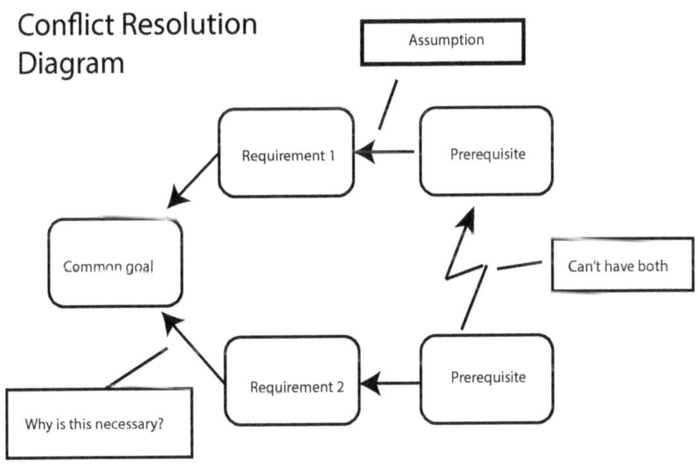


Figure 5-4 Conflict resolution diagram

## Leadership

The agile coach is seen as a mentor to serve the needs of the team, that is, a 'servant-leader' — a concept first developed by Robert Greenleaf and published in his paper, *The Servant as Leader* (1991). The servant-leader employs the following practices.

- **Self-awareness.** The servant-leader has an understanding of who he or she is, including strengths and weaknesses, skills and experiences, how others perceive him or her and the impact that he or she has on other people. The servant-leader takes the time to consider behavior and behave in a thoughtful and appropriate manner.

- **Listening.** The servant-leader listens first before acting. He or she listens in as many ways as possible including, oral and written communications, observing and watching what people are doing, asking questions.

- **Serving the team to serve management.** The servant-leader listens to what the people within the team need and serves them. By listening, the team shares information that's non-biased and complete and the team shares bad news as well as good. Well informed, the servant-leader can better serve top management.

- **Developing colleagues.** The servant-leader creates an environment in which the members can work, grow and learn. This develops the capabilities and experience of the team.

- **Coaching, not controlling.** Servant-leader strives to bring out the best work in the team members. This includes supporting the team to understand the goals of the project and then coaching and mentoring the team to reach those goals.

- **Unleashing the energy and intelligence of others.** The servant-leader encourages all the team members to make their maximum contribution. This includes allowing the team to make its own decisions and team members stepping up as leaders to make decisions and commit to results.

- **Foresight.** The servant-leader has the foresight to look ahead and see where the project is going. Without foresight, the leader is only reacting and this could endanger the project. This foresight allows the servant-leader to stay out front and lead the team.

## Situational leadership

An agile coach needs to coach and mentor the team in understanding the agile values, goals, and methods for realizing the project.

Coaching is the process of providing perspective, insight, and guidance to help an individual or team achieve improvements or changes in performance, learning, or development. Mentoring is transferring relevant knowledge and experience to an individual or team. Coaching and mentoring is all about helping to understand and apply the relevant aspects of the agile framework to achieve the project goals.

The style of coaching should vary depending on the team's maturity with agile practices and the team members' readiness to learn the new practices and unlearn old ones. The situational leadership model, developed by Hersey and Blanchard in 1969, offers a tool that helps agile coaches determine these factors, and choose the coaching style they should adopt.

## Situational leadership model

The following is a description of Hersey and Blanchard's situational leadership model (Figure 5-5).

#### THE LEADER'S BEHAVIOR AND DECISION STYLES

Task guidance describes to what degree the leader defines and directs the activities of the team. This includes setting goals; organizing what's to be done; directing how it's done, when it's done and who does it; and checking that it's done through regular interventions.

Support (Relationship) describes how the leader communicates with the team. This includes active listening, facilitating interactions, giving support, and providing feedback to the team.

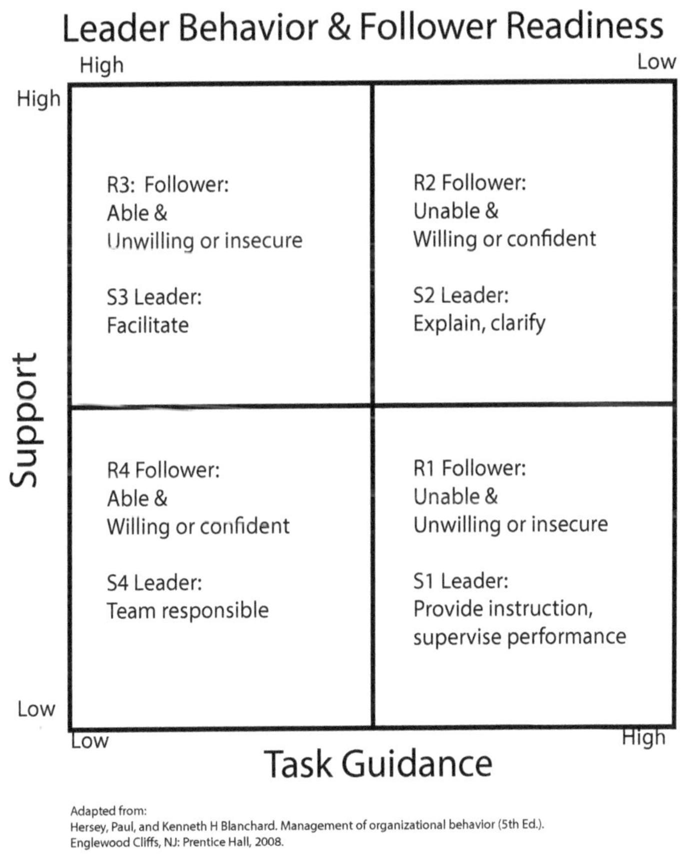


Figure 5-5 Hersey and Blanchard's situational leadership model

#### THE LEADER'S BEHAVIOR

**S1.** Telling—providing specific guidance and training on the agile methodologies and practices, and assessing the ability and willingness of the team members to adapt to the new practices.

**S2.** Selling—explaining, clarifying, and providing support on the agile practices. The team's ability and willingness should be understood. Leader-made decisions with discussion or explanation to the team.

**S3.** Participating—sharing ideas with the team and supporting the team with decision-making by encouraging and collaborating with the team. Team-made decisions with encouragement from the leader.

**S4.** Delegating—all responsibility for implementation is with the team; observing and monitoring the team. Team-made decisions.

#### THE FOLLOWER'S BEHAVIOR

'Ability' defines the team's knowledge, skills, and experience to perform the activity and as well as understand the activity. 'Willingness' defines the team's motivation and commitment to perform the activity, as well as its willingness to assume responsibility.

**R1.** Low—the team is unable, unwilling, and insecure. Training the team members on the practices (a 'telling' leadership style) is required.

**R2.** Moderate—the team is unable, but it's willing or confident.

**R3.** Moderate—the team is able, but it's unwilling or insecure.

**R4.** High—the team is willing, able, and confident in using the agile practices.

Overtime, the agile coach needs to adapt his or her style from teaching and enforcing the agile rules (at the early stages of team development) to coaching the team on applying the rules (in later stages); once the team is 'mature,' the coaches' main role is to provide guidance through different situations and scenarios.

The situational leadership model also describes the decision styles most appropriate for each level of team readiness. Within an agile project, the rules about who makes what decisions are clearly defined. Therefore, the agile coach must avoid making decisions even when the team is at low or moderately low levels of readiness. Whenever the team is responsible for decision making, participatory decision-making practices should be used.

## Active Listening

An agile coach needs to practice active listening. This requires not only hearing what a person says, but also observing the person's body language; understanding and comprehending the meaning, intent and emotion behind what was said; remembering and retaining what was communicated; and providing feedback on what's been heard and understood. The feedback can consist of repeating, paraphrasing, or reflecting upon what was heard; it's a way of confirming whether it's been understood correctly. When providing feedback, the agile coach shouldn't place any judgment on what the speaker has said.

There are different degrees of listening and providing feedback.

#### DEGREES OF LISTENING

- **Selective listening.** The listener hears the words spoken, but focuses on selected words or phrases that fit with their expectations. The listener doesn't try to understand everything that's said, only what's relevant to his or her specific topic.

- **Detailed listening.** The listener hears and tries to understand everything that's said: what's behind or meant by the words, both logically and emotionally.

- **Global listening.** The listener considers absolutely everything, including the words, the speaker's body language, the room temperature, background noise, etc., as well as and the thinking, perception and perspective of other cultures. He or she understands that cultural differences can influence communications exchange (Pisculli 2010).

#### DEGREES OF PROVIDING FEEDBACK

- **Repeating.** The first degree of providing feedback is repeating what was heard. The listener pays attention, remembers what's been heard, and repeats exactly the same words used by the speaker.

- **Re-stating or paraphrasing.** The next degree of providing feedback is adding some thinking and reasoning to what's been heard. The listener reformulates the message using words or phrases similar to those used by the speaker.

- **Reflecting.** The highest degree of feedback, the listener adds reasoning to what was heard, but provides feedback using his or her own words.

The agile coach should develop competencies to practice global listening. That requires the ability to work with people with different communication styles. Feedback should be provided without placing judgment on what's been heard.

## Failure and success modes

There are behaviors that can cause an agile coach to fail or succeed. Lyssa Adkins has documented personas and recommendations for the failure and success modes of agile coaches. We provide here is a short summary thereof:

### Failure modes

- Spends only enough time observing the team to pick up topics for the next retrospective
- Attends the daily stand-ups, gives the team well-intentioned observations or advice, and then leaves
- Often expresses opinions and gets attached to those opinions, losing the objectivity needed to coach the team
- Undermines team ownership by becoming an unnecessary middle man for meeting logistics, access requests and other administrative details
- Acts like the 'center of the universe' for communication between team members and for task-level coordination
- Floats from team to team, staying just long enough to give some piece of wisdom or pose a philosophical question
- Gets so involved in the details of the team's work that he or she gets lost details
- Helpfully reminds the team to start the stand-up, update the storyboard, complete tasks, and so on

### Success modes

- Asks questions that reveal what couldn't be seen before
- Genuinely wonders 'why' and is propelled by a curiosity about life and everything in it
- Hears everything but gives people room to grow by not responding to all of it
- Keeps it fun and light and just a little bit off-balance to jolt people out of complacency
- Asks the dumb question that sheds light on things
- Makes small moves that are imperceptible to the team but relentlessly pull them back, bit by bit, to the core of agile
- Bravely articulates possible futures waiting to be created
- Makes sure all voices are heard, especially those of the oppressed

## Summary

- An agile coach requires a broad range of skills for working with people. He or she has to develop the team from its initial inception through to being a mature, high-performing team capable of self-management. Understanding different techniques for facilitating collaboration, participatory decision making, and conflict resolution are essential methods the agile coach can utilize. One critical success factor is self-awareness, that is, understanding how one's own behavior affects others. Other success factors and tasks include:

- Establishing a clear goal for the team and taking steps to facilitate the team's forming its own identity and start collaborating; this is necessary to take the team from a working group to a team. The project chartering session, co-locating the team, and establishing ground rules are some activities that can be undertaken to form the team.

- Not taking over with problem solving and conflict resolution, which are the responsibility of the team members within a self-organizing team. The agile coach can facilitate problem resolution by coaching and mentoring the team when interpersonal issues arise, as well as by teaching the negotiation and critical-thinking skills.

- Respecting the team's responsibility for its own decision-making. The agile coach can support the team by leading them to practice participatory decision making on a daily basis and in meetings.

## Recommended reading

- Lyssa Adkins' book *Coaching Agile Teams* describes the responsibilities and working methods for the agile coach. She provides details on the skills, techniques and methods that an agile coach can use to develop into a seasoned mentor and coach.

- Jean Tabaka's book *Collaboration Explained* describes the content, structure, techniques, and tools for executing collaborative events.

- Kaner et al. offer practical advice on facilitating decision making in their book *Dynamics of Group Decision-Making.*

# Chapter 6 The Role of the Project Manager

The most popular agile methodologies such as scrum, extreme programming, and lean/Kanban processes, do not include a project manager role. The Agile Practice Guide, issued by the Project Management Institute in 2017, states that the "role of the Project Manager in an agile project is somewhat unknown" (PMI, 2017a, p. 37).

According to the *Project Management Body of Knowledge (PMBOK®) Guide*, "The project manager is the person assigned by the performing organization to lead the team that is responsible for achieving the project objectives" (PMI, 2017, p. 52). The agile coach (called scrum master in the scrum methodology) is responsible for "helping everyone understand Scrum theory, practices, rules, and values" (Schwaber & Sutherland, 2017, p. 7). There's a remarkable difference between the two roles.

The *PMBOK® Guide* sees the project manager in a command and control position over the project and team. The role of the agile coach as a servant-leader was discussed in chapter 5. In agile methodologies some — but not all — of the typical project management responsibilities have been distributed to other roles. The agile coach is not a replacement for the project manager. In fact, the product owner's responsibilities are closer to the project manager than that of the agile coach.

This section identifies the project management tasks that remain outside the agile project roles and are generally the responsibility of a project manager or the project sponsor.

## Project management tasks

Within the limits of a project, research shows that project managers engaged in agile projects have a non-traditional distribution of project management tasks (Miller, 2019). The project sponsor delegates management responsibilities to the product owner and the agile coach. The agile coach supports the team and the product owner with integrating agile practices, removing impediments, and resolving issues. The project team self-organizes to perform the work or tasks to achieve the project objectives. The product owner manages the stakeholders and the product scope. The different delegation and management styles required by different responsibilities is a valid reason to separate the project manager and coaching roles.

The following is a list of project management tasks that are typically retained by the project manager or the project sponsor.

Schedule

- Develop schedule
- Control schedule

Cost

- Estimate costs
- Develop budget
- Control costs

Quality

- Plan quality
- Perform quality control

Communication

- Plan communications
- Distribute information

Procurement

- Plan procurements
- Administer procurements
- Select suppliers

Stakeholders

- Identify stakeholders
- Manage stakeholders

## Summary

- Project managers are engaged in agile projects and continue to perform management tasks with an altered task distribution.
- The project manager and the agile coach are two different roles that should not be embodied by the same person.

# 2 Agile & Project Management

# Chapter 7 Integration

This chapter aligns with the *PMBOK® Guide* Project Integration Management knowledge area. As such, it covers the processes and activities needed to unify and coordinate the project and other knowledge areas. This chapter covers the following topics:

- Developing the project charter
- Developing the project management plan
- Directing and managing project work
- Managing project knowledge
- Monitoring and controlling project work
- Performing integrated change control
- Closing a project or phase
- Case Study: Betfair business case

## Developing the project charter

Agile projects are initiated with a chartering and business case process that's similar to that of traditional projects, and they end with a 'lessons learned' session called a retrospective. The project charter is the document that authorizes the team to conduct the project and guides them in their day-to-day decision-making.

## Chartering

Chartering describes the activities required to define the agile project charter it should include the vision, mission and success criteria for the project.

A chartering session is a very important collaborative event that the team performs to understand the project, the product they'll be producing, and the parameters and context of the project.

An agile project charter document is usually not very long — just a page or so. Nevertheless, it's critical for focusing the team on what they're producing and for understanding the reasons and justification behind the project and the product. The charter is also useful to frame the scope of engagement with the suppliers and vendors that will provide services on the project. The chartering document should include the following elements:

- **Vision**—why the project is being undertaken; that is, its purpose.
- **Mission**—what needs to be done to fulfill the project vision.
- **Success criteria**—the benefits the project should deliver to achieve the objective for which it's being undertaken.

The vision should cover the main characteristics of the product and the work that's needed to deliver the product, i.e. the product scope and the project scope.

Gregory Moore's (1991) "elevator pitch" (Figure 7-1) provides a framework for defining the purpose of the project (i.e. the product that should be produced during the project). It explains in a concise and clear way the purpose of the product, the target audience, and the expected competitive advantage. It's called an elevator pitch because the product vision should be explainable in the two-minute opportunity one gets when an executive steps into the elevator.

Figure 7-1 Geoffrey Moore's elevator pitch

## Project business case

The business case is the justification for performing the project. "Steering committees often categorically reject investment projects where the benefits are primarily qualitative or 'soft,' such as 'increased customer satisfaction' or 'an improved image'" (Ritter & Marburger, 2012, p. 1). Therefore, projects must be justified as good investments from a financial or a governance point of view. That is, while compliance projects are not optional, so they must be undertaken without regard to the financial business case. Other types usually require financial justification.

Creating a business case for most agile projects is not a simple mathematical problem. Projects are initiated for a number of reasons including soft factors such as 'improving customer satisfaction.' To build a quantified business case requires identifying the internal and external factors that influence customer satisfaction, quantifying the impacts of the different factors, and then building the financial model. Johannes Ritter and Frank Röttgers have published a pragmatic approach to building a business case in their book *The Definitive Guide to Getting Your Budget Approved.* The following are some of the justifications for projects, along with their related decision criteria.

#### COMPLIANCE

Compliance is a requirement to meet the criteria established by external regulation or internal governance policies. Projects undertaken for compliance reasons are usually mandatory.

#### RETURN ON INVESTMENT

The return on investment (ROI) is the difference between the gain from an investment and the cost of that investment.

- If ROI is greater than one, the project would add value to a company. Its benefits outweigh the costs. The project should be selected.
- If ROI is less than zero, the project would subtract value from the company. Its costs outweigh the benefits. The project should be rejected.
- If two projects are compared, select the project with the higher ROI.

#### NET PRESENT VALUE

Net present value (NPV) is the value of the investment once all of the costs are taken into consideration. NPV takes into consideration the future cost of money.

NPV = (present value of all cash inflows) - (present value of all cash outflows)

- If NPV is greater than zero, then the project would add value to a company. The project should be selected.
- If NPV is less than zero, then the project would subtract value from a company. The project should be rejected.
- If comparing projects, pick the project with the higher NPV.

#### INTERNAL RATE OF RETURN

The internal rate of return (IRR) is the discount rate where the present value of inflows equals the present value of cash outflows. It's outflows are measured as a percentage.

- If the IRR is greater than the interest rate of money (cost of capital), select the project.
- If the IRR is less than the interest rate of money (cost of capital), reject the project.
- If two projects are compared, pick the project with the higher IRR.

#### PRESENT VALUE

Present value (PV) is the future value (FV) of a payment discounted at the discount rate (R) a number of periods (N), where the discount rate is the interest payment used to calculate the present value of expected yearly benefits and costs.

- If two projects are compared, pick the project with the higher present value.

#### PAYBACK PERIOD

The payback period is the number of years required to recapture an initial investment. The discount rate is not taken into consideration for the payback period.

- If two projects are compared, pick the project with the shorter payback period.

## Developing the project management plan

The methodology used for a specific project engagement must be selected based on the characteristics of the project. It then needs to be customized and tailored to fit the organizational requirements. The project methodology will determine the type of plans required, as well as the phasing for creating those plans.

### Selecting an approach

The first step in planning the project is to select the appropriate methodology. The selection process and the considerations for selection are discussed in Chapter 16. An overview of some software development methodologies is provided as an appendix. The selected methodology will prescribe the practices, artifacts, events and processes for running the project. Nevertheless, none of the methodologies will provide a perfect fit for a specific project: all of them will have to be tailored.

Process tailoring is taking an existing process and changing it to meet your needs. After a methodology is selected, the process should be adjusted to fit the organization and the project requirements. Care should be taken to add just enough ceremony to deliver the project. See Chapter 16 for further information on tailoring the methodology to comply with regulations.

## Progressive planning

The agile methodologies are based on progressive planning, which uses the information that's known at the start of the project to create high-level plans; as more information and details are uncovered, the plans become more detailed. This allows the team to focus on creating plans for just the work at hand and avoid wasting time and effort on details that are likely to change. Agile plans usually have the following planning elements:

- **Roadmap planning** details the long-range planning for the product. It has a time horizon of a year or more and describes at a high level the upcoming releases.
- **Release planning** has a time horizon of quarter years and details the product scope across a number of iterations.
- **Iteration planning** has a time horizon that's equal to the duration of the iterations (usually monthly to bi-weekly). The iteration plan details the features to be included in the iteration.
- **Task planning** has a time horizon of a day and details the tasks that will be completed during the next 24 hours.

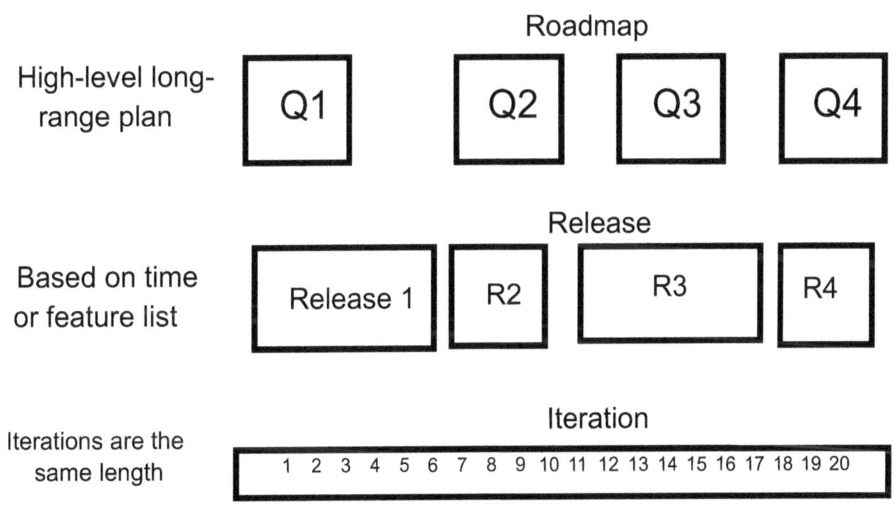


Figure 7-2 Planning roadmap

## Roadmap planning

A product roadmap is a visual overview of future — planned or proposed — product releases. It usually includes a high-level set of features or themes to be included in the product and a rough timeframe (usually quarters or years). It generally extends over two to three release cycles.

The product owner does the roadmap planning. The team supports the process by estimating the relative size of delivering the product themes and helping to understand a feasible delivery timeframe. The roadmap planning may take one or more meetings facilitated by the product owner.

## Release planning

Release planning is an activity to plan the goals, timing, and wish list associated with a release or shippable product. A release usually consists of one or more iterations and has a timeframe of one to three months.

The release plan assigns a date to the product release. The product owner is responsible for the release plan in conjunction with the team.

Release planning normally addresses the following topics:

- Success factors
- Definition of done
- Story estimation
- Decisions on iteration length
- Expected velocity
- User stories
- Selecting a release date
- Stories by iteration
- Number of iterations

The following section describes the topics covered in release planning.

- **Success factor**—the agreement between the parties as to what would make this release a success. The project can be date-driven or feature-driven. A date-driven project must release the product on a specific date with the features that are available at that time. A feature-driven project must release the product once it has a minimally agreed setup of features. The release criteria and any other necessary criteria should be discussed and agreed.

- **Definition of done (DoD)**—The DoD should be agreed to define what a potentially shippable product means to the team and the product owner. Work not yet done is 'undone work' — and it builds up over time. Undone work prevents the product from being shipped, so it should be avoided.

- The DoD may evolve over time. In the first stage, it may not include items that might be available and ready by subsequent iterations. Therefore, consider that the DoD isn't static over the life of the project. For example, stress and load testing may remain undone in the first iteration until the appropriate environment is established, starting only in the second or later iterations.

| Definition of Done |
|---|
| Coding |
| Unit test |
| All other testing |
| Maintenance documentation |
| Training manual |

Table 7-1 Sample definition of done

- **Prioritization**—Prioritize the user stories. (Chapter 8)

- **Estimate stories**—Estimate the size of each user story that may be considered for the upcoming release. (Chapter 8)

- **Risks**—Identify project risks and actions to manage them; prioritize the risk actions into the product backlog along with the user stories. (Chapter 13)

- **Iteration length**—Agree on the duration of the iteration timeboxes. The Agile Manifesto (2001) says "Deliver working software frequently, from a couple of weeks to a couple of months, with a preference for the shorter timescale." The duration should take into account how often the team requires feedback, how long it takes to deliver a reasonable scope, and the availability of the stakeholders to attend review sessions. (Chapter 8)

- **Expected velocity**—Estimate the velocity. (Chapter 8)

- **Select a release date**—Choose a date for the release and select the stories that should be included in the release.

- **Stories by iteration**—Assign stories as appropriate for each iteration. The product owner should select the stories for the first iteration and place them in a category for iteration one. This is a preliminary alignment as it's allowed to change for each release.

- At this time, stories can be optionally assigned to iterations two and later. Doing it at this stage is only necessary if activities need to be coordinated with other teams. Otherwise, it's up to the team to do it at this stage or during iteration planning, when it's likely to be more accurate.

- For large projects, feeding buffers should be included to protect sub-team schedules from slippage. A feeding buffer is a time contingency that's established to ensure that dependent features are delivered when needed.

- **Number of iterations**—Establish the number of iterations needed to deliver the scope.

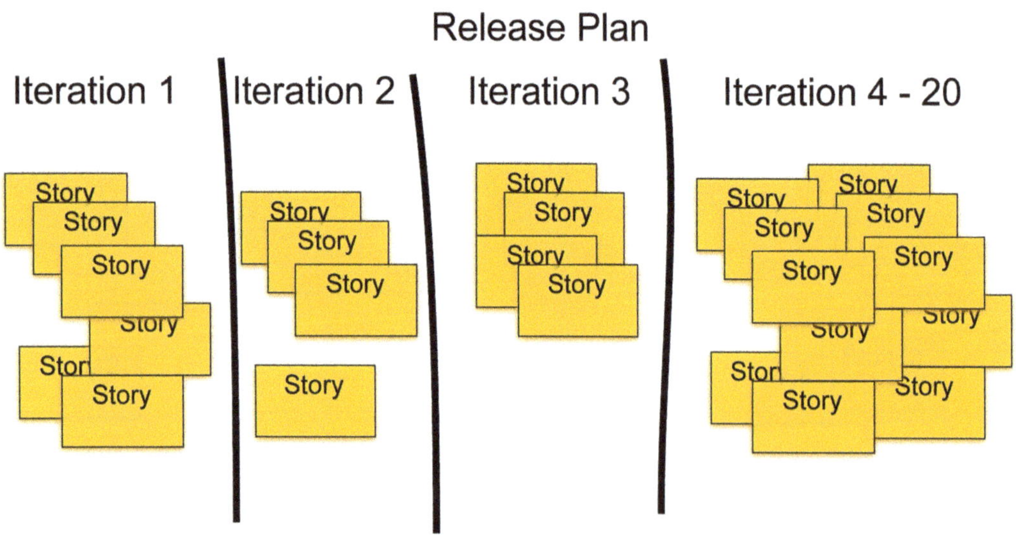


Figure 7-3 Release plan

#### Initial Release Planning

- The initial release planning workshop is likely to be longer and requires a deep-dive into more topics than the follow-on release planning workshops. Therefore, it may take more than a day and contain parallel sessions. The following are some considerations for first release planning:
- **Chartering workshop**—Discuss the project charter, the product vision, the expected business value, and project constraints.
- **Select requirements to study**—Select a subset of the product backlog (Larmen and Vodde recommend using 10 - 20% of the stories). Choose features that are important and cover a breadth of topics.
- **Requirements deep-dive**—Closely examine the selected requirements to understand them and split them into more detailed user stories.
- **Prioritize and size user stories**—Assign priority and size to the stories (in parallel workshops with different teams if necessary).
- **Technical and business risks**—Assign technical and business risks (in parallel workshops with different teams, if necessary).
- **Definition of done**—Define the DoD.
- **Product backlog**—Assign stories in the product backlog to the first release.
- **Retrospective**—Hold a retrospective.

### Iteration planning

The user stories for the iteration are selected, reviewed, and agreed in an iteration planning session. The entire team and the product owner attend the session. Iteration planning can be commitment-driven or velocity driven.

The first half of the iteration planning meeting is conducted with the product owner and team.

- **Establish goal**—The team establishes a goal for the iteration that outlines in a short, clear, focused statement what they want to achieve during the release (e.g. "implement sales reporting").
- **Target velocity**—The team determines its target velocity.
- **Priorities**—The priorities for the stories are adjusted as necessary. This is an activity for the product owner, and it's necessary, because iteration reviews or other events may have adjusted the priorities.

- **Requirements**—The user stories are discussed to clarify their meaning and content, to gather examples, to gather examples, and to make sure the team understands the full requirement.

- **Select stories**—Each user story contains an estimate (usually in story points or ideal days), and the team selects a volume of stories that can be completed in that iteration.

- **Risks actions**—Risk actions should be selected for implementation based on their priority in the backlog.

The second half of the iteration planning meeting is for the project team to determine the tasks and activities needed further to analyze, design, develop, test, document, and deliver the user stories or features. Specifically, the team's DoD is used as a basis for the iteration's activities. At this time, the team estimates the time effort to deliver the user stories.

- **Tasks (for scrum)**—Each task is written on a card with the estimated effort in ideal time, which is the time a person would spend working on the task if he or she had no interruptions and a good work environment.

- According to Mike Cohn "The tasks you create should be of an approximate size so that each developer is able to finish an average of one per day" (Cohn 2006, p. 156).

- **Stories (for Kanban**)—Kanban doesn't break the stories into tasks but prefers smaller stories that can be completed in a couple of days.

- **Story commitment**—the team decides on and confirms the user stories that can be delivered during the iteration.

- For commitment-driven plans, the team selects and estimates the stories one by one; selecting and estimating stories stop when the team capacity is depleted.

- For velocity-driven planning, the team selects the number of stories they can complete within their target velocity based on the high-level story estimates.

- Because velocity-driven planning uses high-level estimation data, it may not be as accurate as the commitment-driven method. Nevertheless, both are reasonable options for planning.

## Directing and managing project work

The project's product is delivered through iterative and incremental project iterations. Each iteration should deliver 'working software' based on the team's definition for delivering a completed product.

### Agile coaching

During the project execution, the agile coach is responsible for mentoring and coaching the project team in the delivery of the product, for supporting the product owner, and for managing the stakeholders.

### Daily stand-ups

A daily stand-up is a daily team meeting in which the team members share the status of the project, discuss the activities to be accomplished in the next 24 hours, and identify issues that are impeding progress. It's one of the key tools for communication among the team members and for ensuring continuous progress towards the project goals.

### Reviews

Demonstrations and reviews with the project stakeholders are held at the end of each iteration. At the reviews, the completed deliverables that are potentially shippable are demonstrated to the stakeholders, who provide feedback; the product backlog and plans for the next iterations are discussed.

### Progress updates

Productivity metrics and progress reporting are provided through burnup charts, burndown charts, and task boards that are managed by the team, as well as through velocity metrics that are measured after each iteration.

## Managing project knowledge

Explicit knowledge is codified in documents or systems using words, pictures, or numbers. Tacit knowledge is personal and not expressed in an easily accessible way. Agile projects offer opportunities to tap into the tacit knowledge through the high level of interaction between project team members and through events such as retrospectives.

## Monitoring and controlling project work

In agile projects, information radiators or big visible charts are used to monitor the work and project performance. The project progress is updated daily and at the end of an iteration to show how the project is proceeding in reaching its goal. This real-time update of information allows the team and the stakeholders to maintain visibility of the project status. The following are some of the progress information that may be used to monitor the project.

### Task board, Kanban board

A task board (or Kanban board) (Figure 4-1) is a visible project board that uses cards to represent a task, story, or feature. These cards are placed on a timeline (that is, the board) that represents the project workflow. The cards are pulled (that is, moved) through the workflow as team members are available to perform the work. Task boards are mounted in the team space or electronically, and they're updated daily by the team.

## Burndown chart

A burndown chart (Figure 4-2) shows planned and actual work remaining by the target end date. The vertical (y) axis measures the work remaining in story points or ideal days. The horizontal (x) axis has marks for iterations (for a release burndown) or the working days (for an iteration burndown) and the target end date. The burndown chart is created at the beginning of a release or iteration and updated with daily progress.

## Burnup chart

A burnup chart (Figure 4-3) shows how much work is included in the project and how much work is completed. The vertical (y) axis shows the work effort and the horizontal (x) axis shows the iterations. A release burnup chart is created at the beginning of the release and updated at the end of each iteration.

## Parking lot chart

The 'parking lot chart' (Figure 4-4), which originated with the feature-driven development (FDD) methodology, is a visual, low-maintenance way to report the progress of feature sets. The original parking lot chart has a box for each theme (a group of features) with indicators for the total number of features, the percentage complete, and the initials of the chief programmer. In FDD, the percentage complete is automatically calculated based on the milestone stage for each individual feature. To use a parking lot with other methodologies, it's necessary to decide how to treat these two metrics. One possibility is to eliminate the chief programmer; the percentage complete would be the number of completed story points divided by the total number of story points for the given theme.

## Velocity cycle time

Velocity (Figure 7-4 and Table 7-2) is a measure of the rate at which teams consistently deliver business value. It's the sum of the estimates of delivered (that is, accepted) features per iteration. A velocity diagram shows the target and actual velocity of the team over time. The vertical (y) axis shows the work effort (in story points or ideal days) and the horizontal (x) axis shows the iterations.

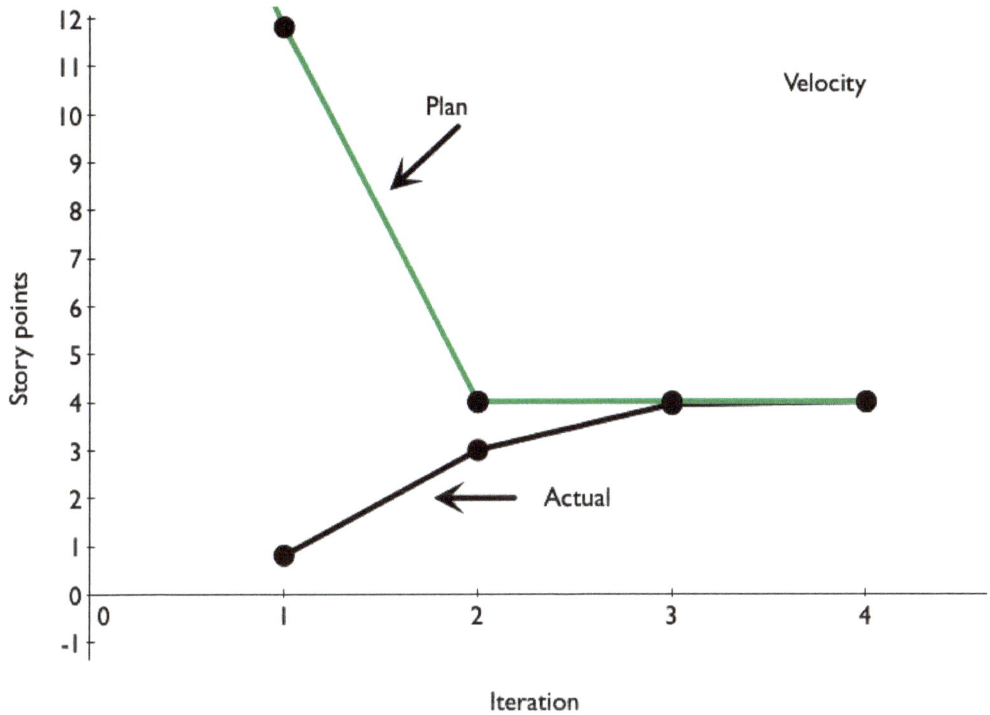


Figure 7-4 Velocity diagram

| Initial estimate | Iteration 1 | | Iteration 2 | | Iteration 3 | | Iteration 4 | |
|---|---|---|---|---|---|---|---|---|
| | Plan | Actual | Plan | Actual | Plan | Actual | Plan | Actual |
| 22 | 8 | 1 | 5 | 1 | 5 | 5 | 5 | 5 |
| | | 5% | | 20% | | 100% | | 100% |

Table 7-2 Velocity data

## Cumulative flow diagrams

A cumulative flow diagram (CFD) is a visualization chart that represents the status of features and stories over time. The vertical (y) axis defines the total number of features, the horizontal (x) axis shows time, and the depth (z) axis shows the status of the story in the project (e.g.

planned, in-progress, done). CFDs are valuable for gaining insights into the cycle times, completion dates, or project issues.

The CFD shows the work-in-progress (WIP), or the work started but not completed. By looking at the vertical (y) axis of the CFD, the number of WIP items can be determined. By looking at the horizontal (x) axis of the CFD, the cycle time can be determined. The cycle time helps to predict when the WIP is likely to be completed.

From a lean processing point of view, WIP is an investment that can only be translated into value when the work is completed. Thus, the number of WIP items should be kept as low as possible and cycle times should be kept as short as possible.

According to the theory of constraints, we should look for the bottlenecks in a system and focus on improving them. Bottlenecks result in limitations on the team's throughput. By separating WIP by activities, the CFD can be used to identify bottlenecks. An area in the CFD between the WIP items and the final activity identifies a bottleneck.

Once a constraint has been identified, it should be addressed. To address it, first understand what is the target throughput is and why it's not being achieved. Determine the changes to make to get the bottleneck point operating at its maximum capacity. This could mean making changes in one or more of the other process steps. If the bottleneck is already at full capacity, then changes may be needed at other process steps to achieve the desired throughput. Other options could include adding more capacity or changing the workflow. Once the changes are made, they should be given time to take hold and then the situation should be reevaluated to determine if further bottlenecks or issues occur.

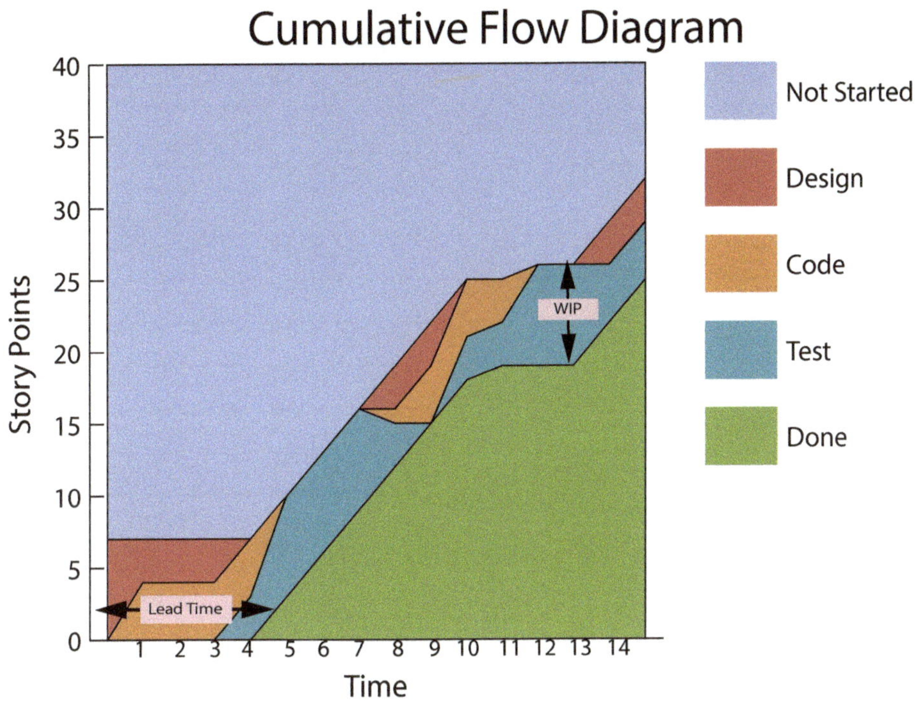


Figure 7-5 Cumulative flow diagram with WIP

## Earned value management

Earned value management (EVM) is not typically used as a management tool in agile projects. However, Tamara Sulaiman and Hubert Smits report that EVM has been proven statistically valid when at least 15% of the features are completed. Consequently, they propose the following strategy for using EVM in agile projects.

- Use the number of iterations, the number of story points, and the budget as the baseline data. If story points are added or removed, recreate the baseline.
- Evaluate the EVM at the iteration boundaries.
- Time to complete is derived from the number of iterations instead of relying on the work breakdown structures (WBS).
- The EVM formulas are adjusted to use the number of completed story points and iterations.

**EVM example case (Table 7-3):** A project has a budget of 735,722 money units, four iterations, and a scope of 120 story points, 60 of which are completed after three iterations with an actual cost of 367,861 money units.

| User Story/Feature | Estimated Story Points | Completed Story Points | Actual Cost |
|---|---|---|---|
| Financial plan by branch | 10 | 10 | 61,310 |
| Financial plan by product | 20 | 20 | 122,620 |
| Plan reconciliation and validation | 30 | 30 | 183,931 |
| Plan breakdown by month | 30 | | - |
| Plan review and acceptance | 30 | | - |
| | 120 | 60 | 367,861 |

Table 7-3 Earned value example data

The following list provides a summary of the EVM metrics using the example in Table 7-3.

**Expected percent complete** is based on the number of completed and total iterations. It's calculated from the number of completed iterations divided by the total number of iterations. Example: 75% = 3 / 4

**Actual percent complete** is the number of completed story points divided by the total number of story points. It represents the percentage of the total scope that is completed. Example: 50% = 60 / 120

**Planned value (PV)** is the value of the planned budget at a specific date. Example: 551,792 = 75% * 735,722

**Earned value (EV)** is the value of the completed story point at a specific date. Example: 367,861 = 50% * 735,722

**Actual cost (AC)** is the cost at a specific date. Example: 735,722

**Schedule performance index (SPI)** is a measure of schedule efficiency. If greater than one, the project is ahead of schedule; less than one, it's behind schedule; and equal to one is on schedule. It's calculated by dividing the earned value (EV) by the planned value (PV). Example: 0.87 = 367,861 / 551,792 (behind schedule)

**Cost performance index (CPI)** is a measure of cost efficiency. If it is greater than one, the project is under budget; less than one, over budget; and equal to one it is on budget. It is calculated by dividing the earned value (EV) by the actual cost (AC). Example: 1 = 367,861 / 367,861 (on-budget)

**Estimate at completion** forecast for **cost** is the amount of money needed to complete the work based on the actual expended cost and the estimate to complete. It can be calculated by adding the actual cost (AC) to the original budget (BAC) and subtracting the earned value (EV). Example: 735,722 = 367,861- 735,722 + 367,861

**Estimate at completion** forecast for **schedule** is the number of iterations that will be needed to complete the release. It can be calculated by dividing the number of iterations by the SPI. Example: 6 iterations = 4 / 0.5

## Performing integrated change control

Flexible change control is one of the principles of the Agile Manifesto. "Welcome changing requirements, even late in development. Agile processes harness change for the customer's competitive advantage." Therefore, the scope remains flexible throughout the project. The project duration and costs may be fixed.

The product backlog — along with feature prioritization, change business rules, and iteration planning — are used to manage the scope.

### Feature prioritization

The product backlog contains the features that should be implemented in the product. Feature prioritization places the most valuable features of the scope are the top of the backlog. Features should be developed based on their priority. The quantity of features delivered is determined by the team's velocity, i.e. the rate at which a feature can go from concept to completion. The prioritization foresees that the most valuable features are delivered with the highest priority.

### Change business rules

Change business rules are established to allow features to be added, deleted, or moved in the product backlog. (Chapters 8, 9, and 10)

The agile methodologies do not allow changes to the agreed work during an iteration or a backlog state. The iteration backlog is frozen once the scope is committed to by the product owner and the team.

### Iteration planning

Decisions on what will be included in the iteration are delayed until the last possible moment to allow for changes in the features to be delivered. Usually the scope of an iteration is decided on at the start of the iteration during the iteration planning.

# Closing a project or phase

## Retrospectives

A retrospective is a meeting where the project team reflects on and discusses a topic, including what was completed, what worked well, and what needs improvement. During the retrospective, the team should agree on what can be improved; the timeline and actions for realizing those improvements should be planned.

### Iteration retrospective

Held at the end of an iteration, an iteration retrospective (Figure 7-9) focuses on reviewing the product delivered and the process used in order to identify opportunities for improvement. The retrospective is attended by the project team and facilitated by the agile coach.

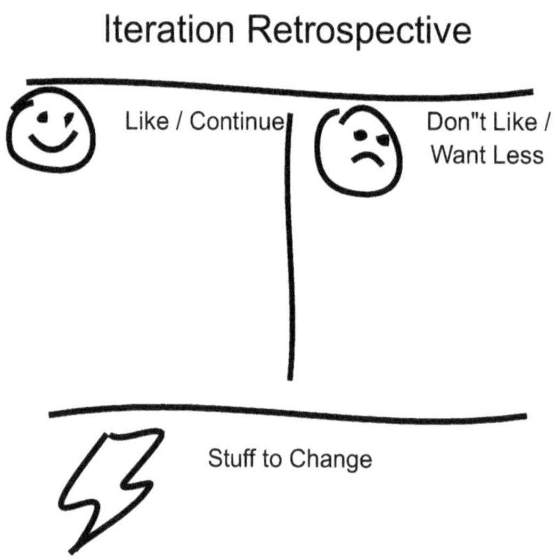


Figure 7-6 Iteration retrospective

### Project retrospectives

A project retrospective is a meeting where the project team reflects on and discusses the project, including what was completed, what worked well, what needs improvement.

### Process for conducting retrospectives

Esther Derby and Diana Larsen, in their book *Agile Retrospective: Making good teams great,* recommend the following process for conducting a retrospective:

1 **Set the stage**—Review the goals and agenda for the session and establish a collaborative working environment.

2 **Gather data**—Create a shared view of the objective and subjective facts. Discuss the facts from the individual team members' perspectives.

3 **Generate insights**—Review the big picture of the information gathered and dive deep into any topics that warrant further investigation.

4 **Decide what to do**—Identify and prioritize improvement opportunities.

5 **Close the retrospective**—Summarize the plans and commitment.

### Abnormal termination

The product owner can end an iteration at any time. Early stoppage of an iteration is called an abnormal termination. The product increment should be reviewed and a retrospective should be conducted.

## Summary

- A project charter is a brief statement that outlines the vision, mission, and success criteria for the project product. It should be used to guide the project team and project procurements.

- A methodology should be selected and tailored to include the right amount of ceremony to fit the project and organizational situation.

- Release planning identifies the stories that should be implemented in the next one to two releases; it assigns delivery dates to the releases. The initial release planning may include the chartering workshop, requirements deep dive, and risk planning.

- Iteration planning is used to agree on the detailed content of the user stories, confirm the user stories for the iterations, and break the stories into the tasks that must be completed during the iteration.

- During project execution, the team uses daily stand-ups, burnup charts, burndown charts, and task boards to monitor and manage progress. They use planning sessions to plan the scope of the iteration, and reviews to demonstrate the deliverable product to the stakeholders.

- Scope is managed by prioritizing features to deliver the most valuable features first, establishing business rules for addressing changes, and deciding on the iteration's scope at the last possible moment.

- Projects may be abnormally terminated for any reason. In all cases, projects close with a retrospective that reviews the lessons learned and opportunities for process improvement.

## Recommended reading

- *The Definitive Guide to Getting Your Budget Approved* by Johannes Ritter and Frank Röttgers provides a systematic guide for creating a financial business case. The book includes examples as well as the methods for using Monte Carlo simulations and sensitivity analysis to create the business case. The methods described in the book can also be used for quantifying risks and project costs.

- Mary and Tom Poppendieck's book *Lean Software Development:* An Agile Toolkit describes lean principles and the types of waste found in software projects.

- Esther Derby and Diana Larsen's book on *Agile Retrospective: Making good teams great* includes guidelines in the form of tools, tricks, and tips for designing and running effective retrospectives.

# Chapter 8 Scope

This chapter aligns with the *PMBOK® Guide* Scope Management knowledge area, and it covers the activities needed to ensure that a project includes the work needed to deliver a working solution. Since agile projects break down work based on product features and not tasks, the 'create WBS' process is not applicable (N/A). This chapter covers the following topics.

- Planning scope management
- Collecting requirements
- Defining and validating the scope
- Controlling the scope

## Planning scope management

There's no big requirements or design document prepared up-front (BRUF) before the development team is engaged. Instead, requirements are collected in small increments and documented as individual user stories or product features. The user stories are progressively elaborated throughout the project to add more details through discussions with developers, test cases, and examples. The user stories are prioritized into a product backlog. The prioritization should identify the minimal set of features to be delivered.

Agile requirements are composed of:

- A user story or product feature that describes the needed capability
- A conversation that occurs between the developer and the customer to add details to the user story
- Examples that illustrate what's expected from the user story

- Tests that define what the developer needs to know in order to determine when the story is done, i.e. the acceptance test for that story.

Once an iteration ends, user stories have no further formal role in the project; they may, however, be retained for future reference. They aren't use cases or IEEE 830 requirements (see Table 8-1). The life spans and definition styles of user stories are different from these items.

| User Story | Requirement | Use Case |
|---|---|---|
| Describes a feature needed by a role | Describes all the requirements the system must have | Describes a process and the user's interaction with the process |
| Created before the analysis stage; contains just enough information to trigger discussion | Detailed definition of what the system must do; documented in requirements specification | Created after analysis; contains complete details |
| Is no longer needed after implementation | Has an indefinite lifespan | Exists as long as the product is in use |

Table 8-1 Comparison of user stories, requirements, use cases

The scope management plan should identify:

- The format and collection method for the user stories
- The prioritization method for the product backlog
- The format for the product backlog

The following section provides details on the content of user stories, as well as techniques for gathering and writing user stories.

## User stories or product features

A user story is a requirement or a feature that should be implemented in the product. It's written from the user's (or customer's) point of view and contains the information needed to estimate the effort required to implement it.

User stories should be gathered in different sizes (level of details) and they will change over time. A theme is a high-level topic that's a collection of related user stories; an epic is a large user story. Individual user stories or features are listed in a product backlog. They're used for planning, discussing details between the customer and developer, and evaluating whether the story is complete.

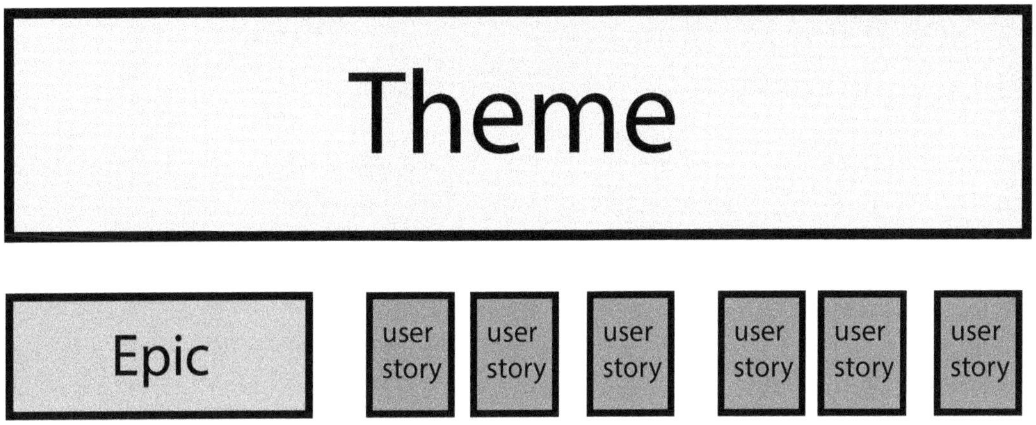


Figure 8-1 User story levels

The product backlog consists of all user stories and features that should be included in the product. The product owner (or customer) is responsible for the product backlog. He or she collects the requirements from the stakeholders and user community. Anyone can add items to the product backlog. An analyst may support the product owner. (See Chapter 12) In any case, the product owner is the single person responsible to the team for providing the requirements.

The iteration backlog consists of the stories that should be implemented in a given iteration. The iteration backlog is agreed on by the team and the product owner during the iteration planning meeting. The team owns the iteration backlog, and only the team can change it.

The following is a description of the content of user stories. In his book *User Stories Applied* (2004), Mike Cohn provides significant insights and details on what user stories are, how to write them, and their characteristics.

**Author.** The customer writes the user stories since the stories should be written in business language and the user knows what features he or she expects in the system. While it may be challenging for a typical user to write a user story, there are specific techniques described later in this chapter to facilitate the process (see 'Gathering user stories'). In addition, the team may have a business analyst that can support the product owner and users in performing this activity.

**Story cards.** User stories are written on cards although they may also be documented in an electronic system. They include just enough information to act as a reminder to the development team and the customer of the functionality needed.

User story cards contain:

- A phrase or two about the feature
- Optionally, notes about issues to be resolved when implementing the user story
- Details are written as tests on the back of the story card.

Cards, rather than electronic systems, are preferred, as it's easier for multiple people to create the cards. They're easy to move around and change during collaborations.

**Tests.** Tests are the way the customer plans to evaluate whether the story meets their requirements. These tests are written on the back of the story card. The tests are used by the development team and the customer to know if a story is finished. An agile tester may support the customer in writing the tests. (See Chapter 11)

**Story characteristics.** User stories must be INVEST-worthy: independent, negotiable, valuable, estimable, small and testable.

#### INDEPENDENT

Stories should avoid being dependent upon other stories. Dependencies between stories cause difficulties with prioritizing the story in the backlog. It can also present problems with estimating and planning. To avoid dependent stories, they can be combined into one larger story and split up again in a different way that makes them independent.

#### NEGOTIABLE

The details about how a feature is to be developed are negotiated between the customer and the developer. The user stories are short descriptions of the feature. The details of a feature emerge in a discussion between the customer and the developer. These details, as they are discussed and agreed upon become the tests that will be used to evaluate when the feature is completed. The tests are written on the back of the card. Items that come out during the discussion that are worth noting may be recorded on the front of the card.

#### VALUABLE

A feature can be valuable to the person who will use the system (the user) or it can be an attribute important to the buyer of the system (the purchaser). The user story should be valuable to either the user or the purchaser. The story should demonstrate the value to one of these audiences.

### ESTIMATE-ABLE

The developer should be able to estimate the size of a user story based on the information on the story card and the discussion with the product owner. This estimation is not necessarily the number of days to implement the story, but a forecast of the effort, complexity, and potential risks in implementing the story.

Developers may not have the domain or technical knowledge to estimate the story or the story may be too large to estimate.

- Lack of domain knowledge requires further discussions with the person who wrote the story to understand the necessary details.
- Lack of technology knowledge may require a 'spike.,' which is a brief investigation or experience to learn about and understand the new topic area.

Stories that are too large to estimate are called epics; they should be disaggregated into smaller stories. Epics can be compound or complex.

- Compound epics are made up of several constituent stories, and they should be split into multiple smaller stories.
- Epics can be complex for different reasons. If it's complex due to a lack of understanding, it may be split into a research story and the actual feature. The actual feature can be better defined after the research, but the product owner should still prioritize it.

### SMALL

Stories should be small enough to use them for planning, but not too small. While too-large stories such as epics should be disaggregated, too small or tiny stories, such as bug reports or user interface changes, should be combined into stories that require between a half-day and several days of work.

A story should be something that can be implemented in an iteration.

In a blog post (2005), Bill Wake described "Twenty Ways to Split Stories" based on how easy or difficult it is to engineer or implement the product features. The categorization method can be used to break large stories into multiple smaller stories or to prioritize the value of the story. The following are a few examples of the splitting topics proposed by Bill.

| | | |
|---|---|---|
| Batch | -vs- | Online |
| Static | -vs- | Dynamic |
| Ignore Errors | -vs- | Handle Errors |
| Single User | -vs- | Multi-User |

Table 8-2 Options for splitting stories

#### TESTABLE

A user story must be testable so that the developers know when they've successfully implemented the features. Nonfunctional requirements may be non-testable. Automated tests should be defined whenever possible — 99% automated test should be the goal.

## Gathering user stories

Agile methodologies promote a participatory design, where the users become part of the team designing the behavior of their software. User stories facilitate participatory design, as the users are required to provide the content for the stories. The following are some techniques for gathering user stories.

### Interviews, observations and questionnaires

Interviews, observations and questionnaires are a few good ways to capture requirements. For the best results, use a combination of these techniques, plus open-ended questions, and involve the team and the customer in a collaborative event.

### Story writing workshops

A story writing workshop involves anyone who can write stories; it relies on brainstorming and a low-fidelity prototype (paper, flip chart, or a whiteboard), innovation games, or story mapping to write as many stories as possible. The prototype and story maps developed during the workshop are used to identify features and show high-level interactions with the system. Innovation games are used to identify user stories and their priority.

## Brainstorming

Brainstorming is a technique for a group to generate ideas. The following is the process for brainstorming.

- Select a topic.
- A facilitator is identified and ground rules for the session are established. Typical ground rules include all ideas are accepted; nothing is out-of-bounds; no criticism of an idea or person is accepted; people should not be interrupted when speaking.
- Every individual thinks about the topic and writes down (or calls out) as many ideas as possible.
- All ideas are captured on a board.
- All ideas are discussed and grouped.
- All ideas are ranked for their appropriateness.

## Innovation games

Innovation games are a technique for engaging the stakeholders in collecting user stories. They're a fun way to collaborate with the customer or user to understand their needs and requirements. In his 2007 book *Innovation Games: Creating Breakthrough Products Through Collaborative Play,* Luke Hohmann describes 12 innovation games; here are a few of:

### THE APPRENTICE

The 'Apprentice' requires a team member to navigate through the system while other team members observe. The team member uses the system the way a customer would so that they understand the challenges and views of the customer. He or she makes observations and comments on the features, functionality, and usability of the system. The goal is to take a fresh look and generate ideas for how it might be improved or changed.

### BUY A FEATURE

In 'Buy a Feature,' stakeholders are given a fixed budget. They're shown features along with their estimated prices, and the stakeholders have to decide which features to purchase for that budget.

### BANG-FOR-THE-BUCK

'Bang-for-the-Buck' is a game in which the stakeholders collaborate to prioritize the product backlog based on value and risk. The goal is to have the stakeholders prioritize what's important and valuable.

**Easy / Less Effort** **Hard / More Effort**

Manual -vs- Automated

#### DESIGN THE PRODUCT BOX

In 'Design the Product Box,' stakeholders design the retail box or carton that they would use to sell the product in retail stores. The goal is to have the stakeholders identify the features that are most important to the consumer.

#### PRUNE THE PRODUCT TREE

For 'Prune the Product Tree,' the stakeholders place the product features on a tree drawn on the whiteboard. The core or main functionality is the base of the tree, bigger features are on the tree's larger limbs, and other features are placed on smaller limbs. The goal is to shape how the product should evolve and grow.

#### 20/20 VISION

'20/20 Vision' places the features in their relative order of importance on the whiteboard. The goal is to order the features from most to least important.

#### GIVE THEM A HOT TUB

'Give Them a Hot Tub' transforms extreme or outrageous features into something the customer would use or buy. The team generates a set of extreme features and discusses them in a collaboration round with the customer. The product's outrageous features are described to illustrate their usefulness. The goal is to transform seemingly extreme features into useable ones.

### Force field analysis

Force field analysis is a way to analyze the forces for and against (or pros and cons) when moving towards a goal. It can be used for planning the solution for or identifying the causes of an issue. To use this technique, describe the current situation and the desired situation, and then use brainstorming to generate ideas for or against the desired situation. Analyze the results and plan a course of action to eliminate or weaken the forces against the solution.

### Root cause analysis

Root cause analysis is a method for evaluating the source of an issue. A cause and effect diagram (also called fishbone or Ishikawa diagram) is drawn to show the different causes of an issue and their relationship.

### Five whys

The 'five whys' is simple: One asks "why?" five times to get to the bottom of a problem. To use the technique, you ask why the problem occurred. Based on the answer, you ask why with regard to the response. The querying continues five times; by the fifth time, you should have reached the root cause.

## Writing user stories

The following are some recommendations and considerations for writing user stories.

**Story format.** One approach is behavior-driven development (BDD), which starts by first identifying the expected business outcome, and then the feature set that will deliver that outcome. Each feature becomes a user story with its own acceptance criteria or tests.

The format should include a title and information on the role of the user, the function they need, and the value they should derive from the function. The following is a sample format (see Figure 8-2):

**As a (role), I want to (function) so that I can (business value).**

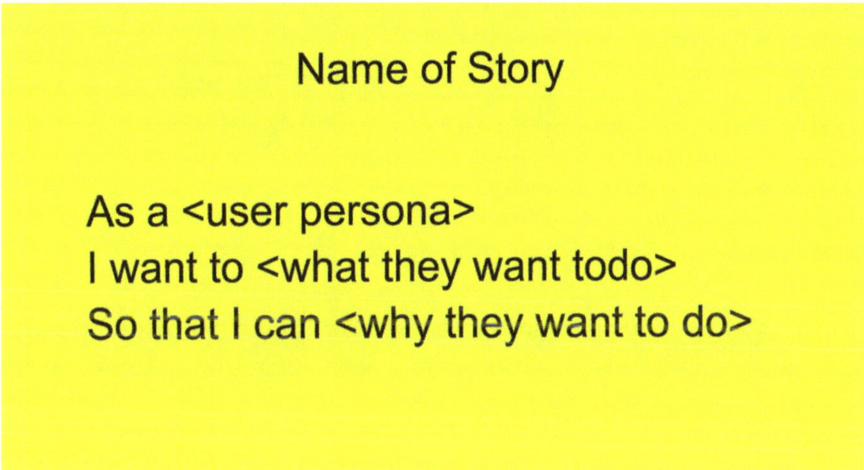


Figure 8-2 Sample story card

**Title** makes it easier to reference the story; it should describe an activity that the user has to perform.

**Role** defines the characteristics or attributes of typical system users and their intended interactions. It could be represented by a persona or an extreme character.

- A persona is an imaginary representative that personalizes a user role to an individual with a personal background, and even a picture. Personas should be created based on market and demographic research to ensure that they represent the target audience.
- Extreme characters are personas that exemplify extraordinary characteristics of the target audience, for example, a 90-year old end user who has never used a computer before. Such a person would have a completely different need than someone who uses a computer on a daily basis. Using extreme characters helps to derive requirements that may not otherwise be identified.

**Function** describes the capability that the user requires. Ideally, the function should finish with a completed activity, not an on-going activity. It should allow the user to feel that something has been accomplished. For example, "As a webmaster, I want to manage a website" is something that never ends. "As a webmaster, I want to add and delete web pages" is a task that can be checked as completed. Stories that end with an accomplishment are called 'closed stories.'

**Business value** should explain the importance of the function or the value it provides.

**Tests (acceptance criteria).** In BDD, the tests are scenarios that describe what should happen based on the feature. The format for the test could be:

**Given (context) when (event), then (outcome)**

There may be more than one scenario for a single feature.

- **Context** describes some background or environment that triggers the feature. The context can be compound and include more than a single statement.

- **Event** describes the feature.

**Outcome** describes what should happen when the feature is used.

**Time horizon.** Stories are worked on and detailed by priority (and not before). Therefore, stories that will be implemented in the near-term have more details than stories that will be implemented in the future.

**User interface.** Details on the user interface should be kept out of the story for as long as possible to avoid mixing requirements with solution specifications.

**Non-user stories**. Not all requirements fit into the story format! Such requirements should be documented in an appropriate format. For example, guidelines that layout the user interface may require examples, widgets, screenshots, etc. These may be documented in a user interface guidelines document.

**Constraint stories.** Constraints are restrictions that must be obeyed. They're not directly implemented in the system, but they're useful reminders to developers and for implementing acceptance tests. Constraint stories are not estimated or planned into iterations. An example would be "Users should never be able to enter an invalid postal/zip code."

**Single user**. Write the story for a single user role, unless it's important to imply that multiple people can perform the action.

**Active voice.** Write using active verbs, not in the passive tense.

**No numbering.** Don't number cards! It may become confusing when stories are split or prioritized.

## Prioritization

Agile prioritization uses one of several techniques to rank the features and user stories in terms of value and risks. Prioritization creates an order of importance, identifying the order in which items should be delivered.

User stories or features can be prioritized according to technical and customer factors:

- Technical—risk
- Technical—impact on other stories
- Technical—readiness of peripheral systems
- Customer—desirability for all users
- Customer—desirability for important users
- Customer—cohesiveness to other users
- Customer—readiness of organization/processes.

The goal of prioritization is to deliver the highest possible value to the business with each project iteration. With the help of the team, the product owner is responsible for prioritizing the user stories and features in the product backlog. Nevertheless, the preference is for customer-valued prioritization. This method engages the customer in the process of prioritizing the features that are incorporated into the product.

The following sections describe some of the techniques for prioritizing user stories or features.

### Story maps

A story map is a two-dimensional view of the product backlog that organizes user stories to show the priority of stories and their relationship to one another.

Story maps, popularized by Jeff Patton (2008) (see Figure 8-3), are a type of product roadmap that shows the importance of a sequence for features by classifying them as 'backbone,' 'walking skeleton,' or 'additional' features.

The key steps for creating a story map are as follows:

- Place the features horizontally in a sequential order that represents usage sequence or workflow. It's a time sequence.

- Place the features vertically to indicate how much the feature is used in the business process (that is, from 'always used/critical' to 'seldom used'). The most-used features go at the top; less-used features go toward the bottom. This defines the order of criticality.

- Identify logical breaks in the business process flow (e.g. by function or user group) with vertical lines.

- Identify groups of features that logically belong together, that cut through business processes. This group of features is called a 'system span.'

- The first system span for release should be the "bare bones minimum anyone could legitimately do and still use the system" (Patton, 2005, p. 22). This small segment of features at the top is the 'backbone.' They must be implemented. The features further down from the top are the 'walking skeleton' and must be prioritized for implementation.

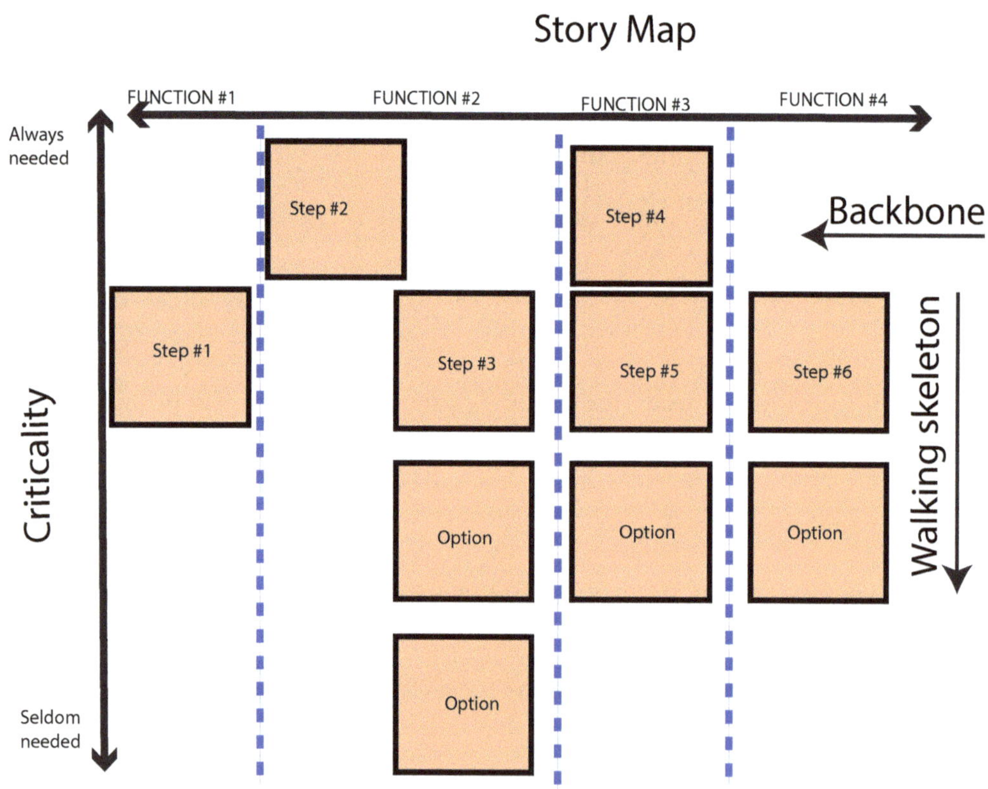


Figure 8-3 Story maps (Jeff Patton)

### Kano Model

The Kano model, developed by Professor Noriaki Kano, (see Figure 8-4) classifies a product's attributes based on customer preferences. The model is very useful in helping a design team to view requirements from a customer's point of view. It focuses on the differentiating attributes rather than basic customer needs.

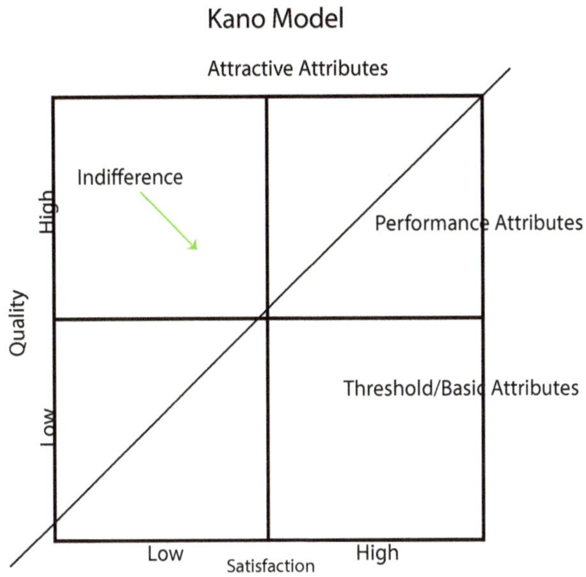


Figure 8-4 The Kano model

Based on quality and customer satisfaction, the model classifies the product features as follows:

**Attractive attributes (exciters)**—These provide satisfaction when achieved fully, but don't cause dissatisfaction when not fulfilled. Since they're unexpected, they delight the customer when present.

**One-dimensional quality (competitive)**—These attributes are expected in the product and are competitive differentiators.

**Must-be quality (basic)**—These attributes are considered baseline capabilities. When they're not present, the customers are dissatisfied.

**Indifferent quality**—Attributes that have no impact on the customer—neither good nor bad.

**Reverse quality (dissatisfiers)**—These are sophisticated attributes that may not appeal to all customers.

The Center for Quality of Management Journal published a special edition on "Kano's Method for Understanding Customer-defined Quality." It describes details as well as examples for applying the Kano model. The following steps are adapted from those recommended by the journal for using the Kano model for feature prioritization.

1 Create a list of product features. They should be written from the customer's viewpoint and address the problems that the product feature solves for the customer. They shouldn't be written from a technical viewpoint of *how* the problem is solved.

2 Formulate the Kano questionnaire using functional (positive) and dysfunctional (negative) questions. The answer key for both types of questions should include the level of 'like', 'neutrality' and 'dislike' for the feature. (See Figure 8-5)

3 The customer should be provided the questionnaire in an interview, focus group, or survey format.

4 The responses should be combined into an evaluation table (see Figure 8-6), the results analyzed for the customer's level of satisfaction or dissatisfaction of the features, and the features mapped to the Kano matrix. Using the frequency of the response is the simplistic method for consolidating and interpreting the results.

5 The classification should determine the prioritization of the features into the backlog. Must-haves would be the first priority, satisfiers next, and then attractive attributes.

| | | |
|---|---|---|
| Functional | How would you feel if the product had feature X? | 1. I like it that way<br>2. It must be that way<br>3. I am neutral<br>4. I can tolerate it that way<br>5. I dislike it that way |
| Dysfunctional | How would you feel if the product did not have feature X? | 1. I like it that way<br>2. It must be that way<br>3. I am neutral<br>4. I can tolerate it that way<br>5. I dislike it that way |

Figure 8-5 Sample Kano questionnaire

Dysfunctional:
"How would you feel if the product DID NOT have feature X?"

Functional:
"How would you feel if the product HAD feature X?"

| Product Feature | I like it | It must be | I am neutral | I can tolerate | I dislike it |
|---|---|---|---|---|---|
| I like it | Q | A | A | A | O |
| It must be | R | I | I | I | B |
| I am neutral | R | I | I | I | B |
| I can tolerate | R | I | I | I | B |
| I dislike it | R | R | R | R | Q |

Kano Response Matrix

Legend: Q-Questionable, R-Reverse, A-Attractive, B-Basic, I-Indifferent, O-One-dimensional

Figure 8-6 Kano response matrix

## MoSCoW approach

The MoSCoW approach is a prioritization model that classifies items in terms of Must-have, Should-have, Could-have, and Won't-have at this time. Rules should be applied to define each category of items. DSDM "Atern The Handbook" (2008) suggests that:

**"Must-haves"** are the minimum features needed to make it legal, safe, and fulfill the business case — or put simply, it's not worth doing the project if those features aren't included. As a rule of thumb, DSDM recommends that must-haves' not exceed 60% of the project effort.

**"Should-haves"** include features that are important, but not vital; it may be painful without them, but the solution is still viable, and a workaround may be needed. The DSDM rule of thumb is that features in this category shouldn't exceed 20% of the project effort.

**"Could-haves"** include features that are wanted or desirable but have less impact if left out. The rule of thumb for could-have features is also 20%.

**"Won't-haves"** at this time includes features that are agreed by the team not to be delivered, but they remain on the list so they're not lost.

### Requirements prioritization model

The requirements prioritization model is a ranking approach that considers both the positive benefit and the negative impacts of delivering a feature.

The steps for creating the model include the following:

- List all the requirements
- Estimate the relative benefit on a scale of 1 to 9
- Estimate the relative penalty (customer impacts of not having the feature) also on a scale of 1 to 9
- Customers rate the benefit score
- Developers estimate the relative cost
- Developers estimate the relative degree of risk (for implementing the feature)
- Calculate the priority number based on these factors
- Sort the list of features in descending order, according to what should be implemented first.

In 1999, Karl E. Wiegers of Process Impact published an article, *First Things First: Prioritizing Requirements,* outlining this method of prioritization.

### Pareto principle

The Pareto principle, also known as the 80/20 rule, is a rule (for most events) that says large percentages (80%) of effects come from 20% of causes. At the XP2002 conference, Jim Johnson (2002) from the Standish Group reported:

- A DuPont study showed that 25% of the product features were needed and 75% were nice-to-have
- A Standish study showed that most product features and function usage are rarely (19%) or never (45%) used

In agile projects, the Pareto principle can be used to select the features that will produce the maximum effect.

### Minimally marketable feature

A minimally marketable feature (MMF) is the smallest set of functionalities that must be realized for the customer to perceive value from the product. Whether 'must-have' as in DSDM, 'basic/must-be attributes' as in Kano, 'backbone' as in Jeff Patton's story maps: each represents a definition for MMF.

## Economic Prioritization

The project's business case and the reason it was undertaken in the first place are important factors when prioritizing features based on their economic value. Therefore, the business case and product vision are necessary inputs before assigning financial values to product features (see "Developing a project charter" in Chapter 7). Since projects are undertaken for many reasons, soft factors such as 'better customer satisfaction' are best quantified by conducting a cost-benefit-analysis that attempts to quantify all positive aspects—the benefits—and all negative aspects —the costs or expenses—to determine if a project will bring a positive financial benefit to the organization. The underlying data in that quantification should also form inputs before assigning economic value to product features.

User stories or product features can be prioritized according to their economic value by considering their revenue potential, operational efficiency, or development costs. This section describes the information you may want to collect to assign economic values to product features. Johannes Ritter and Frank Röttgers's book *The Definitive Guide to Getting Your Budget Approved* provides information on gathering the revenue and cost benefits for a project as well as methods for quantifying the economic values.

**Revenue potential.** The revenue potential of a product feature is based on the revenue that could be produced by having that feature in the product. The underlying question is how the organization's revenue stream would change if that feature were available. Might the product:

- Attract new customers or new markets (acquisition)?
- Reattract customers that defected to a competitor (reactivate)?
- Be upgraded and the price increased (upsell)?
- Retain existing customers that would otherwise defect (retention)?
- Be sold to a new segment of existing customers (cross-sell)?

The revenue potential for each story would depend upon how the feature would affect the organization's revenue. Acquiring new customers and cross-selling to the existing customers could mean new revenue streams for the organization. Retaining customers could mean retaining revenue that would have otherwise been lost. Upselling could mean adding incremental revenue from existing customers. The sales potential for each feature would have to be estimated by the organization's product managers or salesforce to derive the revenue potential.

One also needs a process to collect the data and assign it an economic value. The information could be collected through market research, interviews, surveys, or workshops. The economic value could be assigned by revenue source (acquisition, upsell, cross-sell) or revenue type (new, incremental, retained). The timeframe for the revenue source should also be collected; that is, after the product release how many months, quarters or years would it take before this revenue would be earned? The revenue stream is then normalized based on time (i.e. considering the time value of money) (See "Developing the project charter" in chapter 7).

The product features are then be ranked from highest to lowest based on their impact on revenue potential.

**Operational efficiency.** If the product feature provides efficiency to the organization, it may be quantifiable (e.g. cost savings or avoidance) or non-quantifiable (e.g. better user-friendliness). To assign an economic value, determine how the organization could reduce/avoid spending money that it would previously have spent (i.e. cost savings) or reduce/avoid the use of resources. These figures are usually quantified by evaluating their spending amounts or their fully loaded resource costs.

Information on the operational efficiency of the features can be collected through interviews, surveys, or workshops with project stakeholders, functional and executive managers, and the finance function. The timeframe for cost savings or avoidance should also be collected; that is, after the product release, how many months, quarters or years would it take for the savings to be realized? The cost impact is then normalized based on time (i.e. considering the time value of money).

**Development costs.** Since each user story will require an effort to implement, that effort can be translated into an economic value. Specifically, estimate the size of the story (see *Estimate activity durations and resources* in Chapter 9), the value per unit of size (see *Estimate costs* in Chapter 10), and assign the development cost to feature based on its size multiplied by its cost per unit. For example, if the size is 10 ideal days, and the cost per ideal day is 1000, the development cost is 10,000. This information provides a relative sizing for each feature and allows the product owner (and stakeholders) to make decisions about the features to implement.

## Personal experience: Release prioritization: silence is golden

### —David Moran, Product Manager & Agile Blogger

> An important part of release planning involves setting priorities. Our management team regularly reviews and prioritizes our product backlogs with our product owners, and we've found the affinity technique far superior to debating the merits and priority of each and every feature.
>
> As pre-work, the product owner prepares epic or feature-level user stories on cards. To make sure that we have a common understanding, the product owner quickly reviews the user stories with us, presenting them in what he or she feels is an appropriate priority order. Once each

user story is reviewed, the cards are placed on a table from left to right, with the left-most user story being the highest-priority item. When all cards are on the table; (or this could be a wall if you need the space), we set a time limit; the management team uses the affinity technique to refine the priorities.

The affinity technique requires silence! We begin moving cards around based on what we think their order should be, and a couple of trends always seem to emerge. Generally, there is little doubt about what is a low priority. User stories are moved to the back and stay there. (We always seem to agree on what's not a priority.)

I have personally been involved with moving something up in priority only to have someone else move it down in favor of another user story. In these situations, I wait and see what other items are moved around, and if I still don't agree, I move it back. If another person again places another user story above 'mine', I make a note of it. Once the time limit expires, we all talk about why differences of opinion on some items existed. We've found that the affinity technique allows you to eliminate a lot of unnecessary conversations about things on which you clearly agree. This allows you to focus on the cases where priorities have been 'questioned' by the way the user story cards were moved around; from there it's a simple matter to reach a final agreement on the overall product priorities.

Another tip: Don't try to look too far down the road. We typically perform this exercise on a quarterly basis. We certainly have ideas about what we need to do long-term, but we always defer on definitive prioritization until the last responsible moment—when our teams are getting close to being able to work on what we prioritize.

## Defining and validating the scope

In agile projects, the scope becomes more precise and detailed through the three planning stages roadmap, release, and iteration planning. Table 8-2 describes the content evolution of the user stories through the different stages of planning.

| Stage | Level of Detail | Source |
|---|---|---|
| Roadmap | Theme | Product owner |
| | Release assignment | |
| | Relative size | Team |
| Pre-release planning | Title, role, function, business value, test | User(s) |
| | | Product owner |
| | Priority | Product owner |
| | Iteration assignment | |
| Release planning | Size | Team |
| | Dependencies | |
| Pre-iteration planning | Priority (updated) | Product owner |
| Iteration planning | Examples, test | User(s) |
| | | Product owner |
| | Ideal days, schedule | Team |
| | Tasks | |
| Review | Acceptance | Product owner |
| | | Stakeholders |
| Retrospective | Archive | Team |

Table 8-3 Content life cycle of a user story

Feedback is needed from the product owner and the stakeholders to verify the scope. Demonstrations are critical for determining if there are gaps between what was developed and what the customer expected. The term IKIWISI (I'll Know It When I See It) explains the importance of demonstration in software development.

The following are some tools and techniques for getting user feedback on the proposed product designs and concepts:

- **Simulation**—build a miniature version of the product
- **Wireframe**—make a simple mock-up of the functionality; a wireframe is a drawing or prototype of the user requirement. It shows the basic structure and layout of a screen including content, feature navigation tools, and interactions.
- **Prototype**—build a subset of the product or its features
- **Demonstrations**—preview the product to the customer
- **Evaluation**—provide the customer with the solution for their assessment.

The scope and duration of the iterations can be verified with stakeholders in planning sessions and review meetings.

- The release and iteration planning sessions are conducted with the product owner, and the scope of each iteration is agreed between the product owner and the team.
- The duration of the iterations should be established to ensure frequent sessions to review the product with the product owner and the stakeholders.
- Ideally, the user stories should be written by the users, and the project team should include a user or user proxy for frequent exchange between the team and the users.
- A review meeting is held at the end of each iteration. At the review meeting, the product increment that is completed and potentially shippable or useable by the end users is demonstrated. The stakeholders, including the product users or sponsors, can provide input, insights and guidance on the product to ensure the delivered product meets their expectations. The product backlog and plans for the next iterations are also discussed during the review

## Functional contingency

A functional contingency is defined according to the feature prioritization. It's a reserve of features that may not be implemented if the project can't realize everything due to budget or time constraints.

DSDM suggests that the contingency is the effort to implement any features beyond the must-haves and that the must-haves should represent 60% of the total project effort. In this scenario, the contingency is 40%.

Based on the Pareto principle, 20% of the product features will have the biggest effects. This is supported by a DuPont study that reports that 25% of product features are needed and the remainder is just nice-to-have. That translates to guaranteeing to deliver must-have or minimally marketable features (MMF) within the budget.

This allows the project team to manage stakeholder expectations that, within the established budget, they will accomplish the must-have features. Of course, the goal would be to deliver more than the minimum.

## Controlling the scope

The product backlog is constantly changing with new items being added, and items being prioritized up or down. Along with feature prioritization and change business rules, the product backlog is used to manage the scope. The following items are designed to support controlling the project constraints while allowing flexibility in the features implemented.

**Scope baseline.** The product backlog contains the features that should be implemented in the product in order of their priority. The quantity of features delivered is determined by the team's velocity, i.e., the rate at which a feature can go from concept to completion. The prioritization ensures that the most valuable features are delivered with the highest priority. The MMF, or the smallest set of functionalities that must be realized to perceive value from the product, should be agreed to formulate a scope baseline. The features that compose the MMF may change over time. Nevertheless, the initial estimation and budget are usually based on the initial backlog; thus, this categorization can play a role in defining the cost and schedule baselines.

**Change business rules.** The agile methodologies don't allow changes to the agreed work during an iteration or a backlog state. The iteration backlog is frozen once the scope is committed between the product owner and the team. The change business rules define the impact on the cost and schedule baselines as features are added, deleted, or moved in product backlog at the iteration boundaries. These rules should be specific to the project. The following are examples of change business rules:

- Swapping features—Allow for exchanging one feature for another of the same size to maintain constraints on cost and time. This manages expectations on the available capacity to deliver features within the agreed project constraints.
- Work-in-progress limits—Set WIP limits for change requests based on this time allocation. Allocate time to change requests based on demand. This reduces the availability of resources to add new features.
- Contingency usage—Allow project contingency to be used should the need arise to add features to the product backlog that would require additional budget or iterations. Such a process should be considered as extending the scope, and should be managed in a structured fashion.

## Summary

- User stories are a technique for capturing the requirements for specific product features from the customer or users. The user stories should be INVEST worthy.
- The product owner prioritizes user stories with the help of the users and the team. Story mapping is one technique for grouping the user stories and deciding on the implementation priority. Kano, MoSCoW, Pareto principle, and MMF are also methods for prioritizing the features into the product backlog.
- The scope is verified with the product owner during the planning sessions and with the stakeholders during the review sessions. The scope is controlled by establishing change business rules to maintain project cost and time constraints or renegotiate them with the project sponsors.

## Recommended reading

- In his book *User Stories Applied,* Mike Cohn provides insights and details on user stories, including how to write them and their characteristics. His book *Agile Estimating and Planning* provides guidance on prioritizing user stories.
- Luke Hohmann's book *Innovation Games: Creating Breakthrough Products Through Collaborative Play* describes 12 innovation games.
- *The Definitive Guide to Getting Your Budget Approved* by Johannes Ritter and Frank Röttgers provides a systematic guide for creating and quantifying the economic value for projects.

# Chapter 9 Schedule

This chapter aligns with the *PMBOK® Guide* Schedule Management knowledge area, and covers the activities needed to ensure the timely delivery of the project. The following topics are discussed in this chapter.

- Planning schedule management
- Defining and sequence activities
- Estimating activity durations and resources
- Developing schedule
- Controlling schedule

## Planning schedule management

The schedule management plan should identify:

- the time management model (continuous or timeboxed),
- the task management method (Kanban, Task Board, other),
- the estimation units (story point, ideal days) for the scope,
- the estimation techniques,
- the iteration length, and
- the precision (i.e. range) for forecasting velocity.

### Time management model

There are multiple models for scheduling projects using agile practices.

**Continuous flow.** One model is to have a continuous flow of stories with regular review meetings and retrospectives. This model can be used in projects using a Kanban scheduling system.

**Timebox.** An alternative model is to have the delivery iterations timeboxed so the duration is fixed to usually between one and four weeks. With a timebox the duration time window remains fixed and the project scope, deliverables and activities are adjusted to fit within that time window. The schedule planning includes deciding the length of the iterations, the number of iterations, and the phasing of the iterations. This model is used by Scrum.

## Defining and sequence activities

The activities and their sequence are determined by the release plan, the product backlog, and the iteration backlog. Stories that were discussed and agreed for the specific release are worked on in their order of priority. All the activities needed to deliver a completely tested and functional solution should be included within each iteration. An iteration planning session is used to define the tasks, their duration, and sequence. A task board or Kanban board is used to schedule and monitor the activities.

### Kanban and task boards

Kanban board or task board is used to visualize and track the progress of the user stories. Both are visual boards that track stories through a workflow. However, there are differences in the structure and content of the boards and their operations. Table 9-1 provides a summary of the differences between a Kanban board and a task board.

This section describes the structure and operations of Kanban and task boards.

#### Task board

A Task Board (Figure 9-1) is a visible project chart that represents the project work that has to be completed by the team. The tasks are determined during the iteration planning. Cards are used to represent individual tasks. The board should include columns for the backlog (i.e. to do), in-progress, and done work. The columns should reflect meaningful stages for the team.

A Task Board should belong to one team. However, scenarios exist where a task board connects multiple teams. For example, parts of the workflow are completed by different teams. Or, the product backlog may be divided among multiple teams or between internal and external team members. Furthermore, there could also be scenarios when a task board shares team members at multiple sites. Options for managing multi-team or multi-site task boards are discussed in the Scaling Agile Chapter.

| Kanban Board | Task Board |
|---|---|
| Cards are the user stories that move through the workflow; there should a signal when the next process step can start | Cards are tasks that progress through states, e.g. to do, in-progress, done |
| Work-in-progress (WIP) is limited per process step to maximize throughput | Only stories and tasks that can be completed in an iteration are scheduled |
| Team members pull work based on their availability | Team members work on tasks as agreed in the planning and daily standup |
| Daily stand-ups walk through the board to discuss completed and upcoming work and impediments | Daily stand-ups discuss what was accomplished yesterday, what will be done today, and impediments |

Table 9-1 Differences in Kanban and task board

Task boards should be used visually to inform on the state of the work in progress. They should be dynamic and updated regularly. However, the work of keeping the task boards up-to-date should not be overwhelming for the team. Update the task board using the simplest, most effective way to inform the team members and related teams on the work and its status.

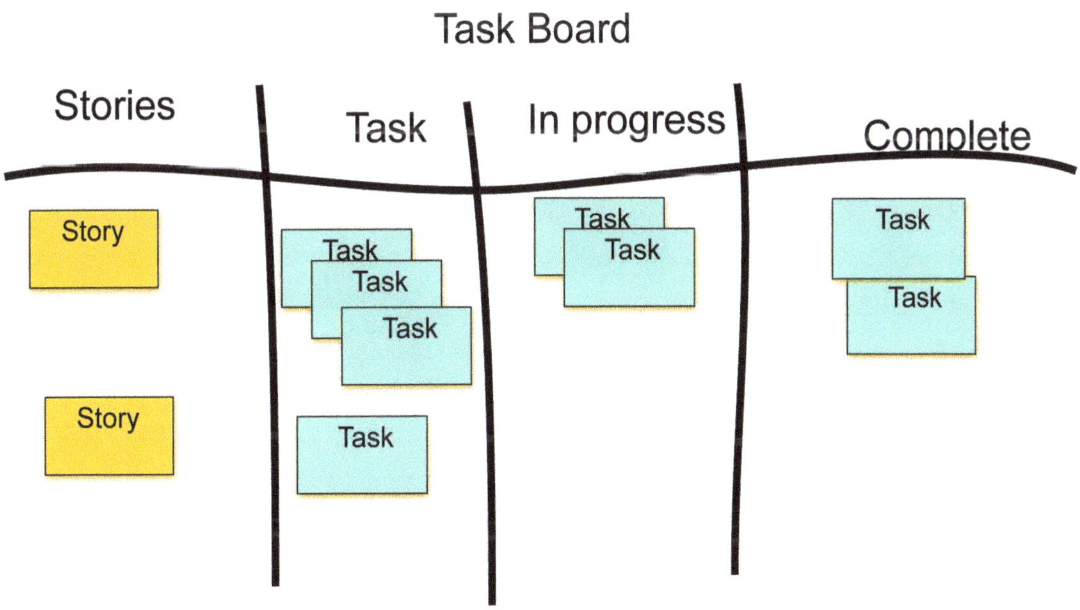


Figure 9-1 Task board

## Kanban Board

A Kanban task board (or Kanban board) (Figure 4-1) is a visible project board that uses cards that represent a task, story, or feature placed on a timeline (that is, the board) that represents the project workflow. The cards are pulled (moved) through the workflow as team members are available to perform the work. There must be a signal that the next step can start and each workflow step must have a WIP limit. The following are the steps and considerations for creating a Kanban board.

1 The first step in creating a Kanban Board is to visualize the workflow. Typically, for software development it includes activities such as analyze, design, develop, test, document, and release. As a starting point, the process should include the process that is actually used and not an ideal process.

2 Next, for each workflow step consider the number of stories that can be accomplished at one time. If a developer could work on one story at a time and the team has three developers, then three stories can be in the develop step at one time. If the team has one tester and the tester can test one story at the time, then only one story can be in the test step. These would become the WIP limits for the different process steps.

3 WIP limits are established based on the capacity of the team, and with the goal to ensure work started can be completed in the agreed iteration. That is, WIP limits are meant to optimize the throughput, not resource utilization. WIP limits are established per process step. Excess WIP is a waste as it:

Consumes resources and means money spent with no return

Hides bottlenecks that slow throughput

Is a risk as it may cause rework

4 The WIP limits should be set realistically based on what is typical. That is, they should not be set too high or too low. They can be adjusted over time.

5 If necessary to reduce WIP, the entire team may be focused on a single user story (also called swarming) before starting on another one.

6 Based on the workflow, draw the Kanban board. There should be a column for each workflow step. The WIP limits should be indicated under the workflow step. The backlog should be added to the Kanban board. The board should be in a visible location and easy to update as work progresses.

7 Kanban boards can be used for tracking different types of work activities, including development, maintenance requests, or software bugs. These can be defined as different classes of services and have rules for how to address them. For example, the Kanban cards may be color-coded or otherwise marked to indicate the different types of activities. The different classes of service may have rules for priority, service levels, and WIP limit impacts.

8 Agree on the rules for the operation of the Kanban board with the team members. The rules should identify such things as the WIP limits per step, the rules for moving a card from one step to the next step, how to prioritize cards for unexpected events, what to do when the WIP limits are violated, and the types of meetings and their frequency.

Kanban is a pull system so as team members become available, they pull a card from the board and begin to work on it. Once the team member starts on the task, it's their task until they complete it and someone else pulls the card to the next step in the process.

The Kanban board should be reviewed for bottlenecks. Bottlenecks occur when the team's work is stopped or delayed because WIP limits have been reached. This will be highly visible on the Kanban board. During review meetings, the team should look for opportunities to improve the process. Lead time and cycle time are two measures that can be used for tracking performance.

**Lead time**—how long it takes to get from a card entering the kanban to delivery

**Cycle time**—how long it takes to complete a card once it's started.

Little's law indicates that the cycle time is proportional to the amount of WIP. The size of the WIP queue can be used to predict completion times.

## Estimating activity durations and resources

User stories should be sized to complete in a single iteration. The estimate for the story and the team's velocity determine how many stories can be completed during an iteration. Therefore, the elements needed to estimate activity duration, include deciding on the iteration length, estimating the user stories, and forecasting the velocity. These topics are covered in this section.

### Iteration length

The timebox length is the iteration length, and it's usually decided in release planning. The following factors should be considered in deciding the length of the timebox.

- By having short iterations, the project team estimates more often which increases their skills estimating and improves the accuracy of the estimates.

- The more unclear the requirements for the solution, the shorter the iterations should be. That is, there need to be more opportunities to demonstrate and review the product to ensure the team delivers the right solution.

- Demonstrations are the best method to show how the team understood the requirements. The iteration length should be short enough to avoid going too long without stakeholder feedback. Alternatively, the iteration length should be the longest period the team could go without validating their understanding with the product owner and keep the release on-track.

- Mike Cohn in his book *Agile Estimating and Planning* recommends having between four to five feedback opportunities with the stakeholders during a release (Cohn, 2006).

- The iteration length should be long enough to give the team time to create a potentially shippable product increment, short enough to allow for frequent feedback from the stakeholders, but not so short that the product owner has no time to groom the backlog in between iterations.

- The length should be based on how often it's possible to get the stakeholders together to attend the review session. Their availability should be considered.

- If the stakeholders tend to request changes that are of the highest priority at each review, the iteration cycle should be shorter rather than longer. That is, how long can the product owner wait for changes or new ideas to be addressed.

- The length should consider the number of instances complete integration and regression testing can be performed. If continuous integration is used and testing is fully automated, there may be a low overhead to the testing activities. However, if not, the overhead will be higher.

- The iteration length should consider the amount of iteration planning sessions the project can afford. This will be a significant decision if there is a distributed team that has to travel or adjust working days to attend the planning sessions. The cost of coordination should be minimized as much as possible. The "coordination costs on projects are any activities that involve communicating and scheduling" (Anderson 2010). This includes the release planning and iteration planning meetings, the daily stand-up, the emails, etc. If the team is meeting to create value—design, test, analysis—, then it's not a coordination cost.

- The length should be an optimal duration to keep the team working towards the goal at a good consistent pace without being too slow or feeling overwhelmed.

- There should be a regular delivery rhythm. This can be achieved by having the iteration lengths consistent across the entire project and preferably of shorter lengths rather than longer ones.

## Estimation units

At the release planning stage, estimates represent the complexity, effort, and risk of the story. At that time, the stories are not defined in enough detail for accurate estimates and they are not broken down into tasks. Furthermore, it is logical to avoid the effort of estimating stories that are not a priority and won't be addressed in the near-term. Thus, at release planning estimates are usually produced in story points or ideal days.

Estimating the duration to complete a story is conducted during the iteration planning. The tasks define the work that has to be completed to realize the story. The hours to complete the task are then estimated or given by their workflow step for Kanban.

#### STORY POINTS

A story point is a unit of measure for the overall size of a user story, feature, or another piece of work. The actual meaning of a story point is determined by the team and can vary widely from team to team. NUTs means 'nebulous units of time.' Joshua Kerievsky (2003) coined this term as an alternative name for story points. It indicates story points can vary from team to team and therefore have no clear meaning beyond the team that estimated them.

Usually, a story points represent some consideration for the time, effort, complexity, or risk of implementing the story. Story points are not effort in terms of work hours or days.

Pair programming has no impact on the number of story points (Beck,1999).

#### IDEAL TIME

Ideal time is the time a person would spend working on a task if there were no interruptions and the person was working in a good environment.

- In 2001, Booch and Brown in the *Collaborative Development Environments* did a study with 50 programmers to determine how programmers spend their time. The average programmer spends 3% of his or her day on phone calls, 7% reading, and 17% in meetings.

- Similarly, Brook (1995) reported that estimation errors in one team could be pinpointed to the team programming and debugging only 50% of the week. The remainder of the time was spent on interruptions, meetings, paperwork, company business, sickness, etc.

The bottom line is that the average team member doesn't spend the whole day on planned activities; team members have a number of planned and unplanned interruptions during the day.

Ideal days can be used as estimates for story sizes. When the ideal days represent story sizes, the following rules apply:

- Overhead activities or absence don't need to be considered since ideal days aren't elapsed time and already take these points into consideration:

- There should be one estimate that encompasses the number of days needed for all activities by all team members (that is, one aggregated number)

- The length of a day in hours should be clear. Is the standard working day 7.5 hours or 8 hours?

#### ELAPSED TIME

Ideal time does not equal elapsed time. By specific example, during a two-week iteration (10 days), one day is spent for planning, one day for review and retrospectives and an estimated one day collaborating on team topics (e.g. estimates, stories, etc.). Therefore, in this two-week iteration there are 10 elapsed days, but there are only seven ideal days before any of the following kinds of activities are deducted from that working time:

- Time off for sick leave, military leave, vacation
- Attending or preparing for meetings, events
- Attending training or seminars
- Phone calls
- Reading (emails, mail, reference materials)
- Switching between tasks
- Peer reviews
- Performance reviews
- Innovation time
- Ad hoc activities.

Team members may require time to try out new ideas or concepts. While there is no standard for how much time should be spent on innovation, 15 - 20% of the time can be used in companies like 3M and Google. Other companies allow a fixed number of days per week or use a break time between iterations. Not all projects or companies allow time for innovation.

The iteration schedule should consider time for unexpected events (such as bugs or maintenance issues). The amount of time needed for such activities will vary throughout the life cycle of the project. That is, at the start of the project, there should be no bugs or maintenance issues while after a few iterations they may start to occur. In addition, depending upon the nature of the solution, such activities may be able to be prioritized in the backlog and wait until the next iteration planning for resolution.

Thus, the time available in the working week must be translated to the ideal time for the team. Table 9-2 is an example of subtracting coordination, innovation time, and unexpected events from an available work-week to calculate the ideal time.

| Weekly calculation of available time | | | Reductions to available time | | | |
|---|---|---|---|---|---|---|
| Staff | Percent engagement | Hours available | Hours of Scheduled Project coordination | Hours of Innovation Time | Hours of other activities | Ideal time |
| Team Member 1 | 100% | 40 | 10 | 4 | - | 26 |
| Team Member 2 | 100% | 40 | 10 | 4 | - | 26 |
| Team Member 3 | 100% | 40 | 10 | 4 | 8 | 18 |
| Team Member 4 | 100% | 40 | 10 | 4 | - | 26 |
| Team Member 5 | 50% | 20 | 8 | 2 | - | 10 |
| Team Member 6 | 100% | 40 | 8 | 4 | - | 28 |
| | | | | | | 134.00 |

Table 9-2 Available time to the ideal time

The project schedule or duration is based on elapsed time.

### STORY POINTS VS. IDEAL DAYS

Story points are a measure of the size, while ideal days are a measure of size and effort. The following are some advantages for each of the methods.

For story points:

- The value remains consistent as the team gains experience
- The values are a measure of the size and do not represent effort; effort may change over time
- Teams are able to estimate story points faster than ideal days
- Story points are independent of a single team member's view on what on an "ideal" day
- Story points are less likely to be intentionally over or under estimated. Ana Magazinius, Sofia Borjesson, and Robert Feldt (2012, p. 29) in their study on *Intentional Distortions in Software Cost Estimation* found " . . . intentional distortion of estimates is both common, has multiple different reasons and leads to either or sometimes both, increased or decreased estimates."

For ideal days:

- Ideal days are understood by people that are not in the team
- They make it easier to predict the velocity
- Teams are able to establish a baseline for estimating faster (at first)
- Estimating velocity for ideal days is easier
- By iteration planning estimates have to be done in ideal days

Unfortunately, there is no formula to translate from story points to ideal days. At the latest during the iteration planning, the team will estimate the tasks associated with a user story in ideal days.

## Estimation techniques

There are several techniques for grouping user stories or features to estimate their effort, complexity, and risk. The methods vary by the technique, the speed at which the estimation can occur, and the precision of the estimation. Therefore, different techniques are more applicable at different stages of the project life cycle. For example, roadmap planning may use relative sizing or affinity estimation while release planning may use Planning Poker®[1].

Accurately estimating time is a challenge for all methodology types. However, speed comes easily to mind when making decisions about velocity. Therefore, the intuitive approach from agile methodologies may have a negative side effect in estimation. Therefore, the use of formal time estimation methods is recommended to avoid bias in the estimate (Fink & Pinchovski, 2020).

The following section describes some of the available estimation techniques.

### Three-point estimate

A three-point estimate captures a minimum, most likely, and maximum value. Three-point estimates are preferred as most people feel comfortable giving a range instead of precise estimates and they take the uncertainty around the estimate into consideration. The estimates are translated into single point estimates using a formula that initiated with PERT, i.e. beta distribution. The estimated value will be the best case (O) plus four times the most likely case (M) plus the worst case (P) divided by six., i.e. PERT = (O + 4M + P) /6). O stands for optimistic and P stands for pessimistic.

### Relative sizing

Relative sizing is estimating the size of work to be completed by comparing it to the size estimated for another piece of work.

- Using this method, take a user story and estimate its size.
- For the next story estimate if it's bigger or smaller than the previously estimated story. Place it to the right or left of the story relative to its size of the previous story.
- Continue this process until all stories are placed in their relative position.

### Planning Poker®

Planning Poker ® is a wideband Delphi estimation method used to estimate the relative size of tasks in software development. It was first introduced by James Grenning (2002). Wideband Delphi is a consensus-based estimation method derived from the Delphi Method that was developed by the RAND Corporation. The characteristics of Planning Poker® are:

- It uses expert judgment as the experienced professionals are performing the estimate
- It uses analogy as it compares the effort to complete one story with the size of other known stories
- It uses disaggregation since the stories are split into small estimable stories
- It involves the people that will perform the work in making the estimate, which support the team's commitment to the estimate
- It involves the complete team in the estimate so all views required for coding and testing the solution are considered
- It is a quick method to gather the estimates as it occurs in a single session
- It gathers the estimate from multiple parties without one individual's opinion influencing the estimate before it's made.

The cards used in planning poker are based on using a Fibonacci numbering system (?, 0, 1/2, 1, 2, 3, 5, 8, 13, 20, 40, 100, infinity). Fibonacci numbers are derived recursively by taking the sum of the previous two numbers in the sequence, (that is, 1 + 2 = 3, 2 + 3 = 5). Since Fibonacci numbers increase in scale and have gaps between the numbers, they reflect the increasing uncertainty that usually comes with larger user stories. The card values represent the estimates, where a 1 is an insignificant story and 20 is a big user story. An estimate of 40 or 100 would be extremely large and would need to be broken down further. A question mark means the person has no idea and need more information.

The mechanics for planning poker are as follows:

- As a reference, the team takes a previously estimated story of small size (e.g. 5 points). Since they have previously worked together, they have an understanding of the effort, complexity, and risks of a story of that size. If the team has not worked together before, they start with a story from a previous project or a new story. This step creates a baseline so that estimates have similar meetings between the team members.

- The product owner reads and explains the user story to the entire team. The teams ask questions until they understand the story. A prerequisite is that the story is an estimate-able size (see INVEST). After everything is clear about the story, each team member turns over a card that represents his or her estimate for the story.

- The team members that estimated the lowest number and the highest number discuss their justifications for their estimates. The remaining team members can ask questions until everyone is clear on the thinking and logic behind the different estimates.

- There is another round of estimating for the same story with each team member displaying his individual estimate. This is conducted until the estimates converge.

- When estimates have not converged by the third iteration, then the highest estimate is taken.

### Affinity Estimating

Affinity estimating (see Figure 9-2) is a team estimation method where features and user stories are grouped based on their relative effort to implement them. The team defines the grouping. It can consist of groups such as large, medium, or small.

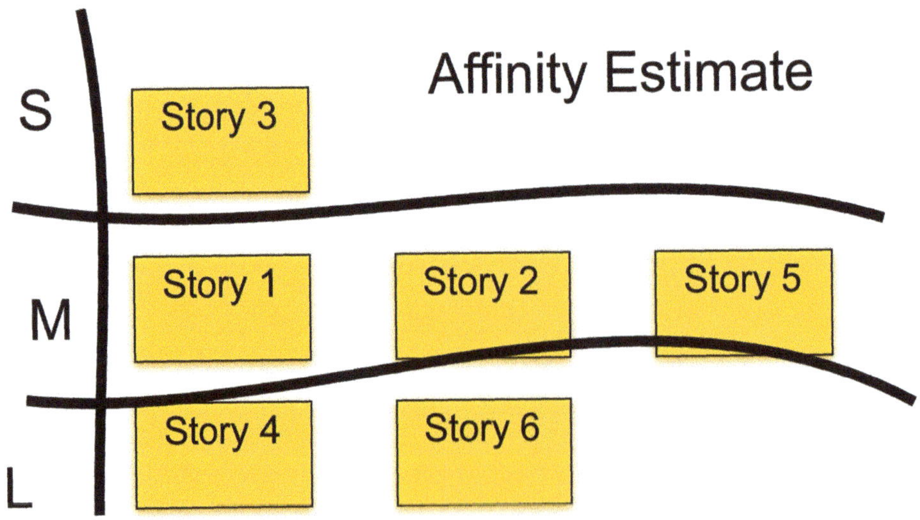


Figure 9-2 Affinity estimate

### Triangulating

Triangulating is estimating a story based on its relationship to one or more other stories. In this case, the team selects a story of a small size for which all members of the team are familiar. The story can be from a previous iteration or a new story that the team can estimate together. The selected story becomes the reference story. For each story, the team compares its size to the size of the reference story.

Triangulation can be used together with other methods such as Planning Poker ®.

## Velocity

To go from the size of the story to the duration estimate, velocity is used. Velocity is a measure of the rate at which teams consistently deliver business value (Figure 6-4 and Table 6-2). It is the sum of the estimates of delivered (that is, accepted) features per iteration.

During estimation, the velocity should be presented as a range since there will be fluctuations in the team's performance for any number of reasons: miscommunications with the product owner, overestimating or underestimating tasks efforts, etc.

### Estimating initial velocity

The options for establishing the initial velocity include using historical values, running iterations, or forecasting the velocity. "Real velocity is not estimated, it is measured" (Larman, Vodde, & Arbogast 2010, p. 184). Therefore, of the following choices running an iteration would be preferred if the historical data represent in the same environment doesn't exist.

#### HISTORICAL VALUES

Historical velocity is best used as an initial velocity when everything about the project is the same: people, technology, content, product owner, etc. To compute the historical velocity, use the average velocity for the previous release. That is, calculate the size (story points or ideal days) completed during the release divided by the number of iterations.

#### RUNNING ITERATIONS

Running a few iterations to measure the actual velocity would be an alternative for establishing the initial velocity. In practice, a team's velocity stabilizes after about three iterations. For two-week iterations, that would be six weeks and for four-week iterations it would be about three months.

Depending upon the project size, six weeks or three months coincidences with the duration of a requirements gathering or feasibility stage of a traditional project. From this point of view, running some initial iterations is a reasonable approach to being able to provide reasonably sound velocity estimates. The Feature Driven Development methodology suggests that its first phase—developing an overall model—is approximately 10% of the project development effort (Palmer and Felsing, 2002, p. 133). This fact also provides justification for running a few iterations to form a baseline for velocity.

#### FORECASTING

Make a forecast by planning a selection of stories down to estimates of hours at the task level; match the estimated effort with the team availability and utilization for an iteration's worth of time. First, estimate the total number of hours each team member and the cumulated team will have available during an iteration. Select a number of stories, break them into tasks, and estimate the number of hours to complete the tasks. Do this until the complete number of available hours of the team members would be consumed. Convert this figure into the velocity.

### Deciding a range for the velocity

Since the velocity is the measure used to determine the project duration, it should be presented as a range, rather than a point estimate. The premise is that early in a project little is known about the size of the project, the details of the target platform, the personnel and team cooperation, and the detailed process specifics. Thus, the estimates become more accurate later in the project as the information is determined through requirements and detailed design.

The velocity is used to determine the schedule and the schedule is used to determine the budget. The velocity should be adjusted based on when and how it's forecasted. At the roadmap stage, very high-level estimation techniques are used, during release planning more accuracy is added, and the iteration planning is based on a calendar so it has the most accuracy.

The 'cone of uncertainty,' rough order of magnitude (ROM), or an uncertainty analysis are methods of establishing the range.

#### CONE OF UNCERTAINTY

The 'cone of uncertainty' (see Figure 9-3) was coined by Steve McConnell (1998) but created by Barry Boehm. It provides the uncertainty ranges based on the phases of a waterfall project.

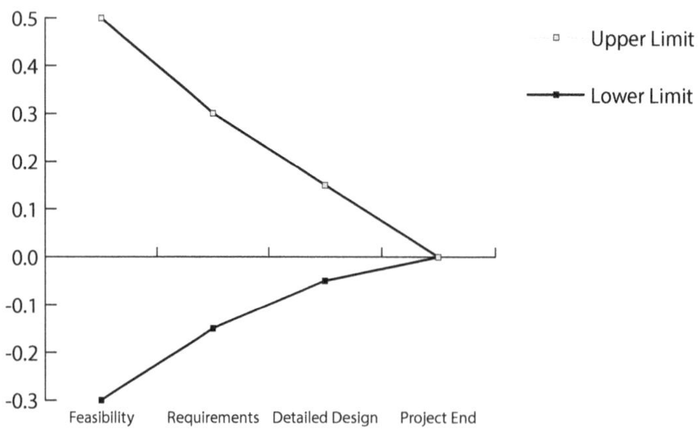


Figure 9-3 Cone of uncertainty

### ROUGH ORDER OF MAGNITUDE

ROM estimates a range that becomes increasingly more accurate as the project proceeds. ROM is one of the methods suggested by the *PMBOK® Guide* (2017). The Advancement of Cost Engineering (AACE) provides standard ROM estimates and some Table 9-3 includes the estimate ranges from National Aeronautics and Space Administration (NASA), AACE and the *PMBOK® Guide.*

Less accurate
Early in lifecycle → More accurate
Late in lifecycle

| | Feasibility | Requirements | Detailed Design |
|---|---|---|---|
| NASA | ± 100% | ± 75% | ± 40% |
| | Class 5: feasibility | Class 3: budget | Class1: check |
| AACE | -20% / +100% | -10% / +50% | -3% / +15% |
| | Order of manitude | Budget | Definitive |
| PMBOK® | -25% / +75% | -15% / +30% | -5% / +10% |

Table 9-3 Industry-standard estimation ranges

### SIMULATION

Finally, uncertainty analysis can be conducted using simulation methods such as Monte Carlo to determine the impacts of uncertainty on the estimate. The project specific assumptions on project size, costs, and risks are input into a project model. The Monte Carlo simulation runs thousands of iterations using random numbers to generate a distribution curve that provides the likelihood of the project being delivered for a specific cost (or schedule)

### DECIDING THE METHOD

The best method to use will depend upon the organizational requirement. Using the cone of uncertainty as well as ROM is the easiest to explain. The cone of uncertainty is specific to the software projects. The AACE ROM and *PMBOK® Guide* models are industry neutral. The simulation model is project-specific. It should be considered when the estimate requires accuracy or the estimates from the other methods are not accepted (perhaps because the costs are too high). The simulation option requires simulation software to produce. *Riskology* is a free option offered by Tom DeMarco and Tim Lister (2004) (http://www.systemsguild.com/riskology).

The result is adding a range to the velocity estimate rather than stating it as a point estimate.

## Schedule contingency

Schedule contingency is a time buffer that is added to the schedule baseline to account for adjustments and fluctuations based on risks or unknown events. The method for estimating the contingency will vary depending upon the estimation method used for sizing the project and a range to the velocity. The simplest method is to calculate the expected project duration and add a percentage of time for contingency (e.g. 20%). For example, if the project was expected to complete in five iterations, a 20% contingency would have it completed in six iterations. The more sophisticated method is to calculate a three-point estimate per user story and risk, calculate a range for the velocity, and add the information into a simulation model to compute an estimated probability of completing the project with a 99% accuracy rate. The decision on the method will depend upon the accuracy needed for the project.

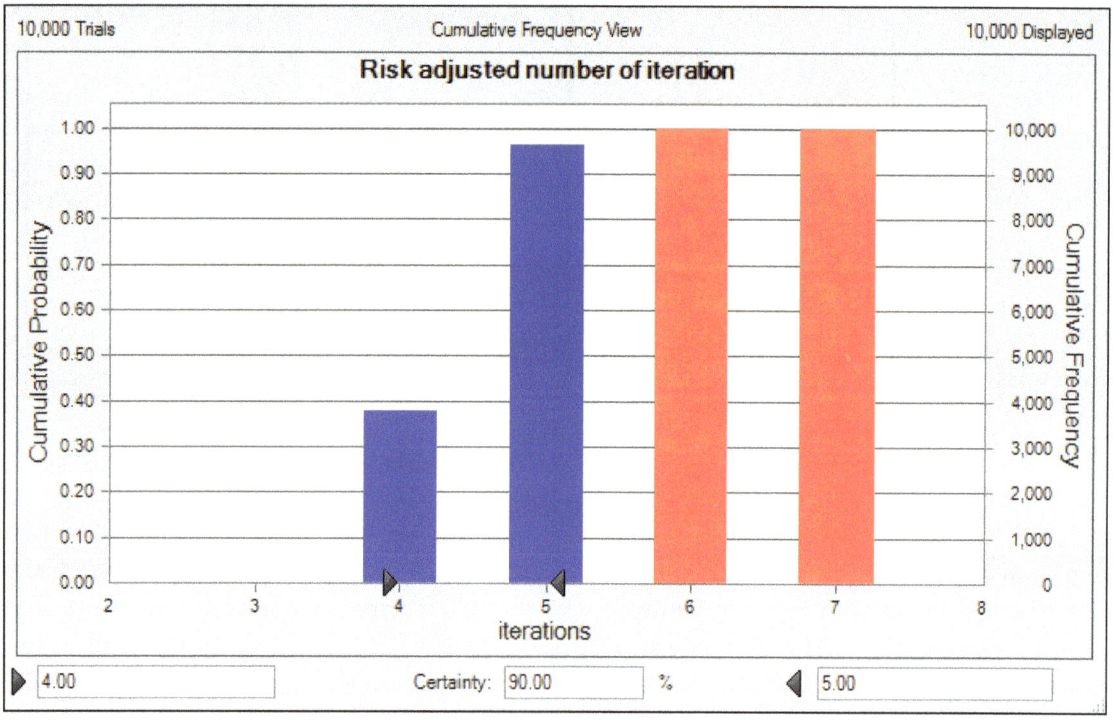


Figure 9-4 Simulation of project duration

# Develop schedule

## Project schedule

The overall project schedule is based on releases that are a series of iterations. The number of iterations required to complete the entire scope is based on the number of features, the size of those features and the velocity of the team. Iterations should be planned back-to-back; however, continuous non-stop iterations may be tiring for the team. It may be necessary to plan a break after a series of iterations.

Rough project duration is computed by dividing the size (number of story points or ideal days) by the velocity and multiplying by the duration of iteration. For example, given a project with 120 story points and a forecasted velocity of 25 to 45, the project would be planned for three and five iterations. If the iteration lengths were 4 weeks, then the duration would be from 12 to 20 weeks.

For a reliable project duration, the iterations should be aligned to a calendar taking into consideration holidays, vacations, and other company events that may play a role in the project duration.

## Iteration schedule

For most agile projects, the time schedule for each iteration is based on the iteration length, and each iteration should be of the same length. For Kanban, the iteration length may vary and should be decided based on the scope of the stories; however, there should be a regular rhythm to the deliveries. While each iteration may have the same elapsed time, the ideal time may vary. The time for holidays, vacations, innovation, coordination, and unplanned events must be subtracted from the available time to work on user stories or product features.

During an iteration, the following coordination meetings may be scheduled:

**Release Planning.** On a regular basis, the product owner will be grooming the backlog and the team is required to support this activity. Grooming the backlog means preparing the backlog for the next iteration, including adding new stories, prioritizing existing stories, incorporating learnings and feedback, and breaking existing stories into smaller stories. The product backlog is groomed to ensure that it's D.E.E.P: Detailed appropriately, Emergent, Estimated, and Prioritized.

- For scrum, a rule of thumb is that release planning is about 15% of the team's time during an iteration. Thus, a release planning meeting may be scheduled during an iteration; it's estimated to require approximately two-hours per two weeks of iteration.

- For Kanban, a rule of thumb is to groom the backlog depending upon throughput and volatility. Domains with low volatility may want a backlog of one year; teams with high volatility may want one month of backlog. A general rule of thumb is to groom the backlog when it contains more than three months' worth of work (Anderson 2010).

**Iteration planning meeting.** Estimated at four hours per two weeks of iteration time. It should not exceed eight hours for a one-month iteration (Schwaber & Sutherland, 2017).

**Daily stand-up meeting.** The daily stand-up should be no more than 15 minutes (Schwaber & Sutherland, 2017). It may be held less frequently than every day; the schedule depends on the team's need to coordinate.

**Review meeting.** It should not exceed four hours for a one-month iteration (Schwaber & Sutherland, 2017).

**Retrospective.** The meeting should be planned for no more than three hours (Schwaber & Sutherland, 2017).

The following are some recommendations on establishing the iteration schedule (see Figure 9-5).

- Preferably, iterations should start in the middle of the week. Mondays are often used to ramp-up after the weekend. Thus, conducting a planning session on Mondays may be counterproductive.
- Don't align iterations to end at the end-of-quarter. Usually at quarter end, the financial books are being closed and there could be activities that distract the team.

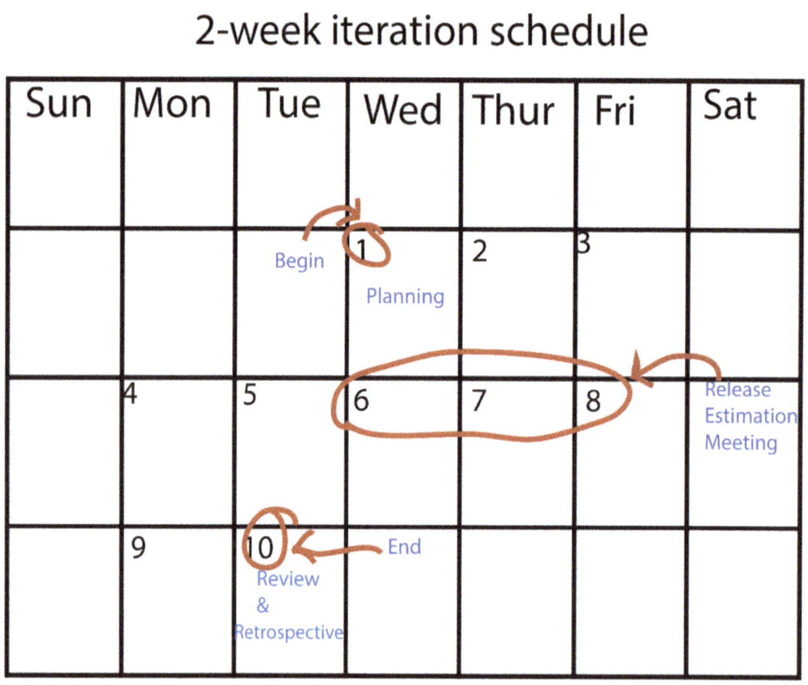


Figure 9-5 Two-week iteration calendar

## Control schedule

The planning meetings, review meetings, task boards, retrospectives, cumulative flow diagrams, and burnup and burndown charts provide tools to monitor the schedule.

**Schedule baseline.** The project size (i.e. story points, ideal days), forecasted velocity, iteration length, number of iterations, and schedule contingency form the schedule baseline. They derive the project duration and thus should be monitored for performance.

**Planning Meetings.** During the release and iteration planning sessions, items in the backlog are reviewed and prioritized. Decisions regarding the release dates as well as other scheduled activities can be adjusted during these sessions.

**Review Meeting.** The reviews provide a control point to evaluate if the project is proceeding according to schedule, to identify and risks, and to commit to continued investment in the project.

**Task Board.** The Task Board provides a view on the workflow and the progress of items through. It can be used to identify resource constraints.

**Cumulative Flow Diagram.** A cumulative flow diagram can be used to gain insights into the cycle times, completion dates, or project issues.

**Burndown and Burnup Charts.** The iteration burndown chart and release burnup chart identify the delivery of completed features against the release or iteration plan. The burndown chart is useful for the team to monitor their day-to-day performance within an iteration. The release burnup chart is useful for management to understand how the project is progressing against the overall project release schedule.

## Summary

- Stories can be estimated in ideal days, a measure of the number of uninterrupted working days, or story points, a measure of the effort, complexity, and risk of the story. Relative sizing, affinity estimating, Planning Poker®, and triangulation are some of the techniques for estimating story size.

- A task board is a visual board that informs on the state of the work in progress. Task cards are moved along a process flow.

- A Kanban board is a visual board that tracks stories through a workflow until they are completed. Kanban is a continuous process and team members pull stories from the workflow. WIP limits are established based on the capacity of the team, and are designed to optimize the throughput.

- The project schedule is based on the iteration length and the number of iterations. Up to 25 % of the team's time may be spent in coordination, including release planning, iteration planning, daily meetings, review, and retrospective. Additional time may be allocated for innovations and unexpected events.

- Project meetings, burndown, burnup charts, and CFD are used to monitoring the work completed and adjust project activities and processes as necessary.

## Recommended reading

- Mike Cohn's *Agile Estimating and Planning* provides guidance on iteration planning, including estimating the effort for user stories.

- David J. Anderson's *Kanban: Successful Evolutionary Change for Your Technology Business* provides the guidance, definitions, and metric calculations necessary to establish an efficient software development flow, including establishing WIP limits.

## Endnotes

[1] Planning Poker® is a registered trademark of Mountain Goat Software, LLC

# Chapter 10 Cost

This chapter aligns with the *PMBOK® Guide* Cost Management knowledge area; it covers the activities needed to ensure the project establishes a budget and delivers within that budget. The following topics are discussed in this chapter.

- Planning cost management
- Estimating cost
- Determining a budget
- Controlling costs

## Planning cost management

The time and resources are usually fixed during the roadmap planning and updated during the release and iteration planning. During each planning activity, there's a focus on prioritizing requirements to deliver incremental value. As in traditional projects, estimate information becomes more accurate as the project progresses. Unlike in traditional projects, the scope is adjusted per iteration. There are no guarantees that the cost will cover the complete project scope. Thus, the cost management plan should identify:

- The degree of accuracy needed for the cost estimate
- The unit of measure for the burn rate
- The unit of measure to size the project scope
- The method that will be used to monitor cost performance.

# Estimating costs

Projects may have direct and indirect costs for infrastructure (hardware, software, facility changes), training and support, labor, contingencies, and risk reserves. The costs should be collected through expert interviews, vendor offers, historical data, the finance department, or other means. They should be collected as a range or using three-point estimates.

## Labor costs

The scope of the project budget should consider everyone engaged in the project, including internal and external team members, any integration teams, agile coaches, agile testers, and fees related to users or user proxies. Each team member, whether internal or external, will have a cost. That can be salary costs that include the direct and indirect cost for the person (i.e. fully loaded) or a consulting rate. The extent to which internal costs are allocated to the project is an organizational decision, and this should be clarified with the project sponsor.

The 'burn rate' is a measure used to calculate the budget and monitor the project costs. It can also be used to value user stories. An iteration burn rate is the cost per iteration. One method to calculate the iteration burn rate is to first compute the labor costs in weeks. Then, the iteration burn rate is calculated by multiplying the iteration duration by the weekly labor costs. The burn rate can be calculated based on the size of the story by dividing the iteration burn rate by the velocity.

For example, there are eight people on the project: seven full-time and one half-time. They have weekly costs of 50,000 money units, and a forecast velocity of 25 story points per iteration. The iteration burn rate would be 100,000 and the story point burn rate would be 4,000 per story point.

| Staff | Fully loaded weekly cost | Percent engagement | Adjusted weekly costs |
|---|---|---|---|
| Agile Coach | 7,188 | 100% | 7,188 |
| Product Owner | 10,482 | 100% | 10,482 |
| Team Member 1 | 7,487 | 100% | 7,487 |
| Team Member 2 | 6,803 | 100% | 6,803 |
| Team Member 3 | 6,948 | 100% | 6,948 |
| Team Member 4 | 5,990 | 100% | 5,990 |
| Team Member 5 | 5,990 | 50% | 2,995 |
| Team Member 6 | 2,108 | 100% | 2,108 |
| | | | 50,000 |

| | |
|---|---|
| 50,000 | = Weekly costs |
| 100,000 | = Burn rate for a 2-week iteration |
| 4,000 | = Burn rate based on 25 story points |

Figure 10-1 Example burn rate calculation

The project labor costs are considered for the entire duration of the project (i.e. number of iterations times iteration burn rate). Determining the duration is discussed in chapter 9.

### Other costs

Other project costs that should be gathered and estimated include items from the following list.

- Course fees for training and certification
- Consulting costs for coaching and mentoring
- Quality costs, including hardware and software costs for new engineering practices, e.g. configuration management environments, automated testing processes, testing hardware, etc.
- Construction and fitting changes to the facilities.
- New technology tools to support the agile process.
- Office supplies, including flip charts, post-its, pens, etc.
- Travel and living expenses for coordination and project activities.
- Hardware, software, and travel costs for working with distributed teams.
- Product-related hardware and software costs will vary depending on the technology used and the deployment requirements. However, this is likely to be the same costs that would apply to non-agile projects.

## Determining a budget

Figure 10-2 provides an overview of the different factors that may be included in the budget. Formulating the budget is a process of aggregating the costs based on the estimates and adding the contingency

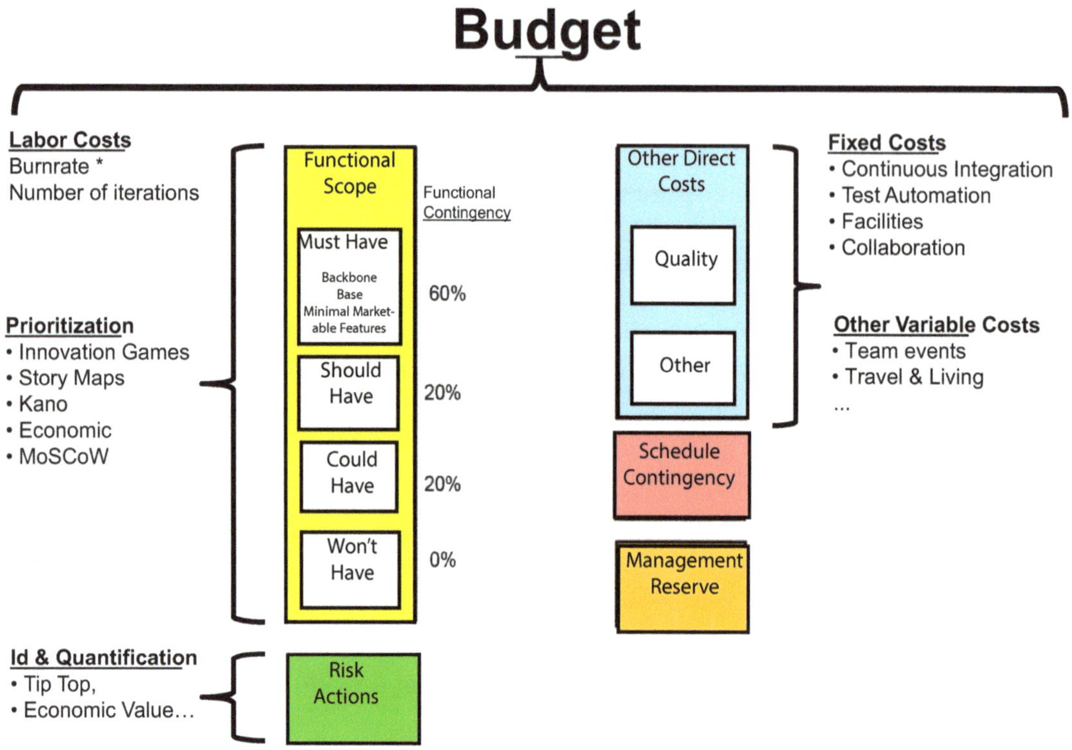


Figure 10-2 Budget composition and functional contingency

High-level estimates for the scope are available once the number of iterations and velocity are established. Therefore, if the costs are fixed based on this information, contingency should be calculated for the schedule (time), the budget (money), and the scope (features). The money and time contingencies protect the project should additional iterations (i.e. time) or money be needed to deliver the scope. The functional contingency protects the project should the scope need to be reduced to fit into the budget or schedule. The budget should be established based upon implementing 100% of the project scope.

The monetary contingency includes a range for other project costs and the risk reserves. If the economic monetary value (EMV) was computed for each risk, then it should be added to the contingency budget as part of the risk reserves. The other costs should be presented as a range. Depending on the project stage when the budget is established, the amount of contingency needed will vary. The 'cone of uncertainty', rough order magnitude (ROM), and simulation methods discussed in chapter 9 can be applied to computing the monetary contingency.

## Controlling costs

**Cost baseline.** The cost baseline includes all the costs and the contingencies, including staff costs and other costs. Since the scope is delivered in iterations, the burn rate per iteration and burn rate per size unit are perfect for evaluating the cost performance. Continuously prioritizing and re-prioritizing the scope and managing functional contingency and risks per iteration are important factors in controlling the project costs. When the budget is at risk, the functional contingencies can be used to adjust the features that will be part of the project and reduce the scope if necessary. Figure 10-2 provides an overview as to how the functional contingencies can be allocated to the budget based on the prioritization descriptions in chapter 7.

**Planning Meetings.** During the roadmap, release and iteration planning sessions, the scope, the overall number of iterations, and scope size are planned, and the actual velocity can be measured. These meetings provide checkpoints where the cost performance can be evaluated and monitored.

**Review Meeting.** The review meeting provides a control point to evaluate the feature delivery against the budget and to commit to continued investment in the project.

**Release burnup Chart.** The release burnup chart identifies the delivery of completed features against the release plan. It provides a variance report of actual to plan as well as information on the trends for the project. It can be used to understand the performance of the project as compared with the budget.

**Earned value management (EVM).** While not traditionally used as a tool in agile projects, since the scope baseline is variable, EVM can be adopted to monitor agile projects. See chapter 6 for further information.

## Personal Experience: Teamwork to a reasonable comprise

### —Edward Krzeminski, Lecturer, Designer, & Continuous Improvement Specialist

In my opinion, developing a project in accordance with the agile principles leads to improved project results and a reduction in project risks, such as delays and budget overrun. The critical success factor is selecting the proper team members. By "right personnel," I mean staff with the necessary professional experience and ability to communicate and guide a team to achieve the most effective solution by a reasonable compromise.

Very often in industrial operations, team members focus on their area of operation and pay little attention to the impact of the solution on the enterprise. This approach results in local optimization and exerts no significant effect on optimizing the functional operations. Project team members are excellent in their narrow professional area. For example:

- Process owners understand the process but not the importance in the supply of materials or services (an important input to the process),
- The scrum master knows and understands the art of teamwork and good organizational practices, but the details of the process are a "black box," and
- The project architect knows about a wide range of tools, but his or her knowledge of the process is based solely on information obtained from the team members.

This situation occurred in one of my projects. The project was for the improvement of an energy media flow measurement system (water and water vapor) in the thermal power plant. The task for the agile team was to adjust the elements of the measuring system (both software and mechanical as well as electrical measuring devices), to automate the measurements, and to ensure the integration of the resulting subsystem with the existing control system throughout the plant.

The core of the problem was that the agile project covered a small part of the plant systems. The designed solution had to be fully compatible with the whole system and the measurements had to be very accurate. Any system failure could result in large losses for the company.

There was a parallel construction of mechanical measuring elements (orifices) on existing parts of the pipelines. The pipelines were relatively short and there was no possibility of extending them. The ISO standards require relatively long straight sections of pipeline to ensure a high accuracy in the measurement.

Consequently, the project had many risks and limitations such as:

- Set the value of the electrical signal; a change would require a redesign of the electrical control system—the risk of budget overruns,
- Redesign and reconstruction of the pipelines to create the sufficiently long straight sections required for the automation of measurement—the risk of exceeding budget and timeframe,
- The accuracy of the measurement—the risk that the solution

would be discarded in its entirety due to lack of functionality, and

- The possibility of exceeding the time frame on the project due to the higher than expected number of iterations (7–8)—at one moment there was a risk that delays in construction and assembly of mechanical components of the measuring system would cause additional downtime throughout the thermal power plant.

Most of the design problems occurred during the initial stages of the iteration. The views of highly skilled team members from different industries -- mechanical, electrical, automation and informatics. were very different from each other. Consensus was not possible.

The pressure of time and the coaching by the scrum master supported the individual members of the design process to make concessions. This facilitated the implementation of the next sprints and iterations.

The project was successful. That is, it achieved the solution and met the expectations of the project sponsors. However, it was not delivered on time, and it exceeded the budget. The cost estimations -- were too optimistic during the strategic planning. Not all aspects of the full complexity of the problem were known those days.

## Summary

- The project costs are determined by aggregating the team costs for the planned number of iterations, plus any other direct project costs. The burn rate is a key metric for calculating team costs.

- The project contingencies suggest that a minimal set of features should be identified that represent no more than 60% of the project efforts. The project should ensure to deliver these features within the project budget.

- The project reserves should be calculated using the cone of uncertainty, a ROM method, or a simulation based upon implementing 100% of the features.

- The project costs should be controlled through the review and retrospective meetings as well as using the release burnup chart.

# Chapter 11 Quality

This chapter aligns with the *PMBOK® Guide* Quality Management knowledge area; it covers the activities needed to ensure the delivered product is of sufficient quality to meet the needs for which it was undertaken. The following topics are discussed in this chapter.

- Planning quality management
- Managing quality
- Controlling quality

## Planning quality management

The quality planning should determine the quality assurance, quality controls, and quality metrics that will be part of the project. Agile methodologies prefer prevention over-detection and therefore advocate frequent verification and validation.

- Verification is determining whether the right feature is being built. The agile verification process involves confirming that the code works correctly and that there's an audit trail and traceability to the requirements. Pair programming is one technique that can be used for verification.

- Validation is determining that the product is being built in the right way. The agile validation process involves evaluating the product increment against the requirements to ensure it performs as intended. Validation is performed mostly through tests.

The test plan should be project-specific and may or may not exist in a separate document. The quality planning process may be supported by a pre-existing test strategy. A test strategy is a long-term plan of action for how testing will occur. It may not be project-specific, but it should be used as a reference by the project. The test strategy should contain items and concepts such as:

- Testing principles
- Defect tracking process
- Test tools
- Test environments

If a test strategy doesn't exist, then the test plan should address the points that would normally be covered by the test strategy. Furthermore, test planning should consider the use of the following practices:

**Behavior-driven development.** With BDD, user stories are written from the point-of-view of the expected business outcome, and then the feature set that will deliver that outcome. The features become user stories with acceptance criteria or tests.

**Iteration planning.** During iteration planning, the user stories are explained and clarified by the product owner. The iteration planning is the right time to start clarifying the story and collecting examples so that tests can be created.

**Acceptance test-driven development**. ATDD can be considered as a method to define the test cases. ATDD defines unambiguous test cases that describe the function or feature inputs and outputs. These test cases become acceptance tests and they can be used to automate tests.

**Definition of done.** The definition of done is a scrum concept where the team must define what it means that the software is fully done for the iteration.

Since each iteration should deliver a potentially shippable product, verification and validation should be performed within each iteration. However, some teams have a separate integration iteration that is used for testing the increment. This should be clarified as part of the planning.

**Continuous integration.** Continuous integration is a software development practice where members of a team integrate their work frequently. In XP, each person integrates at least daily, leading to multiple integrations per day. Each integration is verified to detect errors as quickly as possible (often using automated tests).

**Testing automation.** Testing automation is needed for agile projects, as they have short iterations. Teams with automated testing will have stable velocity over time. Teams with manual regression testing will face challenges and may begin to ignore regression testing after a while.

**Agile tester.** The whole team is responsible for testing and delivering high-quality software. This includes the customer team and thc development team. Nevertheless, the team may have a tester that works with the customer to formulate and execute functional tests. In this case, the testers should be part of the team and be located with the other team members. In addition, dedicated testers are useful at every stage of the product development lifecycle. For example, testers can pair with developers while they write code or automated tests or they can use exploratory testing techniques to offer timely feedback.

## Manage quality

Quality assurance is focused on ensuring that the quality control processes are used. Metrics provide some indications of quality trends and the effectiveness of the quality processes. Furthermore, metrics are useful for understanding the team's progress along the path to an ultimate milestone such as software delivery.

### Quality metrics

Tracking the right metrics can alert the team when there is a problem. Metrics should be used to drive the whole team's behavior and encourage collaboration to make improvements. Metrics should not be used to place blame. The effort or cost of collecting a metric should not be higher than the value it provides.

The following list is a selection of quality measures.

**Defect rate** is the number of open bugs in the system. It can be tracked at different intervals such as defects at the end of an iteration or defects reported in production

**Number of passing tests** involves tracking the number of tests at each level: unit, functional, story tests, user interface, load, etc. The trend is an important factor in this metric.

The progression of story test status can be evaluated by tracking the number of tests written, running, and passing.

This metric is often expressed as a percentage in reports.

**Code coverage** evaluates how much of the code is covered by tests.

**Escaped defects** are defects reported by the customer after all software quality processes have been completed and the system delivered to the customer. Escaped defects are also known as live defects.

**Error feedback ratio** is the number of errors created per fix. It is measured by dividing the number of new errors created by the number of resolved errors.

**Cost of making a change** is more expensive the later the change is introduced in the project life cycle.

At Agile Testing Days 2012, Hartwig Schwier presented a test burndown chart and defect trend chart as two examples used by his team to visualize the testing progress.

The test burndown chart (Figure 11-1) is a cumulative flow chart that includes the number of tests, by module, to be executed in an iteration. The number of remaining tests is visual in this chart.

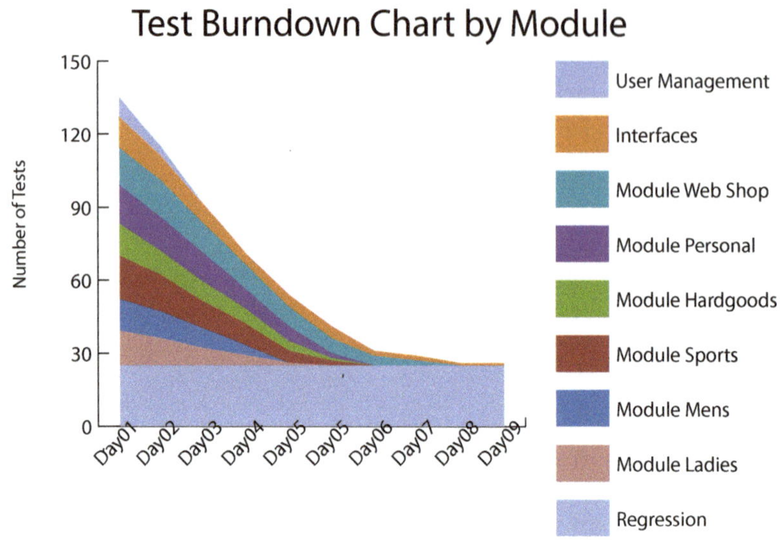


Figure 11-1 Cumulative defect flow

The defect trend chart (Figure 11-2) shows a trend line for the cumulative number of defects open and closed over time; it can also include the number of open and closed defects as bars. The gap between open and closed defects can be seen.

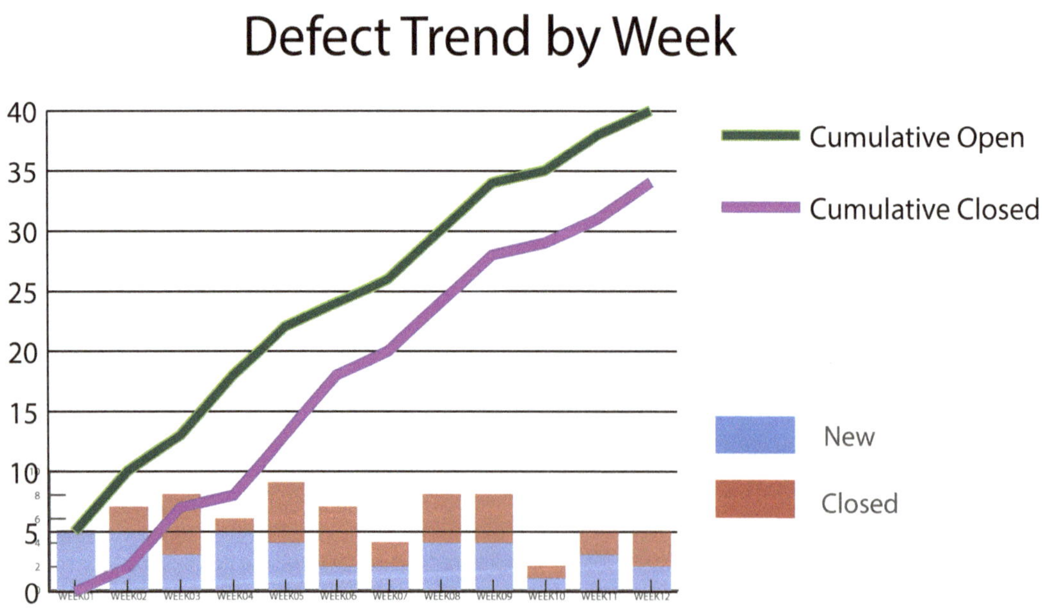


Figure 11-2 Defect trend chart

## Quality assurance practices

Pair programming and coding standards are two practices from XP that also help to ensure that quality is being built into the product.

**Pair programming.** With pair programming, two people sitting at the same computer create the production code. The pairs can include two programmers, a programmer and a tester, or a programmer and the product owner. One person types while the other person thinks (out loud) strategically about the right method to use, the overall approach, cases where the code might not work, and ways to simplify the system. Alternatively, both people can be focused on the same issue discussing tactical and strategic issues simultaneously.

According to Ken Beck (1999), pair programming has the following advantages.

- Encourages face-to-face communications.
- More productive than dividing the work between two programmers and integrating the results.
- Results in higher quality code.
- Encourages or enforces the use of the standards and the application on the tests process.

**Coding standards.** The coding standards define a set of rules that the developers should use to create their code in a consistent way. The standards should be written to prevent duplicate code from being created, to require the least amount of work possible, and to act as a communication tool among the team. The team must voluntarily adopt the coding standards.

# Controlling quality

Agile testing focuses on delivering the quality and value customers require as opposed to just testing conformance to requirements. Each agile project is different and a pragmatic and practical approach needs to be applied to overcome any testing obstacles. In addition, quality control and testing both play a role in minimizing technical debt.

Technical debt is a metaphor for the efforts and costs that are built up when a development team delivers a codebase that's increasingly difficult to maintain over time. Ward Cunningham (1992) created the term by describing a team's delivery of code that included shortcuts and quick fixes as debt that accrues over time. When a code is more difficult to maintain, the cost to change escalates, and the ability to respond to customer requirements decreases.

Ensuring all testing dimensions are considered is one method to minimize technical debt. Furthermore, a user story is done when it's tested at functional and technical levels.

## Agile testing

Brian Marick created an agile testing matrix that identified the reasons to conduct tests. Crispin and Gregory (2009) called it the 'agile testing quadrant' and explained it in their book *Agile Testing: A Practical Guide for Testers and Agile Teams.* On one axis, the matrix divides the tests into technology and business-focused tests, and on the other axis, it focuses on tests that support the team in its delivery work and tests that critique the product.

At the 2012 Agile Testing Days conference, Gojko Adzic argued that the software testing model is more like the pyramid in Maslow's hierarchy of needs. The five levels of the pyramid — from the bottom to top — 'are deployable/functionally ok,' 'performant/secure,' 'usable,' useful, and 'successful.' The tests at the bottom (e.g. unit and component tests) are needed to make sure the system functions. If not, the other tests are irrelevant. At the top of the pyramid is the success of the system. That is, does it achieve the expected business goal. For example, a system that was designed to reach a business goal of 20% but only achieved 10% may not be good enough or successful. Testing and tuning should continue.

Also, at Agile Testing Days 2012, Hartwig Schwier presented a model for testing distributed systems. It groups the tests into categories based on which parts of the systems are tested: code quality, features/ interfaces, behavior, and end-to-end.

The three testing models serve different purposes. The testing quadrant ensures all tests are covered, the pyramid helps to prioritize the tests, and the distributed testing model prescribes parallel testing by multiple teams.

The following section provides a summary of the tests that should be considered. The tests are categorized as either business- or technical- facing as identified in the 'Agile Testing Quadrant,' and they're categorized using the subjects from the distributed testing model. The prioritization and alignment are assumed to be a project-specific decision. Table 11-1 provides an overview of tests and their categorization; as described in the following section.

| Subject | Technical Facing | Business Facing |
|---|---|---|
| Code quality | Unit tests<br>Component tests | Examples<br>Prototypes<br>Simulations |
| Features & Interfaces | Performance<br>Interoperability<br>Compatibility | Functional tests<br>Story tests |
| Behavior | Scalability<br>Maintainability<br>Reliability | Exploratory scenarios<br>Usability testing |
| End-to-End | Security testing<br>Installability | User acceptance testing<br>Alpha/beta |

Table 11-1 Business and technical testing by category

## Business testing for code quality

The business tests help the development team, and they define the external quality and the features the customer wants. Customer tests are used to define what's expected from the code as well as to manage risks.

**Examples** are used to understand the value and functionality of a user story.

Examples are important for building tests and ensuring the deliverable meets the customer's requirements. Asking questions and using examples are important to understand what the customer expects. Checklists, mind maps, spreadsheets, mock-ups, flow diagrams, and software-based tools are some of the methods for eliciting examples from the customer.

**Prototypes** are demonstrations of a subset of functionality.

**Simulators** create data that mimics the key aspects of the data system that will be used in production.

**Emulators** recreate the functionality of the system so that it acts as the system under test.

## Business testing for features

This suite of tests keeps the team focused on ensuring the system is delivered with the desired features. It includes negative testing of the system's functionality.

**Functional testing** is business tests to analyze the way the system will work in its real application.

**Stories** show what the user wants and are the basis for the tests. Conditions for satisfaction or acceptance for the story should be drafted.

**Exploratory testing (ET)** is when small tests are designed, executed immediately, and then further tests are defined based on their results. The project charter should be used as a basis for starting exploratory tests, as it says what the system should do and gives some ideas about what and where to explore.

- Exploratory tests rely on the tester's skills, knowledge, and inquisitiveness to identify the tests and interrogate the system.
- Session-based testing is a timeboxed and structured form of exploratory testing.

## Business testing for behavior

This suite of tests keeps the team focused on ensuring the system is delivered to a user state with the desired behavior and interactions. The tests follow the typical use cases and workflow that will be used by the customer.

**Scenarios** are workflows or cases that mimic end-user behavior. One technique is to use a real-life scenario, exaggerate it, and compress it into a quick sequence of events. Called 'soap opera testing' by Hans Buwalda (2004), it's similar to the way TV soap operas exaggerate behavior and emotions.

Think about questions like "What's the worst thing that can happen, and how did it happen?"

**Usability testing** scrutinizes the use and usability of the system. Personas and intuition are required to put the system through its paces with the end-user in mind:

- Navigating through the system
- Comparing the system with the competition
- Testing the interfaces to the system
- Testing the reports
- Testing to support the creation of user documentation.

## Business testing of the end-to-end system

Business testing of the end-to-end system is an evaluation before the system goes live or is offered to the public. The system should function correctly, be performant, and include the features that the customer wants.

**User acceptance testing (UAT)** is a user or customer evaluation of the features in the system. They may identify future changes and new ideas. For end-user products where a UAT may not be applicable, alpha and beta tests may serve.

**Alpha testing** is the evaluation of an early version of the product. Since it's the first real end-user test and may have a high number of bugs, a limited number of customers do alpha tests.

**Beta testing** is the evaluation of a stable version of the new product that may still have bugs. Customers selected for beta testing usually understand the risk of hitting bugs and agree to report them.

## Technical testing for code quality

Test-driven development (TDD) or test-driven design is a core agile concept. With TDD, one test is written; it's run to make sure it fails; the programmer writes the minimum code necessary to pass the test and; refactors the code; and the process repeats. This allows the programmer to test the internal quality of the code.

**Unit tests** support the team, are technology facing, and are part of TDD. Unit tests verify a small subset of the system.

**Component tests** support the team, are technology facing, and are part of TDD. Component tests verify a larger part of the system than unit tests.

## Technical testing of interfaces

Technology tests of the interfaces analyze non-functional requirements for how the product functions in its technical environment.

**Performance testing** evaluates how the system responds from a temporal point of view. Tests are performed to identify bottlenecks and establish baselines for future comparison.

**Interoperability** considers the heterogeneous systems, organization, and data working together and sharing content as required.

**Compatibility** considers the system working with the various software and hardware versions with which the system should function.

**Interfaces** consider the exchange including the loading or exporting of data

## Technical testing for behavior

Tests for behavior analyze how the product functions under different circumstances.

**Scalability** checks that the system continues to function as expected when more and more users are added to the system.

- Stress testing evaluates the system under a higher-than-expected user load.
- Load testing evaluates the system response with more and more users on the system.

**Maintainability** in agile projects is promoted via techniques such as pair programming and coding standards.

**Reliability** means the system consistently works as expected under normal and abnormal circumstances. The industry metrics for reliability include:

- Mean time to failure—the average time until the first failure.
- Mean time between failures—the average time between two failures.

## Technical testing from end-to-end

End-to-end technology tests the security and install-ability of the system. If not already executed it should include all other necessary non-functional tests.

**Security testing** analyzes the confidentiality and integrity of the system and the required business rules. This includes authentication, authorization, and user identification.

**Install-ability** considers the installation and set-up of the system.

## Personal experience: The testing mindset

### —Adrian Stokes, Agile (Transition) Coach & ScrumMaster

What would happen given every possible practical scenario?

The skill of you and your team is to reduce this broad spectrum down to the most valuable activities based on experience, existing knowledge, risk, and ROI. Testers are knowledgeable about and experienced with many test techniques from boundary value analysis to exploratory testing. These skills, brought to bear at the beginning of the process, help prevent many an issue by never allowing them to happen. This experience will save you the big bucks.

Everybody tests, all the time. Like the first sip of your coffee in the morning — making sure, it's not too hot. So, why wouldn't you test your product from the moment the idea forms? You don't have to have masses of the process behind this decision or fully adopt test-driven development to have a conversation about whether a requirement is:

- Singular
- Consistent
- Current
- Unambiguous (in context)
- Prioritized
- Traceable
- Testable
- Realistic
- Achievable

The original list from software engineering also had 'complete' and 'correct.' We should know by now that complete can only be known by the end of the project. To paraphrase James Bach (testing thought leader), 'correct' is a human notion because 'things' can only be correct in context. Within any agile adoption or project, you can't underestimate the value that a skilled tester can bring to your team and the improvements that can be made by thinking about testing from the outset.

## Summary

- The test plan should consider using continuous integration, test automation, and an agile tester as part of the quality processes. These practices are necessary to maintain a high throughput of user stories, minimize the build of technical debt, and deliver a high-quality solution.

- Quality metrics such as defect rate, the number of passing tests and code coverage are useful for analyzing trends and altering the team when there's a problem. The cost of collecting the data should be considered before defining the quality metrics that will be used by the project.

- Quality control should include a full suite of testing that provides feedback to the team on the technical quality of their code, provides feedback to the users on the correctness of the features, and ensures the system's usability, performance, reliability, and maintainability once it's in production.

## Recommended reading

- In their book *Agile Testing: A Practical Guide for Testers and Agile Teams* (2009), Lisa Crispin and Jane Gregory describe the testing that should occur in agile projects along with the considerations, techniques and roles involved in testing.

# Chapter 12 Resources

This chapter aligns with the *PMBOK® Guide* Resource Management knowledge area; it covers the process from of designing, staffing and managing the team. The following topics are covered in this chapter.

- Planning resource management
- Estimating resources
- Acquiring resources
- Developing team
- Managing team

## Planning resource management

In agile projects, everyone necessary to deliver a working solution is part of the project team, which is a self-organizing unit that's empowered to make decisions and is accountable for the decisions they make. Such a human resource philosophy requires a special physical setup, new and changed responsibilities for the team members and the stakeholders, and new team competencies.

### Team characteristics

The composition of the agile teams is assumed to be highly skilled, cross-functional professionals. However, this assumption must be adjusted to fit with the actual profiles of the available professionals. The following section describes the characteristics of agile teams.

**Co-location.** Agile favors team colocation, open workspaces, and face-to-face meetings. Co-location means having the whole team sit in close proximity to one another. The key justification for team co-location is osmotic communications and the setup of several agile practices. Thus, a distributed team may require special logistics for meetings and collaboration technologies. Team space for co-located and distributed teams is discussed in chapter 13.

**High emotional intelligence.** Team compositions with high emotional intelligence (EI) are ideal for effective communications and interactions. EI is the ability to understand, identify, assess, and control the emotions of oneself and others.

**Self-organizing.** Agile teams should be able to organize themselves and the work tasks to achieve the project objectives. They share a common focus and trust and respect one another. They collaborate and make decisions. They learn to manage uncertainty and ambiguity that comes with software development.

**Cross-functional.** Agile teams should contain all the people needed for the development of the product. In extreme programming (XP), a real user or user delegate is considered part of the team. In scrum, the product owner and the scrum master are not considered part of the team.

**Empowered.** Agile teams are empowered to make decisions and commitments on the scope and their daily activities. This empowerment requires leadership skills such as participatory decision-making, active listening, and problem solving.

**Generalist vs. specialist.** Agile teams should be staffed with generalists who are able to play multiple roles on the project team. They should be able to pull work from the backlog as they are available. Each individual should be focused on doing whatever it takes to deliver the product without regard to job title, seniority, or hierarchical position.

**Systems development and agile experience:** In his book *Agile Software Development*, Alistair Cockburn divides the people learning new skills into three levels. Boehm and Turner further refine the levels to support distinguishing between agile and traditional methodologies. (See Table 11-1.)

| | |
|---|---|
| **Level -1** | Individuals that are unable or unwilling to collaborate or follow shared methods. (They may be technically capable.) |
| **Level 1B** | Individuals that, with training, are able to perform procedural method steps. |
| **Level 1A** | Individuals that, with training, are able to perform discrete method steps. |
| **Level 2** | Individuals that are able to tailor existing methods for new situations. |
| **Level 3** | People that are able to work in unprecedented situations; revise methods and break them into rules. |

Table 11-1 Cockburn's levels as adapted by Boehm and Turner

Agile teams should include people who have experience building systems, good communications and interpersonal skills, and some familiarity with agile development methods. Having systems development experience is more important than agile experience. Lindvall et. al estimates that the team should be composed of 25% to 33% competent and experienced people, or at least 10% if pair programming is being used.

**Small teams**

Agile prefers small team sizes with five to nine team members. This fits with the recommendation of Fred Brooks in his book *The Mythical Man Month*. Brooks describes the ideal team as small and sharp, with fewer than 10 people.

- The lower limit of the team size is based on having enough team members to produce results and warrant the overhead of applying the agile practices.
- The upper limit of the team size is justified by team productivity and communication limitations.
- Sackman, Erikson, and Grant have done research on the productivity of programmers and found that 'good' ones maybe 14 times more productive than poor ones.[1] Such productivity factors suggest that a small group of really good programmers can produce as much as a large group of average programmers.
- With their productivity statistics, Sackman, Erikson, and Grant were most likely referring to people at Cockburn's Level 3. However, given the scarcity of 'really good programmers,'[2] teams have to include members with a range of skills.
- Team meetings and events are used to train members on the project's goals, strategy Larger teams are less able to have collaborative and interactive sessions — it's possible, but more difficult.
- Pair-wise communications between people increase exponentially for each additional team member. The team has degrees of freedom to define code according to standards. However, communication is needed with the architect and other team members for interface specifications, usability design, etc. Barriers to communications like distance and access complexify interpersonal relations.

For large projects, multiple teams are suggested since small teams can't develop really big systems.

## Large teams

For agile to work with large projects and hundreds of team members, multiple agile teams are required. The dependencies between the teams should be minimized. Some examples of how dependencies may be reduced are performing rolling look ahead planning, sharing team members, and dedicated integration teams.

The topic of scaling agile projects is discussed further in chapter 19. Nevertheless, the following are some of the human resource aspects that should be considered.

- There should be one person accountable for the overall product. The product owner should work on a maximum of two teams. To scale agile beyond two teams, a hierarchy of product owners should be created.

- Some team members may be required to serve on more than one team to support coordination, knowledge sharing or product consistency between teams. They should perform the same role in each team.

- When there are time differences, teams or team members may be required to travel for specific meetings or for whole iterations. Alternatively, they may be required to adjust their working hours to have an overlap in the workday. There should be a balance so that no one set of team members has to make all of the adjustments.

## Estimating resources

The resources include the people and materials required to complete the work. The number of teams and team members, and the duration and number of iterations, depend on the scope of the work to be performed. In this regard, see the discussion on the roadmap, release and iteration planning.

## Acquiring resources

Agile projects require similar project roles to traditional projects. However, the ways the people work together, as well as some of their authorities and responsibilities, are different. In addition, a new engagement model for the product's customer creates a new role and the project manager.

There is a lot of variety of role definitions and implementation in various environments. The generic suggestion is to form the team as one unit working in the same team space, include all roles needed to deliver a functioning and useable product, and to balance the roles to avoid or limit bottlenecks (i.e. team roles that are completely stopped while waiting for the output from other roles.)

The following list describes the new and changed roles in agile teams from a software development perspective. It also gives some guidance on acquiring experienced team members.

### New roles

Agile projects have two roles that are not found in traditional projects. They aren't just new names for previously existing roles, but have different responsibilities and authorities.

### Agile coach

The agile coach is a servant-leader who supports the product owner and team in delivering applying the agile practices. The agile coach is not a new name for the project manager role. The agile coach has no command authority over the project team. The agile coach's role is discussed in detail in Chapter 5.

### Product owner

The product owner is accountable for setting priorities for the project team and defining the product features to deliver the maximum business value. A product owner is a single person. The analyst role may take on some of the responsibilities of the product owner. However, the product owner role has more authority over the project team than would be the case for a traditional analyst role.

The individual must have the skills and time to dedicate to the required activities. The time required varies depending on the agile method: XP requires an on-site customer (read as almost full-time and a real user) and scrum requires the time for grooming the backlog, attending half-day planning and half-day review sessions, as well as being able to support the team throughout an iteration.

## Changed roles

Given that agile teams favor generalists who can fulfill a range of activities needed to deliver working software, several of the traditional project roles will change. For example, position titles are no longer relevant. Each person is considered a team member. People are expected to perform tasks when they're available. There are no hierarchical levels within the team and no specialists who perform a single activity. Further role changes are described in the following section.

### Analyst

In traditional projects, the analyst collects the requirements in advance and records them in requirements and functional specification document; this person also, acts as the intermediary between the team and the users, and may perform the functional testing.

In agile projects, the traditional analyst may become the product owner. In this case, they take on the responsibilities defined for the product owner description. Otherwise, the analyst focuses on the activities needed in the current iteration.

Analysts may become the delegate for the product owner to write user stories. However, they don't spend their time writing user stories that will be needed two or three iterations in the future; instead, they work on topics relevant to the iteration at hand. When time permits, they may focus on user stories for future iterations.

They aren't the intermediary for the project team to the product owner or users, although they may coordinate details on the user stories and features with the product owner.

## Architects

In traditional projects, the architect role designs the technical architecture, taking into account the long-term considerations for technical requirements such as scalability, interoperability, standards, etc. They plan the architecture before the team starts its development.

Non-programming architects are not part of an agile team.

The architect doesn't make architectural decisions up-front, but defines the architecture during the iterations. The goal is to delay architectural decisions, so as not to lock the team into a specific path until the last possible moment. The architect must collaborate with the product owner to understand the business needs and work close to the market, users, and customers for decisions on the technical direction that the architecture will take.

## Data professionals

In traditional projects, data professionals (including data architects, database administrators) are used for building data models of the comprehensive (enterprise) data requirements before implementing data designs.

In agile projects, data professionals perform their work during the iterations. This involves working with data requirements for the current iteration or at a maximum one iteration in advance.

Data professionals must also take on a wider role that also includes the non-data aspects of designing, testing, and documenting.

Data professionals are expected to work in an open office space and spend lots of time working and collaborating with other team members.

## Functional line manager

In traditional projects, the functional line manager is responsible for human resource management including professional development, compensation, performance reviews, assigning individuals to projects, etc.

In agile projects, the functional line manager keeps human resource management responsibilities. However, if he or she previously assigned tasks to individual team members, this responsibility is eliminated in agile projects. Furthermore, performance reviews need to account for team contributions and performance rather than individual contributions and performance.

## Instructors, trainers or documentation specialists

To roll out the software to a user community or consumers, the users may require training, help systems, or user documentation. Therefore, instructors, trainers, or documentation specialists may be required to participate — actively or passively — in planning and review sessions or iterations.

## On-site customer or user proxy

The team should include real users to represent different user groups or personas. User proxies are people who may not be users themselves but represent the user. In the case of scrum, the product owner represents the users; in the case of XP, a real user is recommended.

The user proxy must be a dedicated, knowledgeable, and authoritative person who is responsible for maintaining feature priorities, writing tests for how features will be accepted, and reviewing and accepting the product. He or she must be available to clarify requirements, clarify issues, and support the project team.

Boehm and Turner refer to the agile customer or user proxy role as a "Collaborative, Representative, Authorized, Committed, Knowledgeable (CRACK) customer." (Boehm and Turner, 2003, 33)

## Programmers

In traditional projects, programmers are responsible for writing and unit testing their code. They may also be responsible for some or all aspects of the design and the integration testing, and they work from a written specification or design document.

In agile projects, programmers are responsible for all aspects of delivering working code from designing and writing to testing (all kinds) and documenting their code.

Programmers are expected to:

- Be responsible for discussing the user stories and features and requirements with the product owner, customer, and users.
- Work in an open office space and spend time collaborating with other team members.
- Adopt the agile technical practices that are established for the project team.
- Participate in team decision-making.

## Project management office (PMO)

In traditional projects, the responsibilities of a PMO vary from being a support organization to directly managing projects. It can be responsible for defining standards and monitoring compliance with those standards, coordinating cross-project communications and resources, and coaching, mentoring, training, and oversight. A PMO can also take on stakeholder responsibilities such as initiating, deploying project results and terminating projects.

In agile projects, some agile methodologies (scrum and XP) start the project with release planning and end with the solution delivery. That means, the activities to initiate the project should have already occurred and someone else is responsible for deploying the solution. Thus, the PMO may be responsible for organizing the initiation, rollout, and termination activities.

For large projects or enterprise-wide agile transitions, one recommendation is to establish a dedicated team to facilitate the training, coaching, and transition support. The team should include cross-functional team members, who coordinate the cross-team activities. See chapter 19 for more information on large projects.

In the oversight and governance of agile projects, the PMO will have to adjust the project reports, measures, and metrics to those that can be provided by an agile project. The metrics and reports typical for an agile project are discussed in chapter 7.

## Project Managers

In traditional projects, the project manager is responsible for managing what the project delivers according to agreed cost, time, and quality. This usually involves managing the team's activities, for example, assigning tasks, controlling deliverables, and ensuring those actions are completed.

In agile projects, a project manager role may or may not be required, depending on factors like project size. The project manager may also play the role of 'tracker' from XP. A tracker keeps track of the overall project as well as estimates and diverse results (e.g. tests, defects). In this case, the project manager will be responsible for the appropriate role description. The project manager shouldn't take on the role of the agile coach, nor vice versa; these roles are discussed in earlier chapters.

## Stakeholders

Stakeholders are not part of the project team. In agile, people are divided into those involved in the project and those involved in and accountable for project tasks.

Scrum uses an analogy of 'pigs and chickens'[3]: Pigs are accountable for tasks and chickens may be involved in the project, but are not accountable for getting work done. The team members are pigs and the stakeholders are chickens.

There are rules for the chickens:

- They can attend the daily stand-up meeting, but they're not allowed to contribute to the discussion.
- They're not allowed to change the priorities of the team or direct their task activities.
- The agile coach should support the team in managing the interference of the stakeholders in team activities.

## Agile testers

Based on the principles of some agile methodologies, the team members are responsible for testing and there's no specific tester role. Nevertheless, within software projects there are lots of non-development activities that require the skills and capabilities found in individuals who have traditionally played a testing role.

Thus, an agile tester is "a professional tester who embraces change, collaborates well with both technical and business people, and understands the concept of using tests to document requirement sand drive development." (Crispin and Gregory, 2009, 19)

Agile testers are responsible for working with the product owner, customer, users, and other sources. They collaborate to define feature functionality and acceptance criteria. The acceptance criteria are used to determine when a user story or feature is complete.

Agile testers may be delegates for the product owner or customer to write the acceptance tests. They perform different kinds of functional tests.

Agile testers require an independent mind, but separating them into a different team is counterproductive. They're expected to participate in team decision making as well as planning and review sessions. Ideally, agile testers should be part of the team and be located with the other team members.

The number of agile testers depends upon the complexity of the application, the skills of the tester(s) and the tools used for testing. There's no right tester-to-developer ratio. (Crispin and Gregory, 2009)

### User interface designers

User interface designers work in parallel with the development activities and may work one iteration ahead of the development team.

User interface designers are expected to be part of the team, to sit in the same open space as the other team members and participate in the team decision making.

## Acquiring experienced team members

Agile projects should include some team members who are experienced with agile practices; besides learning new practices, inexperienced members must be guided on changing practices that they've previously performed, for example, going from having all requirements explained in detail before starting a project to working with user stories — a big change for most technical people! The following are some of the options for finding experienced agile team members:

- Splitting an existing agile team into multiple agile teams.
- Adding inexperienced agile team members to an existing agile project to grow the experience base. Once the team is large enough, split it back out into multiple teams.
- Placing experienced team members from one team on another team to coach them.
- Hiring an external agile coach who can bring in experience and lessons learned from other agile projects. An external coach can recognize common patterns to help avoid pitfalls. In addition, some people are more comfortable receiving feedback from external experts rather than from colleagues.

## Developing a team

The first team development activity is for each member to understand what it means to be agile. Some methods for introducing agile include:

- Reading copies of agile books (team members and stakeholders)
- Attending external training courses for specific agile roles, e.g. scrum master training, product owner training, lean-Kanban training
- Attending an internal training session to introduce the team members to agile concepts
- Attending skill-specific agile training, e.g. estimating or story writing
- Coaching and mentoring from the agile coach
- Creating peer-to-peer coaching

The next team development activity is to ensure that each member understands that everyone in the team is expected to act as a leader, to solve problems, and to follow the rules. This understanding is developed through coaching and mentoring by the agile coach and by the team practicing the agile principles on a daily basis. The following behaviors are expected from the team members.

**Delivering a working solution.** Agile teams are accountable for delivering a working solution, including decision-making scope commitments and their daily activities, as delegated to them as a unit.

**Leadership.** Everyone on the team is responsible for foreseeing problems and making sure they are brought to the forefront to be addressed.

**Decision making.** Agile teams must include everyone needed to make decisions, which must be made in a timely fashion.

Team members should be aware of the discussions going on around them. They should participate in decision-making without being prompted. They should also understand that others will make decisions as well.

**No blame.** There should never be an occasion to place blame on a single team member. Team members won't make decisions if they feel they'll be blamed when the outcome is different from expected.

**Following the rules.** Each agile methodology has a set of practices or rules. To be truly agile and not chaotic, team members must follow those rules. For example, the daily stand-up should have a structure, be held at the same time every day, and last no more than 15 minutes. It's a place where team members can keep informed and bring-up issues that need resolution. Following the rules of the daily stand-up is one way to be engaged as a team member. Not attending or not following the structure reduces the ability for the team to function as a team in addition to reducing the productivity of the team.

See chapter 5 for more information on mentoring and coaching an agile team.

## Managing a team

Keeping the team motivated and achieving assumes that they'll be highly productive and achieve the project goals. Use the rules, events, and artifacts defined in the agile methodologies as tools and methods to motivate the team members. The following aspects support the concept of team motivation:

- Team members involved in planning and review sessions
- Team members get to know one another
- Form trust through a no-blame culture
- Engaging team members in the entire process
- Empowering the team to make decisions
- Frequent feedback
- Coaching the team member to understand the rules, practices and processes
- Encouraging expected behavior

### Assessing team performance

Since an agile team as a whole is responsible for producing results, performance evaluations should focus on assessing team performance. The daily stand-ups and information radiators are a method for monitoring performance. Retrospectives and self-assessments are methods for optimizing performance.

**Daily stand-ups:** During the daily stand-up, the team members share status reports. The daily stand-up is one of the key tools for monitoring the project's progress. As such, it's also a performance management tool.

Challenges that may require coaching include getting individuals:

- Who don't like to speak publicly to contribute
- Who doesn't like to attend meetings
- Who like to expand the scope of a meeting to stay on topic

**Information radiator:** Just one method of providing feedback on how the team's progressing against the project objectives. The team should maintain most of the information radiators, e.g. burndown charts, task boards, etc.

Challenges that may require coaching include:

- Getting the team to recognize the need to keep them current
- Finding the right format and content to make them meaningful to the team

**Retrospectives:** One of the main tools the team can use to learn what works and what doesn't, provide feedback, resolve issues, and manage change in performance.

Challenges to overcome may include:

- Discussing both positive and negative findings
- Scheduling and prioritizing the actions

**Self-assessment:** Part of a retrospective conducted to identify development needs, understand the opinions and commitment levels of the individuals in an agile team. Its purpose is to stimulate learning and growth by identifying improvement needs and opportunities.

## Knowledge sharing

Agile projects promote knowledge sharing through the team's structure, rules and practices. The following are some of the agile practices that promote knowledge sharing:

- Cross-functional teams
- Daily stand-up
- Colocation of the team
- Planning with the entire team
- Pair programming

Furthermore, team members may belong to a community of practice outside the project team. A community of practice is a group of individuals with similar interests who share experiences and knowledge around a specific theme with members of a community.

## Personal experience: Traditional management or the death of empowerment

### —Dr. Thomas Juli, Certified ScrumMaster & PMP

As the principles of empowerment, agile, and lean methodologies become increasingly popular, more and more managers embrace these ideas. They claim to be honestly interested in trying them out in their organizations and teams.

A good example is the CIO of a German internet service provider. Excited about the huge potential of agile and self-organizing teams and the returns they could yield for his company, he set out a new corporate motto of 'empowering people' and promoted the idea of 'strong teams.' The CIO consequently instructed his managers to empower their people and teams.

While the idea was laudable, the execution failed. Not because no one followed the new guidelines — lots of teams on the operational level did. As a matter of fact, at least two out of the five departments had recently introduced agile product development approaches. The problem was that few middle managers understood and supported the motivation, requirements, implications, and opportunities of this strategic move. They were stuck in their old ways of management by directive. They were used to telling their subordinates what to do, and how and when to do it. Therefore, while they were officially following the new corporate directive, they didn't actually change their management style.

The result was that those individuals who fully embraced the idea of empowered and strong teams didn't have the necessary backing of their own managers, who meddled with the team's activities and thus undermined team morale. It's one thing to set out the direction of empowering people, or of welcoming strong and self-organized teams; it's another to make sure that the whole management team understands the motivation and vision, as well as the possible pitfalls and impediments of the process, and that it supports the teams on the operational level by removing these impediments.

There are many obstacles to overcome along the way: vanity, the desire for power and influence, insecurity—and a closed vs. an open mindset. The latter is characterized by the willingness to make mistakes and a drive to help other people and the organization succeed for the better of all. Management, on the other hand, maintains and sustains the status quo, executes what's dictated from above, and allows micro-management — which, in turn kills motivation and creativity. This is why traditional management is the death of empowerment.

**References:**

Juli, T. (2011). Leadership Principles for Project Success. New York: CRC Press.

Juli, T. (2012). The Power and Illusion of Self-Organizing Teams. 2012 PMI Global Congress Proceedings. Vancouver, BC, Canada: Project Management Institute.

## Summary

- Agile projects favor small teams of highly productive people or multiple small teams for large projects. Each team should have all the people needed to deliver a working solution and make decisions.

- Teams should be co-located in the team space to facilitate communication or additional technologies; otherwise, activities should be undertaken to include distributed teams or team members in the communications.

- If pair programming is foreseen at least 10% of the team members should be experienced with agile practices; otherwise, at least 25% of the team members should be experienced. Splitting teams, training, and coaching are effective methods for incorporating experience into the project team.

- Form the team by including all the roles necessary to deliver a functioning and useable product; balance the roles to avoid bottlenecks.

- The project management office may play a role in initiating, rolling-out the results, and terminating agile projects. For large projects or enterprise deployments, it may also provide coordination, mentoring, training, and coaching.

- Team management requires revising performance measures to account for team results; use the agile practices to motivate and coach the team.

## Recommended reading

- In his book *Succeeding with Agile,* Mike Cohn describes different aspects of organizing agile projects and people.

- In his book *Agile Software Development,* Alistair Cockburn describes the considerations for organizing team space, working with different team sizes, and incorporating people of different skill levels.

## Endnotes

[1] The actual finding was that there is a 28:1 ratio between good and bad programmers. That data has since been reviewed and corrected for mistakes in the analysis and the measuring methodology. The published result is a ratio of 14:1. (Prechelt 1999)

[2] According to the CIO magazine, Computer Technology Industry Association reported that 93 percent of 502 survey respondents indicated they have an IT skills gap. (Levinson 2012)

[3] The concept of pigs and chickens comes from this story. "A pig and a chicken are walking down a road. The chicken looks at the pig and says "Hey, why don't we open a restaurant?" The pig looks back at the chicken and says "Good idea, what do you want to call it?" The chicken thinks about it and says "Why don't we call it 'Ham and Eggs'?" "I don't think so" says the pig, "I'd be committed but you'd only be involved."

# Chapter 13 Communications

This chapter aligns with the *PMBOK® Guide* Communications Management knowledge area; it covers the process for the flow of information from collection through information disposition. This chapter covers:

- Planning communication management
- Managing communications
- Monitoring communications

## Planning communication management

The communications planning should determine the types of documents needed for the project as well as the role that the agile practices, events, and artifacts will play in communication.

Intermediate project documents are used to transfer information between project team members or from one process step to the next process step. In a traditional project, these would include documents such as the requirements specification or the design specification. The agile methodologies are designed to limit intermediate documents as much as possible. The product backlog, including the user stories, is a required document in an agile project life cycle. Other document requirements should be agreed between the project team and the product owner.

The 'product documents' cover the usage, operations, and maintenance of the product. The level of detail required in these documents is determined by the product owner and agreed with the project team, which takes place when the 'definition of done' is decided. Product documentation such as user manuals, and maintenance manuals are prioritized into the backlog and completed like any other requirement. This method of addressing documentation focuses the team on understanding its uses and its importance in delivering the overall product.

Table 13-1 provides a mapping by the role of the communication events, artifacts, and information radiators that should be considered in planning communications.

| Role | Communication Events, Artifacts, Practices |
|---|---|
| Team | Team space, daily stand-up meeting, retrospective, review, release planning, iteration planning, backlog, iteration burndown, task board, pair programming |
| Product owner | Release planning, iteration planning, review, backlog, release burnup, parking lot charts |
| Users | Backlog, product increment (collaboration), review |
| Other stakeholders | Release grooming, review, backlog, release burnup, parking lot charts |

Table 13-1 Project communication channels

## Managing communications

The following section provides a description of the agile team environment, the events, artifacts and information radiators and their role in the communication plan.

### Team space for co-located teams

Agile favors team co-location, open workspaces, and face-to-face meetings. Co-location has the whole team in close proximity to one another. The key justifications for team co-location are 'osmotic communications' and the setting up of several agile practices.

Osmotic communication describes gaining information by (over)hearing background discussions from other team members. It's a form of information flow that allows individual team members to be involved with and understand key discussions, activities, and decisions about the project based on hearing the communications around them.

Osmotic communication occurs when the team is physically located in the same room — a 'war room' or 'team space.' The team space should be an open area shared by all team members with no barriers to communication. Walls or partitions are barriers to communication.

The agile practices of daily stand-up meetings, big visible charts, and limited intermediate project documents rely on frequent, face-to-face interactions. These interactions happen more easily when people are co-located.

The team space should balance human, social, environmental, economic, and personal factors. It should have an area for private calls and one-on-one meetings. Making a team space available may require the acquisition of new facilities or the alteration of existing workspaces.

When one product is being developed by multiple teams or when one team has members in multiple sites, the teams are called 'distributed'. Additional efforts must be undertaken to include distributed team members in the osmotic communications. Details on working with distributed teams are discussed in chapter 17.

## Monitoring communications

From time to time, one should check that the planned communications are effective in meeting the stakeholders' needs. Conducting retrospectives with key stakeholders is one interactive method for evaluating the effectiveness of events, artifacts and practices.

## Artifacts

Engaging real users in the project and having the team collaborate with users and the product owner to collect requirements reduces the need for intermediate documents to transfer product information. This collaboration also gains the interest, buy-in and commitment of the people working together on the project's outcome. Table 13-2 provides a mapping of the groups that may take an interest in the project artifacts.

The artifacts are co-created with the interested parties or shared with them during one or more of the communication events.

| Artifacts | Interested parties |
|---|---|
| User stories include high-level descriptions of the feature requirements. | Product owner<br>Users<br>Team |
| The product backlog contains the user stories that should be included in the product. | Product owner<br>Stakeholders<br>Users<br>Team |
| The roadmap provides details on the long-range planning for the product. | Product owner<br>Stakeholders<br>Users<br>Team |
| The release plan communicates the high-level plan for the user stories (or themes) for multiple iterations and their forecasted release timeframe. | Product owner<br>Stakeholders<br>Users<br>Team |
| The iteration plan details the features that will be included in the iteration. | Product owner<br>Team |
| The product increment is the software solution that's developed, tested, and documented during an iteration. | Product owner<br>Team<br>User<br>Stakeholders |

Table 13-2 Artifact interested partics

## Communication events

Communication events are designed to move the development of the product forward and include the stakeholders in the development process. By making them collaborative events, information is exchanged between the team and the other participants. This feedback is useful to the team to ensure that the right product is being developed. Table 13-3 provides an overview of the typical events in an agile project, their role in managing and controlling communications, and the typical participants.

| Event | Participants |
| --- | --- |
| A chartering session at the start of the project to understand the project, the product that will be produced, and the parameters and the context of the project. | Product owner<br>Team |
| Story writing workshops, user interviews, and other events to gather user requirements. | Product owner<br>Users<br>Team |
| 'Backlog grooming' is an activity the product owner performs to add, change, delete, and prioritize items in the product backlog. | Product owner<br>Stakeholders<br>Users |
| The release planning meeting is a collaborative event to make decisions regarding the release dates and the user stories per iteration. It usually occurs during an iteration to prepare for future iterations. | Product owner<br>Team |
| The iteration planning meeting is used to discuss, understand, estimate, and commit to the user stories that will be developed during the iteration. | Product owner<br>Team |
| In the daily stand-ups the team shares the status of the project, discusses the activities to be accomplished in the next 24 hours, and identifies issues that are impeding progress. | Team |
| The review meeting is at the end of an iteration; it's an opportunity for the team to demonstrate the work that's been completed, confirm acceptance, and discuss the next steps. | Product<br>Owner<br>Team<br>Stakeholders |
| A retrospective is at the end of an iteration and allows the team event to reflect on what was completed, what worked well, and what needs improvement. | Team |

Table 13-3 Communication event participants

## Information radiators

The project progress information should be displayed, either in a visible place in the team space or electronically. The charts should be maintained and be up-to-date. The product owner, team, and stakeholders should be able to view the status at any time. Table 13-4 describes how each information radiator should inform its target audience.

| Information Radiator | Target Audience |
|---|---|
| A task board (or Kanban board) communicates the project workflow during an iteration and uses cards to represents the process step for each user story. | Team |
| An iteration burndown chart shows planned and actual work remaining until the target end date. | Team |
| A release burnup chart shows how much work is included in the project and how much work is completed. | Product owner<br>Stakeholders |
| A velocity diagram shows the planned and actual rate at which teams deliver business value | Product owner<br>Team<br>Stakeholders |
| A parking lot chart reports the progress of feature sets, including the total number of features and the percentage complete. | Product owner<br>Stakeholders |
| A cumulative flow diagram communicates the status of features and stories over time, including work-in-progress (WIP), or the work started but not completed. | Product owner<br>Stakeholders |
| A risk burndown chart communicates the project risks and their potential impact on the project over time. | Team<br>Product owner<br>Stakeholders |

Table 13-4 Information radiators target audience

## Summary

- Communication planning should address the intermediate project documents, as well as the agile practices, events and artifacts that will be used to inform the interested parties.
- Team space should be organized to facilitate free-flowing communications among co-located and distributed team members. This may require adapting the facilities, using collaborative technologies, or undertaking additional activities.
- The collaboration events should include the right participants to ensure two-way communication and frequent feedback between the project team and the stakeholders.
- The project artifacts should be produced by collaborating with the users and the product owner. This collaboration also plays a role in keeping them informed on the project status.
- The information radiators that identify the project status should be kept up-to-date and be highly visible, so that team members and stakeholders can gauge the status of the project.

## Recommended reading

- In the *Collaboration Explained: Facilitation Skills for Software Project Leaders*, Jean Tabaka explains the communication events, their structure and content, and provides techniques for facilitating the sessions.

# Chapter 14 Risk

This chapter aligns with the *PMBOK® Guide* Risk Management knowledge area; it covers the processes that reduce the impacts of negative risk and increase the impacts of opportunities. This chapter covers:

- Planning risk management
- Identifying risks
- Performing qualitative risk analysis
- Performing quantitative risk analysis
- Planning risk responses
- Implementing risk responses
- Monitoring risks

## Planning risk management

Risk management involves making a plan for how the project will address risks (negative project impacts) and opportunities (positive project impacts). The scale of the plan has to be adjusted based on the requirements of the project and the risk tolerance of the organization. The risks must be identified, qualified as to their importance to the project, quantified as to the costs of responding to the risk, addressed as part of the project, and finally, monitored, and controlled.

Before discussing risk management within agile projects, a word about the impact of agile practices on project risks. Agile projects reduce risks because they:

- Break the scope into segments and deliver it in small increments

- Allow frequent chances to inspect and verify that the scope meets the requirements
- Allow payment schemes to be aligned to the increments and thus the extent of the payment can be limited to the delivered scope
- Can accommodate late changes in scope which is inevitable in software projects
- Specify clear rules about obligations, expectations, and deliverables
- Reduce the unnecessary features

Conversely, agile projects increase risks when they are being tried for the first time because they represent a change in the way of doing things. This risk should be added to the register so that it's thoroughly discussed and mitigated in initial agile projects.

In an agile project, the artifacts are responsible for recording risks and their responses; the events identify, analyze and plan risk responses and monitor risks; the project team manages the technical risk; and the product owner manages the business risks (Miller, 2019; Tavares, Silva, & Diniz de Souza, 2019). The risk actions in Table 14-1 are incorporated into agile events and artifacts.

| Risk Action | Event or Artifact | Description |
|---|---|---|
| Risk identification and analysis | Release planning | The risks should be identified, qualitatively and quantitatively analyzed during the roadmap or release planning (See chapter Integration). The result is a risk register (list of risks). |
| | | New risks can be added at any time. |
| | | Risks should be sized and prioritized into the backlog for action. |
| Risks responses | Iteration planning | The risks responses should be planned and scheduled for action during the iteration planning. |
| Monitor risks | Daily stand-up | Monitor risks and risk responses. |
| | | Identify risks and risk responses. |
| Control risks | Retrospective | A specific risk retrospective can be conducted and risks can be discussed during the team retrospectives. |
| | Information radiator | A risk burndown chart can be used to monitor the state of risks within the project. |

Table 14-1 Risk action events or artifacts

## Identifying risks

Risk identification requires the team to determine the potential negative or positive events that could occur in the project. A negative risk would cause harm to the project such as delaying requirements, causing additional rework, or adding to the cost. A positive risk is an opportunity that could add value to the project such as quicker delivery. A 'top tip' or brainstorming session can be used to identify potential risks. If each risk is written on a card during the identification process, then the cards can be used as story cards, for performing qualitative risk analysis and scheduling risk actions.

### Top tip

Top tip is a collaborative exercise from the DSDM methodology (2008) that uses a Champion-Challenger[1] approach to identify risks and potential responses. In top tip:

- The team is split into groups and given the scenario that it's implementation plus one day. They're given the assignment of identifying a list of potential events that would make the project a disaster.
- Once each group has produced their list, they swap lists. Using the other's list, each group defines the potential issues that could have caused the disaster.
- Then they swap lists again. Each group comes up with strategies to avoid or minimize the risk.
- Repeat the champion and challenger routine to refine the mitigation and use the results as the project's risk register.

### Brainstorming

An alternative to top tip is to identify a list of potential risk categories, and in a brainstorming session have the team identify the potential risks under each category. The risk categories can be created based on the risks from a previous project or by using a list of software risks from another source. The Software Engineering Institute Technical Report (Carr, Konda, Monarch, & Ulrich, 1993) includes a *Taxonomy-Based Risk Identification* (see Table 14-2) that can be used as a basis for risk categories.

| Product Engineering | Development Environment | Project Constraints |
|---|---|---|
| Requirements | Development process | Team |
| Design | Development system | Contract |
| Code and unit test | Management process | Project interfaces |
| Integration and test | Management methods | |
| Engineering specialties | Work environment | |

Table 14-2 Software risk categories

As an alternative, to 'top tip' or brainstorming, Mike Griffiths has developed a set of collaborative games for risk management. He suggests a 'doomsday' clock as a method for identifying and categorizing risks, 'karma' day for collecting opportunities, and 'post an ad' for the qualitative analysis of the risks.

The result of the risk identification is a list of potential project risks.

## Performing qualitative risk analysis

During the qualitative risk analysis, the team places the risk in categories by indicating their impact on the project and their probability of occurring. A color-coded probability and impact matrix or a quadrant can be used as a tool for the placement of the risks.

### Risk probability and impact matrix

Based on the probability and impact matrix from the *PMBOK® Guide*, a color-coded matrix can be used to classify risks. The color-coding makes the intensity of the risks visible. Figure 14-1 is an example of a color-coded risk matrix using the *PMBOK® Guide* risk scores.

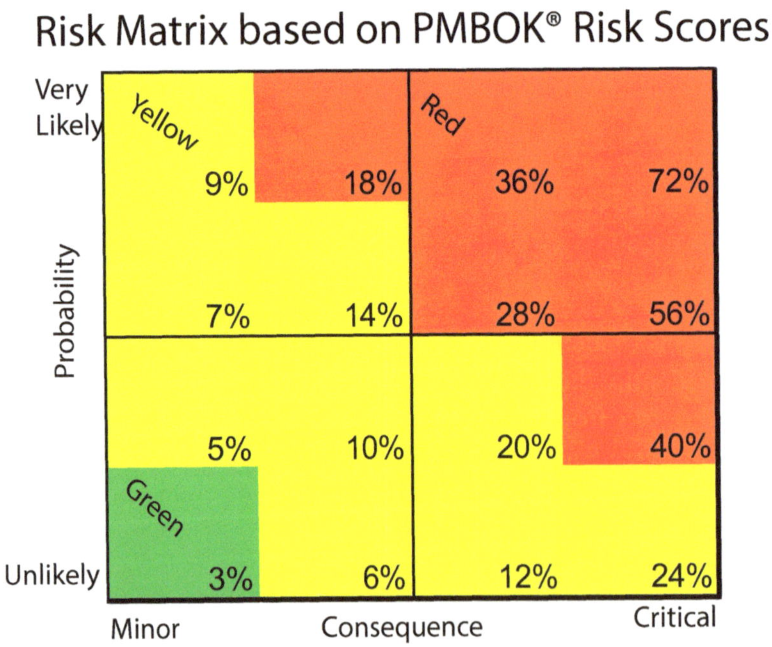


Adapted from:
Project Management Institute. A Guide to the Project Management Body of Knowledge (PMBOK® Guide - Fifth Edition). Newtown Square, PA: Project Management Institute, Inc., 2013.

Figure 14-1 Color-coded risk matrix

A project-specific classification scheme should be created to map the impact and probability percentages to a meaningful description. The following tables are examples of how the impacts (Table 14-3) and probabilities (Table 14-4) might be classified.

| | Impact rating (%) | Consequence | Description |
|---|---|---|---|
| 1 | 0- 20 | Minor | Small cost/schedule impact; all requirements will be met |
| 2 | 21—40 | Moderate | Moderate cost/schedule impacts; no impact on "must have" requirements; may impact other requirements |
| 3 | 41—80 | Serious | Major cost/schedule impact; May impact "must have" requirements; may not deliver other requirements |
| 4 | 81—100 | Critical | Major cost/schedule impact; Will not deliver "must have" requirements |

Table 14-3 Risk impact rating description

| | Probability (%) Risk Will Occur | Description |
|---|---|---|
| 1 | 0- 40 | Unlikely |
| 2 | 41- 60 | Possible |
| 3 | 61–85 | Likely |
| 4 | 86–100 | Very Likely |

Table 14-4 Risk probability of occurrence rating description

The risk score from the matrix is determined by multiplying the impact by the probability. A general rule of thumb for the matrix color-coding and response levels is in Table 14-5.

| Risk Score | Color Coding | Description |
|---|---|---|
| Less than 5% | Green | Risks with a low probability and low impact are coded; these risks should be monitored. |
| Between 5%—17% | Yellow | Risks in the middle may be acted upon to reduce their probability of occurring or their impacts should they occur. |
| Higher than 18% | Red | Negative risks with high probability and high impact; they are considered critical and should be aggressively managed. |

Table 14-5 Risk matrix color coding scheme

The matrix can be drawn on the board (with the color code or as a quadrant) and risks placed into the corresponding position on the matrix. The matrix has the probability on the vertical (y) axis and consequence on the horizontal (x) axis. Using the matrix, the team places the risks in their relative position on the quadrant.

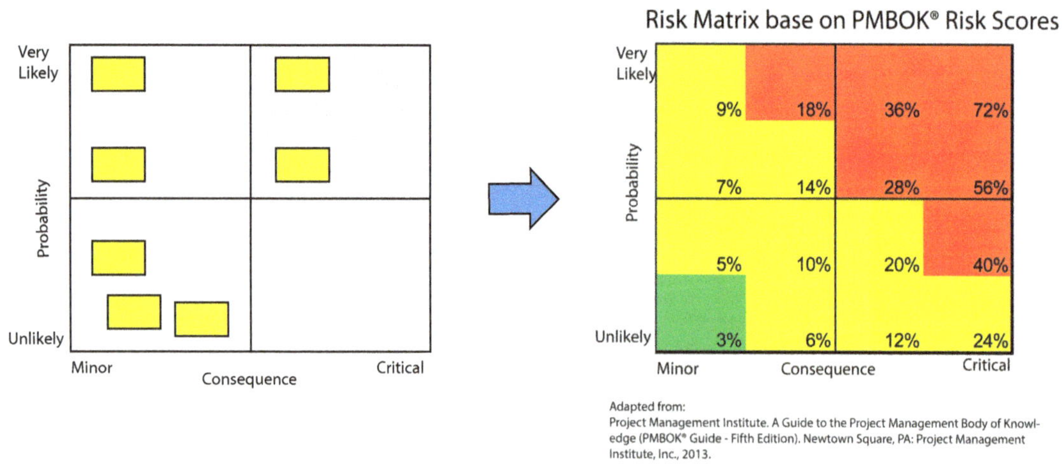


Figure 14-2 Quadrant risk matrix with severity overlay

The risks are placed in their relative position, which means they don't have an exact probability and impact level. (see Figure 14-2) Nevertheless, their relative positioning should provide sufficient information to categorize them for action. If precision is required, the team can assign them a probability and impact percentage.

## Performing quantitative risk analysis

Quantitative risk analysis assigns a numerical value to the consequences of the risks on the project objectives. Sensitivity analysis, expected monetary value (EMV), Monte Carlo simulations, and decision trees are some of the techniques used for the quantitative risk analysis.

Quantifying the risks in financial terms is an optional step as the risks can be prioritized based on their risk score (impact x probability). However, if the backlog is prioritized in financial terms, a financial measure makes it easier for the risk to be prioritized into the backlog. In addition, the financial value can be used to decide on the size of any financial risk reserves.

### Expected monetary value of risks

For each risk, create an estimate for the financial impact of the risk should it occur. These estimates can be based on historical data, interviews, or expert opinion. Three-point estimates, story points, or ideal days may be used as the basis for estimating the scope of the risks. The estimates can be captured in person-day impacts (e.g. 10 days' delay) or monetary impacts.

| Risk Short Description | Best Case | Most Likely | Worst Case | PERT |
|---|---|---|---|---|
| Hardware capacity | 5,000 | 10,000 | 20,000 | 10,833 |
| Design too complex | 5,000 | 20,000 | 60,000 | 24,167 |
| Not able to reclassify data | 10,000 | 20,000 | 60,000 | 25,000 |
| Late hardware delivery | 1,000 | 5,000 | 10,000 | 5,167 |
| Poor performance | 5,000 | 10,000 | 20,000 | 10,833 |
| Team not experienced | 5,000 | 10,000 | 20,000 | 10,833 |

Table 14-6 Example of a three-point estimate for risk impacts

The EMV of risks is the financial impact on the project. The EMV is calculated based on the estimated financial impact of a risk multiplied times its probability of occurring, and adding the products together. For negative risks, it's a negative number and for positive risks (opportunities), it's a positive number. The project EMV is the sum of the individual risk EMVs.

The EMV can be used to size the contingency reserves. This topic is discussed in chapter 10.

## Sensitivity analysis

Sensitivity analysis can be used to determine the significance of the individual risks on the project outcome. Sensitivity analysis would evaluate the impact of each individual risk on the project outcome while holding the other risks constant. The analysis is most often displayed using a tornado diagram. The tornado diagram makes visual the assumptions that have the biggest impact as well as the highest degree of uncertainty.

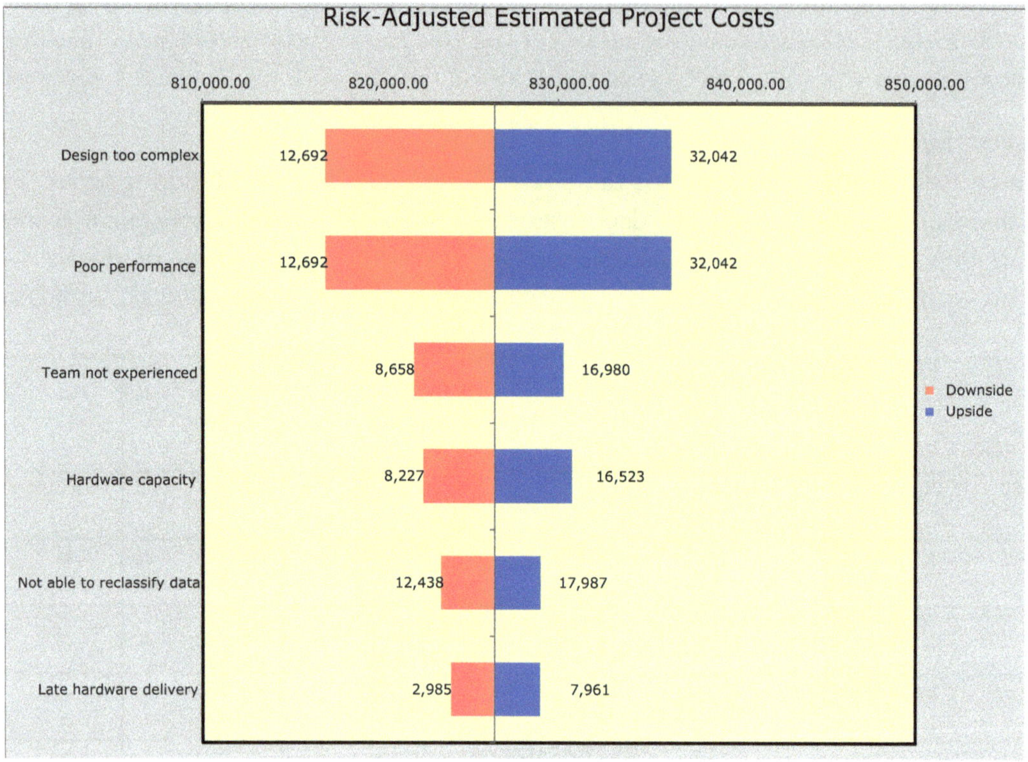


Figure 14-3 Tornado diagram risk-adjusted project estimate

For example, from Table 14-6 the risk for "design too complex" and "poor performance" could result in spending between 5,000 and 60,000 for reworking functionality. In addition, there are other risks that might have an impact such as "late hardware delivery", the "team not experienced," etc. The sensitivity analysis indicates the "design too complex" and "poor performance" have the highest variability relative to other risks, and they will each probably range between 12,551 and 31,908 in costs. (see Figure 14-3) With this information, the team would know to focus on addressing these risks.

## Monte Carlo simulation

The likely project costs (or schedule) can be calculated using statistical methods such as the decision tree or Monte Carlo simulation. The information is supplied into a Monte Carlo simulation engine as a project model. The model runs several iterations (usually hundreds) using random numbers to generate a distribution curve that provides the likelihood of the project being delivered for a specific cost (or schedule). Monte Carlo simulation is valuable in providing probabilistic estimates when there is uncertainty around the project schedule or costs. In agile projects, it recommended when there are inter-dependencies between multiple project teams since the overall project would be impacted should dependencies not be delivered when needed.

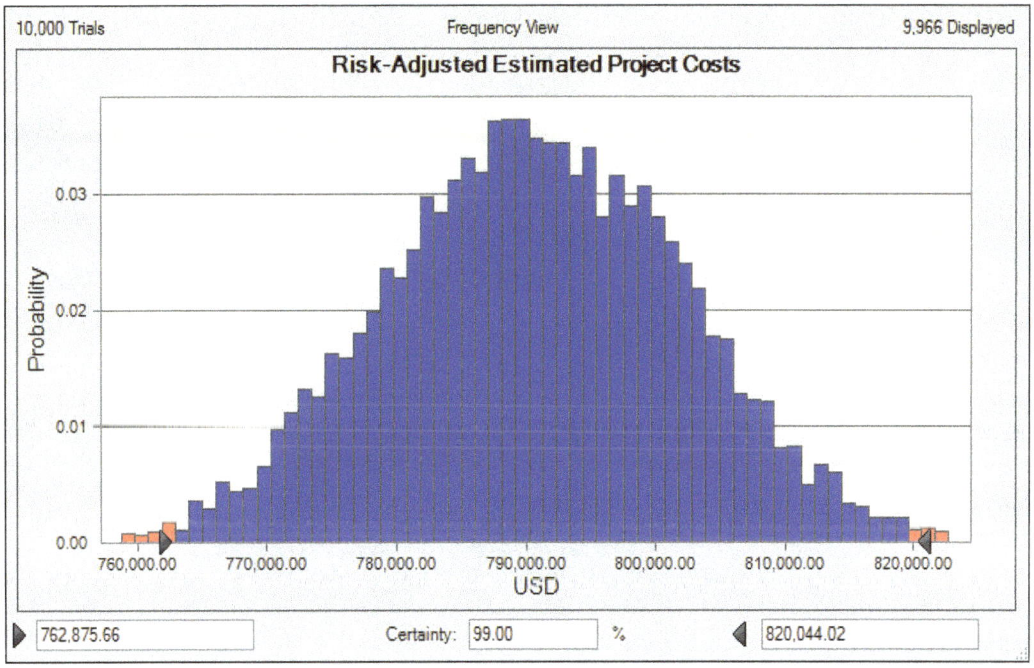


Figure 14-4 Risk-adjusted project cost estimate

Tom DeMarco and Tim Lister (2004) offer a free excel spreadsheet that estimates the duration (time window) you would need to cover the uncontrollable risks in the project. It uses a number of risks factors for projects and Monte Carlo Simulation. The spreadsheet is called *Riskology* and is available free from their website.

The sample out from a Monte Carlo module in Figure 14-4 indicates that the project has a 99% chance of costing between 762,875.66 and 820,044.02 USD.

## Planning risk responses

The next step is to plan the responses to the risks. For each risk, the team needs to decide the actions for addressing the risk. The options from strongest to weakest response are as follows (see Figure 14-5).

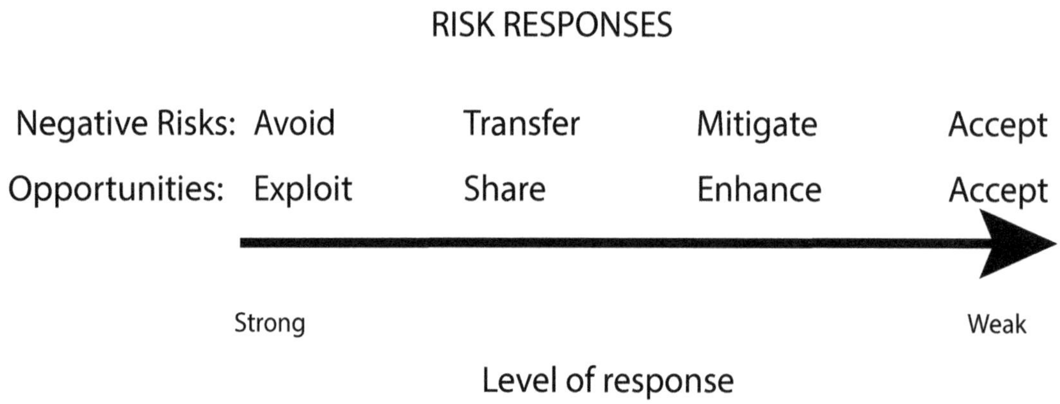


Figure 14-5 Risk Responses

**Avoid**—incorporate activities so that the risk doesn't occur

**Transfer**—ask a party outside of the project to manage the risk

**Mitigate**—take actions to minimize the chances that the risk occurs.

**Accept**—don't take action at this time, but address the issue if it occurs.

Positive risks are opportunities in the projects, and the following are some possible responses:

**Exploit**—ensure opportunity is realized

**Share**—allocate responsibly to a third party that can capture the opportunity and benefit the project

**Enhance**—change the size of the opportunity by identifying key drivers and take steps to increase the probability and impact

**Accept**—do nothing; take advantage if it occurs.

The consequences of the decisions are that the product owner may have to include risk responses in the product backlog for action, monetary reserves may be added to the budget, actions may be delayed until a later stage, or someone outside of the project may be requested to address the risk. However, taking action to respond to risk may not eliminate all risks; there may be residual risks or secondary risks. Residual risks are risks that remain after the action is taken. Secondary risks are new risks that are created after the risk action is taken.

### Risk report card

The risk report card (see Table 14-7) is a list of the risks, the chosen response, and the net EMV. The net EMV is the EMV value minus the impacts of any secondary or residual risks. The risk report card can be used as a tool with the product owner to place the risk actions in the product backlog.

| Risk Short Description | Risk Rating | Risk Action | EMV | Secondary or Residual Risks | Net EMV |
|---|---|---|---|---|---|
| Hardware capacity | Yellow | Accept | (11,339.75) | | (11,339.75) |
| Design too complex | Red | Mitigate | (21,291.71) | | (21,291.71) |
| Not able to reclassify data | Yellow | Accept | (17,071.07) | | (17,071.07) |
| Late hardware delivery | Green | Transfer | (5,256.58) | | (5,256.58) |
| Poor performance | Red | Mitigate | (21,291.71) | | (21,291.71) |
| Team not experienced | Yellow | Accept | (15,606.60) | | (15,606.60) |

Table 14-7 Risk responses and EMV

## Implementing risk responses

The product owner prioritizes risks into the product backlog. Getting the risk response actions into the backlog is how the risks are scheduled for action. Risks can be prioritized into the backlog based on their EMV or their risk score. The result is a Risk-Adjusted Backlog.

If EMV is used, the risks are inserted into the correct relative position in the backlog based on their relative financial position.

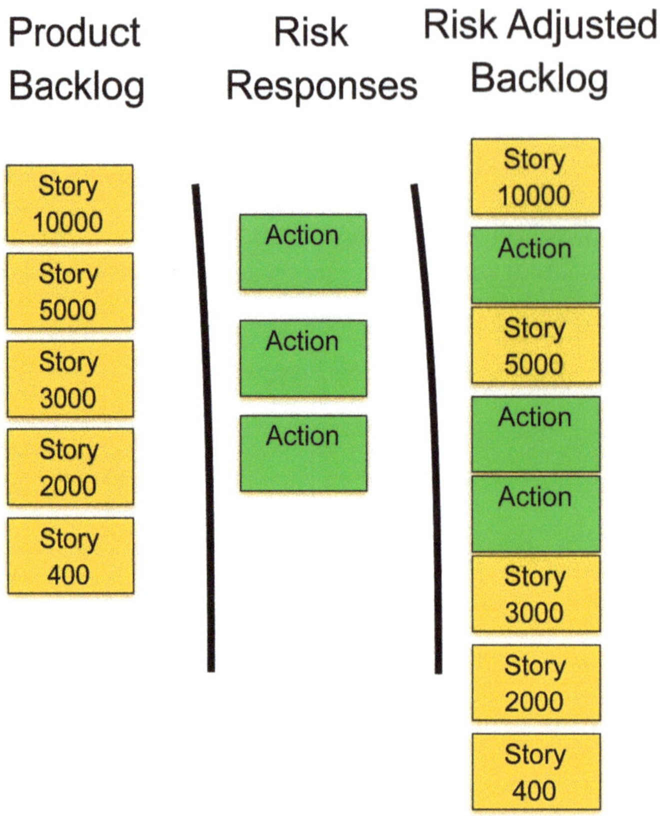


Figure 14-6 Positioning risk in the product backlog

If the risk score is used, a mapping should be created to align the risk score, classification, or color-coding to the backlog prioritization. Table 14-8 provides an indication of how the risks classes might be mapped to the MoSCoW prioritization levels.

| Risk Score | Risk Classifications | Risk Classification | Backlog Prioritization using MoSCoW |
|---|---|---|---|
| Less than 5% | Low | Green | Could or Won't Have |
| Between 5%—17% | Medium | Yellow | Should Have |
| Higher than 18% | High | Red | Must Have |

Table 14-8 Mapping risk scores to backlog priority

# Monitoring risks

A Risk-Adjusted backlog includes risks into the product backlog prioritized by their risk EMV or risk score. The risks are worked on and addressed as part of the normal course of running the project. Risks are discussed and revisited in the iteration planning workshop. This method makes risk management a continuous part of the project and not an activity that may be overlooked.

## Risk burndown chart

A risk burndown chart (see Figure 14-7 and Table 14-9) is a visual chart of individual risks cumulated to total risk on the horizontal axis (x-axis) overtime on the vertical axis (y-axis). The changes in the impact, probability, and risk score are tracked over time and plotted into a stacked graph of cumulative project risk scores. The risk burndown graph makes it easy to identify the trend, identify new or escalating risks. The risk burndown chart can be used as a tool for informing the stakeholders on the risk situation in the project.

| Short Risk Description | Iteration 1 | | | Iteration 2 | | |
|---|---|---|---|---|---|---|
| | Impact | Prob. | Risk Score | Impact | Prob. | Risk Score |
| Hardware capacity | 1 | 2 | 2 | 1 | 2 | 2 |
| Design too complex | 3 | 2 | 6 | 3 | 4 | 12 |
| Not able to reclassify data | 2 | 1 | 2 | 2 | 1 | 2 |
| Late hardware delivery | 1 | 1 | 1 | 1 | 1 | 1 |
| Poor performance | 1 | 3 | 3 | 1 | 3 | 3 |
| Team not experienced | 1 | 4 | 4 | 4 | 4 | 16 |

Table 14-9 Risk burndown table

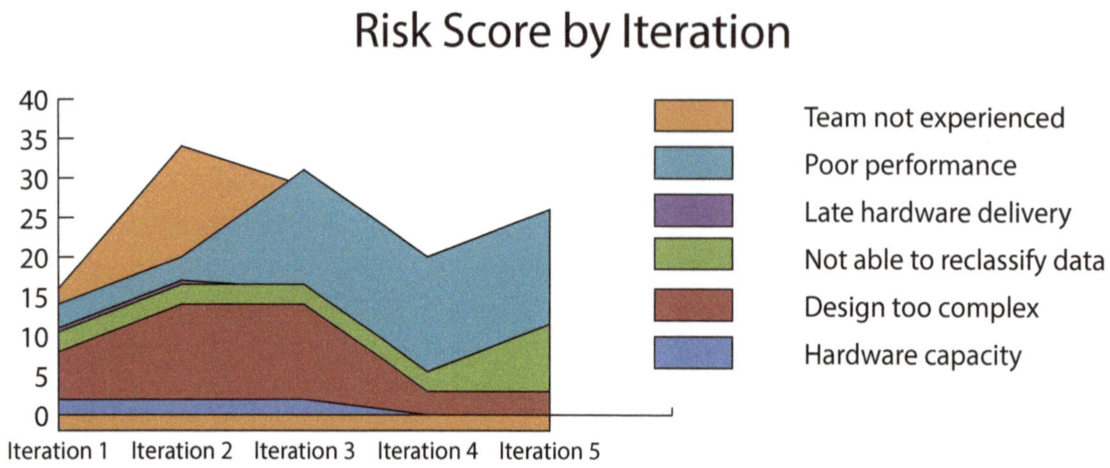


Figure 14-7 Risk burndown chart

## Risk retrospective

A risk retrospective is a review and lessons learned session for the risk artifact, processes, and team's capability in this area. It should be conducted periodically similar to the retrospective at the end of the project iteration. The review should consider what worked well, what should be improved or stopped, and what is the performance of the risk metrics.

## Summary

- Agile project processes can be a method of mitigating project risks as they break projects into small deliverable increments and can accommodate changes. However, the first application of agile practices should be included as a risk and managed in the first implementations.

- Brainstorming and 'top tip' are two techniques for engaging the team in identifying risks, their impacts on the project, and some potential actions.

- Their economic value or risk score should prioritize the risks. It is not important to be precise about assigning risk scores. It is important to understand the impact of the risk on delivering the requirements and on the schedule and costs.

- Risks are scheduled for resolution by placing them in the product backlog during release planning, planning the risk actions during the iteration planning, and working on risk during the project iterations.

- Risk quantification with simulation techniques may be required if there are many interdependencies in the project between sub-project teams.

## Recommended reading

- Mike Griffiths in *Collaborative Games for Risk Management* provides a structure and content for engaging the team in risk management activities. http://leadinganswers.typepad.com/leading_answers/2012/06/collaborative-games-for-risk-management.html (accessed 09 25, 2012)

## Endnotes

1. Champion-Challenger is a methodology for a new idea—the challenger—to test the current leader—the champion. The concept originated in the analytical field. It provides a strategy for continuous improvement by challenging the current champion.

# Chapter 15 Procurement

This chapter aligns with the PMBOK® Guide Procurement Management knowledge area and covers the processes for acquiring and managing products and services from a third party for the project. The processes for conducting, controlling, and closing procurements are similar for agile and traditional projects. Therefore, those processes are not covered in this chapter. This chapter covers:

- Planning procurement management

## Planning procurement management

Agile projects are not suitable for contracts that fix the price, duration and costs since the scope of what will be delivered is usually decided during the project. The business goal of the project, the project methodology, the team, the way in which the scope is decided, and the acceptance process are known at the start of an agile project. Thus, optional scope contracts as proposed by Kent Beck and Dave Cleal (2009) are suitable for agile projects. Other than the details around the contract type, scope and pricing, agile contracts are managed similarly to other project procurements.

### New contracting concepts

Craig Larman, Bas Vodde, and Tom Arbogast (2010) in their book *Practices for Scaling Lean & Agile Development Large, Multisite, and Offshore Product Development with Large-Scale Scrum* recommend that efforts be taken to introduce the lawyers that will construct or negotiate agile contracts to the agile methodology that will be used. Other procurement personnel may also need to be introduced to agile concepts. Some of the key points that should be discussed with them include the following topics:

Agile projects:

- scope evolves during the project and is not agreed in advance,
- reduce risk by delivering the small product increments,
- allow payment schemes to be aligned to the increments and thus the extent of the payment can be limited to the delivered scope,
- have clear rules about obligations, expectations, and deliverables.

The consequence of these points should be that the traditional contract models that were used don't apply and agile projects will result in lower risks, easier acceptance, and manageable costs.

## Contract terms and conditions

Agile contracts contain the same general terms and conditions as non-agile projects. However, the content for some of the terms and conditions are likely to change to allow for a flexible scope. (Table 15-1)

The following information on contracting and agreement adaptations for agile projects is provided from a project management point of view and not a legal point of view. Definitely get legal or contract specialists involved and educated before entering into any agreements.

| Impact of Agile Projects on Contract Terms and Conditions | | |
|---|---|---|
| Will not change | May Change | Will Change |
| Indemnification<br><br>Confidentiality and data protection<br><br>Intellectual property | Limitation of liability<br><br>Warranty<br><br>Timing of payment | Delivery cycle<br><br>Scope<br><br>Change management<br><br>Termination<br><br>Acceptance<br><br>Deliverable or work product<br><br>Pricing |

Table 15-1 Agile impact on contract terms and conditions

## Terms that will not change

The following contract terms will most likely not be different for agile contracts:

- Indemnification
- Confidentiality and data protection
- Intellectual property

## Terms that may change

The following contract terms may change for the following reasons:

**Limitation of liability**—Delivering and accepting a "shippable-product" in increments means the project can be stopped at the end of an iteration. This has the impact of reduced costs, exposure, and damage to goodwill.

**Warranty**—Warranty is established on the product. Nevertheless, the incremental acceptance of the product increments may reduce the risk of issues requiring resolution after delivery.

**Timing of payment**—The timing of the payment can be similar to traditional agreements: monthly, at a major milestone (which is each iteration in an agile project), or a progressive scheme for shared risk-reward. The timing of the payment may correspond to the pricing option, but not necessarily. For example, there could be a Time and Materials (T&M) agreement that is paid at the end of the iteration.

## Terms that will change

The following contract terms will change for agile projects:

**Delivery cycle**–Agile projects deliver deployable product increments in short timeboxes. The duration and team may be fixed but the scope is variable. The nominated product owner and user representative(s) must be available for the project team. The definition of done, timebox duration, team size, and customer availability requirements are worth noting and agreeing.

**Scope**–The scope of the final delivery is variable and is decided during the evolution of the project. The project chartering session should have established a project vision that can be used to frame the scope of the agreement. Larman, Vodde, and Arbogast suggest that a Geoffrey Moore Elevator Pitch (1991) style vision be used to define the scope in the agreement. See the chapter Integration for a discussion on chartering. The variability in how much of the scope will be delivered is addressed through the contract pricing and type.

**Change management**—Changes are a welcome part of agile projects. Therefore, don't include mandated change control boards, special change processes, and formal contractual scope change requests. The variability in the scope that will be delivered is addressed through the contract pricing and type scheme.

**Termination**–Agile projects should be able to be stopped after each iteration. Therefore, define an early termination clause. Early termination should have a variable scale of penalty for the customer that is reduced over time.

**Acceptance**—Each product increment is reviewed for acceptance at the end of an iteration. Thus, the contract should stipulate a framework for acceptance that covers the acceptance per iteration and at the end of the project. The definition for completeness (definition of done) should be defined in the acceptance framework. Avoid rigid, detailed artifact acceptance criteria normally found in the statement of work or quality plan.

**Deliverable or work product**–The focus of agile projects is on delivering working software. Do include a list of the necessary items that should be delivered as part of the solution, for example, source code, maintenance document.

## Collaborative pricing

There are several Time and Material (T&M) and Fixed Price alternatives for pricing agile projects (Figure 15-1). Some of the alternatives are more suitable for agile projects since they require less pre-specification of project details than the other types of agreement. The pricing options best suited for agile projects encourage collaboration towards achieving the project goals at an acceptable level of risk for the supplier and the project sponsor.

Suitability

Pricing Models & Features

High

| | Scope | Time | Cost |
|---|---|---|---|
| **Graduated fixed price per unit of time (e.g. day, hour)** | Variable | Fixed | Variable / UoT |
| **Incentive pricing** | Variable | N/A | Fixed / Project |
| **Time & material per UoT** | Variable | Variable | Fixed / UoT |
| **Capped time & materials per UoT** | Variable | Fixed | Fixed / UoT |
| **Fixed price per iteration** | Fixed / Iteration | Fixed | Fixed |
| **Fixed per unit of work (e.g. story point, use, feature)** | Fixed / UoW | N/A | Fixed |
| **Fixed price per project** | Fixed | N/A | Fixed |

Low

Figure 15-1 Suitability of contract pricing options to agile projects

**Graduated fixed price**—With a graduated fixed price, promoted by Thorup and Jensen (2009) the hourly rate is scaled depending upon early, on-time or late delivery. Early delivery has a higher hourly rate; on-time has a standard rate and late has a lower rate. For example, with a standard hourly rate of 100 money units, early delivery would pay a rate of 120 money units, and late delivery would pay a rate of 80 money units. All hours are paid. This pricing model is very similar to T&M pricing, but the rate is variable.

**Incentive Pricing**–Incentive pricing sets a target price for the project. If the project is delivered for less than that target price, the savings from the lower project costs are split between the client and supplier. The client doesn't expend the funds and the supplier receives additional money without the corresponding resource investment.

**T&M**—T&M pricing includes pricing per hour or day depending upon an agreed rate for the resources and materials. T&M fits best with the concept of incremental delivery.

**Capped T&M**—There are variations of T&M based on the degree of trust and the relationship between the supplier and the client. Specifically, capped T&M per iteration—the price is set at a maximum for the iteration—and capped T&M per project per release—the price is set at a maximum for the project. The cap can drive these types of pricing arrangements to set expectations similar to fixed price with the potential disadvantage that the scope is not clarified before setting the price.

**Fixed price per iteration**—With a fixed price per iteration pricing, an estimate is provided by the supplier for all efforts related to the iteration. This model could work for agile projects when the scope of the iteration is defined and agreed before the iteration or the time-period is fixed without regard to the delivered scope. When the pricing is fixed based on an agreed scope then the agreement takes on the characteristics of a standard fixed-price contract and the supplier will most likely add a contingency to the price.

**Fixed price per unit of work**—An UoW includes a running, tested, and deployable software. The price can be fixed per story, per feature point, or per use. While potentially interesting, these models introduce nuances about the value of a unit of work versus its cost. Determining the percise value of a point is a mixture between science and art.

**Fixed price per project**—Fixed price per project agreements have an impact on the entire operation of the project. They are not consistent with the values of agile projects and generally tend to result in an agile project taking on the characteristic of a traditional project.

## Optional scope contract types

Optional Scope Contracts, a concept introduced by Kent Beck and Dave Cleal (2009), are contracts that fix the time, cost, and quality and allow the scope to evolve during the project. The type of contract defines the combination of the terms and conditions, including the timing of payment, and pricing option. Mary and Tom Poppendieck (2003) in their book *Lean Software Development* summarized the characteristics of Open Scope Contracts that are best for agile projects as follows:

**T&M contracts**—An ideal contract construct is a T&M contract. Specifically, iterations management is agreed in the contract as follows:

- the requirements and software are developed in parallel,
- the highest priority features get prioritized first,
- a working, tested, integrated system is the delivered of each iteration,
- each iteration uses the same timebox duration and
- the timebox durations are agreed on in the contract.

This contract definition allows the customer to manage costs through each of the iterations and allows the supplier to demonstrate value as a justification to continue iterations. This contract type assumes T&M pricing.

**Multistage contracts**–A multistage contract includes an umbrella agreement and separate scopes-of-work per iteration. The umbrella agreement defines the terms and conditions that will be used across the entire project. Each scope-of-work defines the scope for a specific iteration. The iteration scope should be similar to those discussed for T&M agreements. Each contract could use a different pricing model, e.g. T&M, capped T&M, price UoW, incentive.

**Target cost contracts**–A target cost contract requires that the project staffs for the supplier and client collaborate to deliver a working, tested, and integrated solution within a target price. Both parties have the responsibility to maintain the costs fixed while the scope remains adjustable by the project. It differs from a fixed-price contract since the scope is not agreed in advance. The capped T&M, guaranteed fixed pricing, fixed price per iteration pricing models would be options for this type of contract.

**Shared benefit contracts**–shared benefits contracts split any savings derived from lower project costs between the client and supplier. The client doesn't expend the funds and the supplier receives additional money without the corresponding resource investment. The motivation for realizing the maximum scope benefit by the client and maximum profit by the supplier drives a collaboration to benefit from the project. The incentive-pricing model and graduated fixed price would be suitable for this type of contract.

## Summary

- Agile projects should reduce project risks by providing flexibility in defining and adapting the scope based on frequent feedback and by allowing late scope changes. However, they require changes to the terms and conditions within services contracts as well as an appropriate pricing model.

- The scope, change management, acceptance, termination, and deliverable sections of agreements should be adjusted to fit the operations of an agile project, including evolving scope, adapting to change, and early termination.

- Terms such as warranty, limitation of liability, and timing of the payment will be impacted by agile projects, but may not change the terms included within an agreement.

- Optional scope contracts allow the scope to evolve and change throughout the project while agreeing on the pricing, terms, and conditions that will be used during the project. T&M contracts are favored for agile projects. Other contract options include multistage, target cost and shared benefits contracts.

## Recommended reading

- Craig Larman and Bas Vodde in their book *Practices for Scaling Lean & Agile Development Large, Multisite, and Offshore Product Development with Large-Scale Scrum* have collaborated with lawyer Tom Arbogast to include a contract primer. They have outlined the common topics of agile contracts as well as contract models from the perspective of lawyers and non-lawyers.

# Chapter 16 Stakeholders

This chapter aligns with the *PMBOK® Guide* Stakeholder Management knowledge area and covers the process for identifying and engaging stakeholders in the project. The following topics are discussed in this chapter.

- Identifying stakeholders
- Planning stakeholder management
- Managing stakeholder engagement
- Monitoring stakeholder engagement

## Identifying stakeholders

A stakeholder is anyone with a positive or negative interest in the project. Table 16-1 provides a list of the typical stakeholder groups and a subset of their potential interest in the project (Turner & Zolin, 2012).

## Planning stakeholder management

There are different aspects to planning of stakeholder management.

- First is structuring the project to adequately engage the stakeholders and meet their requirements.
- Second is getting what is needed from the stakeholders to deliver the product.
- Third is managing the stakeholder's expectations about the project, product, and agile practices.

| Stakeholder Group | Project Interests (partial list) |
|---|---|
| Investors or owners | That a useful prototype of the product's proposed capabilities is provided |
| | That they realize an earned value from their investment |
| Project sponsors | Performance efficiency of the project with regards to time, cost, and quality |
| | That the stakeholders are adequately engaged in the project and generally satisfied with its progress |
| Product purchaser | That a useful prototype of the product's proposed capabilities is provided |
| | That the specifications for what will be developed meet the requirements |
| Product users | That the specifications for what will be developed meet the requirements |
| | That the product will have a good product performance |
| Project manager and project team | That the work environment and job is satisfying |
| | That they are recognized for their contribution |
| Supplier as the prime contractor | That the project doesn't waste resources |
| | That they gain a profit from the work provided |
| Supplier of products, goods, materials, services | That they comply with the contract requirements |
| | That they gain a profit from their work |
| Public at large | That the delivered product balances social costs and benefits |
| | That the delivered product has an acceptable environmental impact |

Table 16-1 Stakeholders and their interests

Managing stakeholder expectations about the project, product and about using agile practices will vary from person to person and project to project. This topic is discussed further under controlling stakeholder engagement.

The agile methodologies very eloquently engage the stakeholders at pivotal points to understand and meet their requirements and to provide events for the team to get what they need from the stakeholders. Thus, applying the agile practices as designed goes a long way towards stakeholder management. For example:

- Prioritizing the backlog based on value and incrementally delivering to the solution is designed to minimize time to market and deliver incremental value
- The reviews and information radiators provide transparency and visibility of the project status
- The story writing and review meetings provide the opportunity for the stakeholders to influence the product specifications
- Using users for testing and test-driven development influence the product features and performance
- Focusing on using a sustainable pace for delivery and having self-organized teams are steps toward providing the team with a satisfying working environment.

The stakeholder planning should attempt to understand what stakeholders are important to the project, the participation they should have in the project events, and the information radiators that would be relevant for them. See the chapter on Communications for further information on stakeholder communications.

## Managing stakeholder engagement

Successful agile projects rely heavily on having frequent feedback from the stakeholders. The stakeholders are needed at the following pivotal points.

- During story writing workshops, user interviews, and other events to gather user requirements. The users or user proxies are needed to ensure that the product features are adequately identified.
- During backlog grooming, to ensure the appropriate value is placed on each user story so that they are correctly prioritized.
- During the development for clarifying requirements, testing and test-driven Development.
- During the review meeting when the product is demonstrated to provide feedback on the product, accept the product, and discuss the next product increment.

Every effort should be made to ensure that the right people participate in the project. If the stakeholders are not adequately participating, conduct a retrospective with the stakeholders to determine why and adjust accordingly.

## Monitoring stakeholder engagement

A key aspect of stakeholder engagement is ensuring that the non-project team members don't interfere with the team's work or information flow. This is a key responsibility for the agile coach.

The second aspect is managing the stakeholder's expectations about how and when the project will deliver. The information radiators—including the burn-up chart, velocity chart—will assist with this aspect of expectation management.

The third aspect is relevant when introducing agile practices for the first time. In his book, *Succeeding with Agile* Mike Cohn (2010) discusses the importance of managing expectations for organizations new to agile practices. The following are some of the topics where expectation management is important:

**Project progress.** There will be expectations that agile projects should deliver quickly. This expectation is set since fast delivery is defined as a key benefit of agile. In reality, initially the project will be slower while people learn about the new practices and adjust to the working methods. However, the project will deliver faster than a traditional method. Nevertheless, it won't deliver as quickly as people expect.

**Predictability.** When agile teams first get started, they overestimate what they can deliver. In reality, the team's velocity will stabilize by the third or fourth iteration. Thus, initially the team will appear to produce unpredictably.

**Reliability.** Some iterations may not deliver a product increment. It could happen that no features pass through the entire design, development, and test phase. The reasons and justification for this can be wide and varied, for example, the features failed testing. When this happens, the reliability of the agile practices will be called into question. This is a normal occurrence. It will most likely correct its self in the next iteration.

**Attitude.** Agile projects will introduce new practices that require learning new ways of doing things. It also means changing from how things were done in the past. There will be many complaints from all corners of the organization. The common complaints should be anticipated and responses applied.

Even people with a good attitude and willingness to try the new practices will need time to adjust. Distinguish between the people who complain because they need time as opposed to those that complain as a form of resistance to the new approaches.

**Involvement.** The involvement of the business function and stakeholders will change and their expectations in this regard must be managed.

For example, the product owner, who should be from the business organization, will have new responsibilities. These responsibilities will require a time investment on a daily basis as well as a new series of activities.

The stakeholders that have directed the activities of the team or some of the team members in the past will have to adjust to working with a self-managed team. Management and performance reports that previously had a specific format may not be available any further.

The involvement and attitudes of these stakeholders have to be managed.

**Role confusion.** The concept of self-organizing teams, no management hierarchy, and no job titles will be very confusing and unsettling at the start. The immediate tendency will be for people to join the team and continue to carry the role distinction forward. This should be avoided. Eventually things will settle down and people will fall into working as a team.

## Personal Experience: Project revitalization

### — Augusto Evangelisti, Test Engineer

The project was to create a Credit Information Management System using Java (Spring), Tomcat, HTML, jQuery, SOAP, Oracle ESB.

**Before the "Revolution":** Our organization had been going through a transition to Scrum for around one year. In the process of transitioning, we had delivered a couple of software projects. Such projects had been seen as a failure by our Product Owner for not delivering business value, and by the development team for failing to deliver a quality product.

**The goal:** The software development department needed a big success to justify continuing the transition to Scrum and we were all determined to deliver a great product to our customers to demonstrate how much we had learned from our own previous failures. The Product Owner was extremely skeptical about continuing with Scrum and did not refrain from showing his feelings.

**The Plan:** One Scrum team was created to work on the "Project Revolution." Our goal was to deliver in a short period of time quality software that would exceed customer's expectations and drive them back to embracing agile development.

**The Focus:** For the very first time we religiously adhered to Scrum practices, we focused our efforts on Software Quality practices and built a solid relationship between the development team and the Product-Owner.

**How we did it**: We engaged with the Product Owner from day zero and we tried to infect him with our enthusiasm for software development and quality. Before the start of the projects, we gave a demonstration of our Quality plans and new software development approach: Acceptance Test-Driven Development (ATDD).

The Product Owner showed interest in our approach beyond our expectations; he was blown away by the power of the tests ubiquitous language and clearly understood its potential value.

He was also reassured by the demonstration of the Software Quality infrastructure we had built to harness the development of our application and took a large interest in how acceptance tests were run and results reported. The development team discovered that something that seemed only a technical matter was very valuable to our Product Owner.

The Scrum framework was followed rigorously by everybody including the Product Owner that in previous projects was somehow cut away from the core of the Scrum team. This time we really started to discover Scrum's real benefits of fast feedback and continuous improvement. The ATDD approach gave great benefits by allowing front-loading the discussions over incomplete or ambiguous requirements at acceptance test creation (the very start of development). We discovered quickly how front-loading such discussions would on the one hand slow down development but on the other hand would allow us to develop only once and only what was really required rather than get to the final product by continuously fixing defects. Having a large bed of acceptance and unit tests gave the development team the confidence of refactoring freely and we were able to see the positive in the fast feedback of our builds.

**Transparency**: A full transparency policy was adopted, we were all part of one team, and there were no secrets among us.

**Collaboration brings success**: Slowly the Product Owner started gaining confidence in our work and when at the demonstrations he started saying things like "This is a fantastic job guys!" or even "You've done in a two weeks sprint what in the past we were used to getting in three months and at a level of quality that is not even comparable."

It is easy to understand that when our Product Owner started trusting us, we were able to go even one step further and propose our alternative solutions to him. While in the past such solutions were categorically refused and a command and control approach was used by the Product Owner, we were now at a stage where full collaboration was the norm and feedback was working both ways.

**Fun**: The product was delivered in time with an excellent level of quality, the products' business value exceeded the Product Owner's original expectations, and best of all we all had great fun in developing it.

Project Revolution was an amazing experience.

## Summary

- The project stakeholder will have different interests in the project and will come from inside and outside the organization. Map the interests of stakeholders onto the project events, artifacts, and information radiators that will be used to engage them in the project or inform them of the status.
- Monitor the stakeholder engagement in the project to ensure adequate participation and frequent feedback. Conduct a retrospective with the stakeholders if their participation level is not sufficient.
- Manage the multiple layers of stakeholder expectations. That includes expectations related to their access to and influence on the team members, the progress of the project, and the introduction of agile practices.

## Recommended reading

- Rodney Turner and Roxanne Zolin in their articles "Forecasting Success on Large Projects: Developing Reliable Scale to Predict Multiple Perspectives by Multiple Stakeholders Over Multiple Time Frames." describe indicators within a project that forecast project success and stakeholder satisfaction.

# 3

# Going Agile

# Chapter 17 Selecting an Agile Project Approach

The definition of agility doesn't prescribe any specific methodology. In fact, a project or an organization could develop their own methodology by applying the agile values and principles. However, it would be a waste of time, effort, and resources to ignore or avoid the learning and experiences of others. This chapter covers the following options for adopting an agile approach.

- Choose the most popular agile methodology
- Customize a plan-driven or agile methodology
- Implement individual agile practices
- Adapting to regulations

## Choose the most popular agile methodology

Scrum or a Scrum/XP Hybrid is the most popular agile methodology, and Scaled Agile Framework® is the most popular scaling methodology. This could be for any number of reasons such as:

- It is a project management process and applies to any business market.
- It is easily combined with other methodologies and practices (such as extreme programming).
- It is a lightweight methodology with a few practices, clearly defined roles, and easy practices to implement.
- There is widespread availability of professional training and certification[1].
- There are numerous books that describe the intricacies of working with scrum or combining scrum with other methodologies.

## Customize a plan-driven or agile methodology

Boehm and Turner suggest to decide on a type of methodology, and then customize it. First, decide between using a plan-driven methodology (e.g. waterfall) or an agile methodology. To make this decision, Boehm and Turner propose assessing the project characteristics based on criticality, personnel, dynamism, size, and culture. The assessment should determine if the project should be based on an agile methodology or a plan-driven methodology. The following list describes the factors to consider when selecting a methodology and the base methodology with which to start.

**Criticality.** Degree that the functionality and capabilities that the product will deliver would affect the life, safety, or well-being of the organization or society. The more critical the solution the more it requires formal reviews and validations. Examples of critical systems would include those addressing healthcare products, nuclear plants, satellites, etc. Base methodology: High criticality (loss of life), plan-driven. Low criticality (loss of comfort), agile.

**Team size.** The number of people who will be involved in the project. The more people involved the more sub-teams that will be needed. The more sub-teams the more coordination is required across the teams. Base methodology: Large team (300+ people), plan-driven. Small team (10), agile.

**Skill and experience of the team.** The degree of experience and skill the team has to work with the technology and the subject matter. The fewer experienced people, the more the senior people will have to mentor and coach the junior people. The team will be less productive than if it had all experienced people. Base methodology: Low experience (15% Cockburn Level[2] 2&3), plan-driven. High experience (35%+ Cockburn Level 2&3), agile.

**Stability of requirements.** Degree to which the requirements are likely to change in a two- to four-week period. Projects require frequent feedback cycles when the customer only knows what they want once they see it. Base methodology: High stability (1% change per month), plan-driven. Low stability (50%+ per month), agile.

**Customer availability.** The availability and frequency of interactions with the customer. The more the customer can be involved in the day-to-day project activities, the better the communication, and the less the need for intermediate documents. Base methodology: Low availability, plan-driven. High availability, agile.

**Company culture.** The degree to which the company culture can tolerate and adjust to delegating decision-making, allowing negotiations on delivered features, agreeing to a certain amount of uncertainty on exactly what will be delivered. Base methodology: High management control needed, plan-driven. Low management control needed, agile.

**External dependencies.** The degree to which the team can work independently without relying on other teams or service providers for inputs, resources, or services. High dependence requires lead-times and coordination with other parties, and it creates unpredictability. High dependence, plan-driven. Low dependence, agile.

After selecting a methodology, form a working group that should add elements to de-risk an agile method or adds more agility for a plan-driven methodology.

In his book *Agile Software Development,* Alistair Cockburn makes a similar recommendation to Boehm and Turner. Cockburn suggests that you select one methodology to manage and govern the project management practices and add agile practices to reach the desired level of requirements flexibility, planning dynamics, technical quality, and customer collaboration based on the available team and company culture.

Of course, there are risks in customizing a methodology without having experience in its application. Teams can select some parts and skip others that demand effort or require changes they don't like.

Alistair Cockburn suggests a Shu-Ha-Ri philosophy[3]: learn it, internalize it, and then change it. That is, it's better to select a methodology, stick as close to the formal definition as possible, and after gaining experience adapt it.

Value stream mapping is one technique for analyzing a process to identify optimization opportunities. It can be used to evaluate and adapt the selected methodology process. A value stream is the end-to-end delivery steps (e.g. from customer request to delivery) required to complete a process. The term, value stream, is borrowed from lean manufacturing where a value stream normally consists of the flow of materials, the transformation of materials, and the flow of information.

A value stream map is a visual diagram that shows the value stream. It is useful in supporting team decision-making, creating a common language, understanding, and identifying areas of waste.

The steps for creating a value stream map include:

- Identify the product or service to map.
- Understand the icons and symbols to use for your map.
- Map the value stream starting from the customer.
- Consider the following items: the flow of information, production activities, material flow, customer value, push systems, pull systems, any waste, available working time, and lead-time
- Verify the map. It should match the actual process, not the desired process.

- Create a lead-time chart at the bottom of the value stream map to show value-add and non-value-add lead-time.

- Review the map for waste.

Waste is an activity that uses resources but creates no benefit. Mary Poppendieck and Tom Poppendieck have converted the wastes from the lean process to the equivalent software-related wastes. (see Table 17-1)

| Waste | Waste in software projects |
|---|---|
| Task switching | Multi-tasking between several projects when there is a context penalty for switching tasks |
| Extra features | Extra features not required or are thought to be nice-to-haves |
| Motion | Communication or moving information or documents around |
| Waiting | Delays waiting for reviews or approvals |
| Partially done work | Work started, but not completed |
| Extra processes | Extra work that adds no value |
| Defects | Defective documents or software that needs correction |

Table 17-1 Types of waste (Poppendieck & Poppendieck)

David Andersen (2010) defined the waste based on their economic cost to software development.

**Transaction costs** include the activities that are not seen or valued by the customer, but necessary to set-up or clean up the project. They include activities such as release planning, budgeting, etc. The customer would prefer not to pay for such costs.

**Coordination costs** are for the activities to schedule, coordinate or assign people to tasks; they are necessary when there are more than two people involved. They include such activities as daily stand-ups, emails, etc.

**Failure load** is project work that could have been avoided by higher quality work earlier in the project. That is, it's work created by defects in the system, poor quality, poor design, etc. It takes away the capacity for other value-add work.

The value-added work is any activity needed to produce a working solution. It would include some coordination activities, (e.g., meetings where design or analysis are the main themes), testing, coding, etc. The overall goal is to increase value-add activities and decrease waste.

Process Cycle Efficiency is a measure of the value-added time in the process divided by the cycle time for the process. It helps to identify how much of an entire process adds value.

**Process Cycle Efficiency = (Value-added Time / Cycle Time)**

The value stream map should be reviewed for opportunities to eliminate waste by reducing transaction and coordination costs and minimizing failure load.

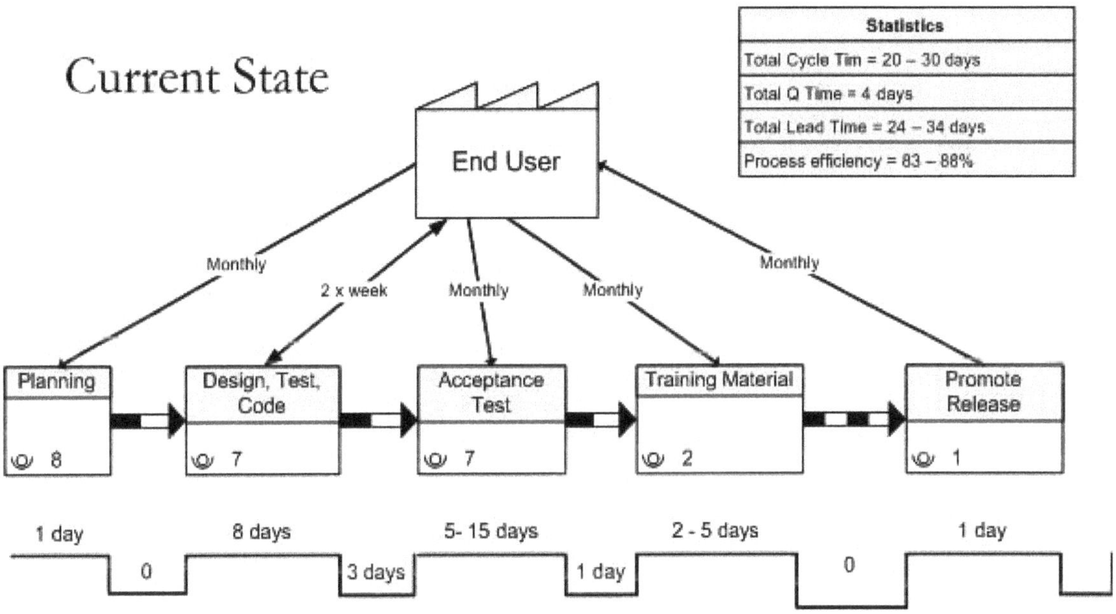


Figure 17-1 Example value stream

# Implement individual agile practices

The 'Sidky Agile Measurement Index' (SAMI) is a five-level maturity model to measure the organization's level of agile adoption. It was published in 2007 by Ahmed Sidky in his dissertation on th *Agile Adoption Framework*. The model is independent of any specific agile methodology.

Within SAMI, each maturity level identifies a set of agile practices that, when collectively implemented, place an organization at that level of maturity on the SAMI maturity model. The model evaluates the organization according to five agile principles, derived from the agile values and principles. Level one is the lowest level of agility and level five is the highest.

SAMI provides a tool for measuring the potential for agility in an organization and building a road map to reach a target agility level.

The SAMI model for assessing the desired agility level and mapping a plan can help with deciding which of the agile practices to apply An overview of the model is provided in Table 17-2. The agile practices are described in Chapter 4.

| | Agile Principles | | | | |
|---|---|---|---|---|---|
| Agile Prin-ciples | *Embrace Change to* | *Plan and Deliver* | *Human-centric* | *Technical Excellence* | *Customer Collaboration* |
| Level 5 **Encompassing** *Establishing a* | Low process ceremony | Agile project estimation | Ideal agile physical setup | Test driven development<br><br>Paired programming | Frequent (collocated) face□to□fac e interaction between |
| Level 4 **Adaptive** *Responding to change through* | Client driven iterations<br><br>Continuous customer | Smaller and more frequent releases (4-8 weeks) | | Daily progress tracking meetings<br><br>Agile documentatio | CRACK Customer immediately accessible<br><br>Customer |
| Level 3 **Effective** *Developing high quality, working software in an efficient an* | | Risk driven iterations<br><br>Plan features, not tasks<br><br>Maintaining | Self organizing teams<br><br>Frequent face□to□fac e communicati | Continuous integration<br><br>Continuous improvement (refactoring)<br><br>Unit tests | |
| Level 2 ***Evolutionary*** *Delivering software* | Evolutionar y requireme nts | Continuous delivery<br><br>Planning at different | | Software configuration management<br><br>Tracking | Customer contract reflective of evolutionary development |
| Level 1 **Collaborative** *Enhancing communicat ion and* | Reflect and tune process | Collaborativ e planning | Collaborative teams Empowered and motivated teams | Coding standards<br><br>Knowledge□s haring tools | Customer commitment to work with developing team |

Table 17-2 SAMI matrix with agile practices

## Adapting to regulations

If an agile project must comply with regulations (internal or external), the recommendation is to read and interpret the regulation and then take a pragmatic approach to compliance.

**External regulation**—external regulators are an external government organization or industry watchdogs that require an organization to comply with a set of rules, regulations, or laws.

**Internal regulations** are regulations or policies adopted by the organization, but not imposed by an external entity. Examples of these are Capability Maturity Model Integration (CMMI®) or International Organization for Standardization (ISO900x).

The *CMMI® for Development, Version 1.3 Technical Report* provides a reference model for activities in developing products and services. It includes guidance on applying the CMMI® to agile projects.

## Personal experience: Customizing the methodology

### —David de Francisco, Software Engineer

I am in favor of the Shu-Ha-Ri philosophy: learn it, internalize it, and then change it. I have often seen how teams take what they like from agile methodologies without understanding a word about their value. In this sense, I have seen things like:

- Teams of four full-time people with two programmers, one scrum master, and one product owner. The scrum master was organizing meetings and the product owner was writing requirements based on a documented meeting. The scrum master and product owner had enough work for 20% of their time. They couldn't program, because "Scrum says this is the responsibility of the team." Well, scrum is value-driven, and no value was extracted from this team. (The project was closed.)
- Teams that skipped documentation, requirements management, and even technical design because, to their way of understanding, agile promotes code over documentation. While the value is in code, the emphasis is on the quality of the code. No result will be extracted from a poorly designed software system.
- Teams that 'adapt' daily meetings to have technical discussions as well. The consequence is a one-hour daily meeting. (I've been in two-hour daily meetings as well). This completely thwarts the rationale of daily meetings and alters their purpose and value.

- And, many more examples I've suffered.

Methodologies can (even should) be customized to extract more value. To my understanding, they can only be customized when they are understood and applied several times. Otherwise, you face the risk of having teams exposed to a shop where they can buy some parts and skip others that demand effort or difficult changes.

## Case study: Adapting scrum to CMMI®

Carsten Jakobsen and Kent Johnson made a presentation on how they applied the CMMI® practices to a scrum project. At a high-level, they conducted the initial planning as a 'sprint zero' and focused on quality. In detail, the project had the following activities and structure.

- In sprint zero, they produced and estimated the initial product backlog. The requirements were broken down into user stories to produce the product backlog. The estimation included three-point estimates. They identified, qualitatively analyzed, and quantified the risks using three-point estimates. They analyzed dependencies between the product backlog elements, the stakeholders, and the risks. The project plan and solution architecture were presented to management for approval.
- The 'definition of done' was made explicit with a quality plan of a few pages. The quality plan included a quality assurance schedule with story inspection, code reviews, document reviews, tests to produce, and acceptance tests scope. The project environment included automated tests, continuous integration, and a standard production line. The production line included development, build, and test servers.
- During the project, the project manager managed the overall project plan and the team tracked and managed the sprint progress. They conducted 10 to 15-minute bi-weekly meetings to review risks.
- They enforced disciple by measuring and auditing. They performed monthly audits of one to two hours of the configuration management system to build a habit of good configuration management discipline. They measured and reacted to fix-time-after-failed-build to establish the habit of fixing broke builds immediately. That is, they performed daily builds. When a build failed, all developers were signaled. They stopped working (i.e. stopped the production line) and focused on fixing the build.

**References**

Jackobsen, Carsten Ruseng, and Kent Aaron Johnson. "Mature Agile with a twist of CMMI®." Agile 2008 Conference. IEEE, 2008. 212-217

## Summary

The application of the different practices as well as the terminology varies depending on the agile methodology. The right methodology for a given company will depend on organizational factors such as culture and team skills. According to Lindvall et al.(2002), the critical success factors for running agile projects include:

- The organization should provide cultural support in order to adapt work practices; delegate authority and responsibility to the team; allow the negotiation of priorities; and facilitate rapid communications.
- The team should include competent members who have experience building systems, good communications and interpersonal skills, and some familiarity with agile development methods.
- The projects should be managed with a high volume of communications and interactions among the team members, as well as close and frequent interactions with the customer or product owner.
- The choices for selecting a methodology are 1) select the most popular methodology; 2) evaluate the project and organizational characteristics then select and customize a methodology; or 3) decide on a desired level of agility and implement agile practices to reach that level of agility.

## Recommended reading

- *Agile Software Development* by Alistair Cockburn describes the details of developing and selecting a methodology for any type of project.

## Endnotes

[1] As of April 2013, 221,798 people certified as scrum masters by the Agile Alliance.

[2] Cockburn Level refers to the experience levels in Table 12-1.

[3] Shu-Ha-Ri is the level of learning from Aikido. Shu-Ha-Ri means *learn-detach-transcend.*

# Chapter 18 Going Agile

Agility can be implemented at multiple levels within an organization: organization-wide, practice or department-wide, individual teams, or individual projects. This book focused specifically on agile projects. Therefore, it doesn't address how to make an organization or department agile. This chapter covers:

- Introducing change
- The challenges going agile
- Getting started
- Selecting a pilot
- Case study: agile adoption & transformation

## Introducing change

Agile projects and teams will have an organization-wide effect. Specifically, there are new technical skills, new collaboration methods, new team working arrangements, and new organizational requirements. These changes require the cooperation of many people, and change processes and practices outside the agile team or project.

### Find the (burning) platform

First, there has to be an awareness that indicates the current practices no longer work. That awareness has to be sufficient to motivate action and justify the change. The awareness can be driven by dire circumstances where the organization must change, i.e. a burning platform. Alternatively, awareness can be that the current practices don't measure up and create a dissatisfactory situation for the team and the stakeholders, i.e., an improvement platform.

Convince the management that staying with the current practices is more dangerous than trying to go agile. Use the different agile surveys, case studies, customer references and your own internal organizational failings to build the case.

The desire to change has to be significant enough for people to act in a different manner than previously, for management to invest in the changes needed to realize the agile project and everyone to trust that agile can solve the problem.

## Find a friend

Form a coalition of people that are willing to take the leap of faith and try going agile. You need a motivated team that is willing to try the new method and a willing business user that will invest the time and effort. Going agile won't be easy as it changes ideas and concepts previously held as the best (or only way) to deliver projects. People have to be willing and motivated to stick with applying the processes even when it seems overly uncomfortable or difficult.

## Engineer success

Select a pilot project or projects where a successful delivery will be highly visible within the organization. One where the organization is willing to invest in the best team, reorganize workspace, hire in outside agile coaches, bend what was traditional organizational norms or rules. That is select an important project, but be sure you can deliver.

## Promote results

Promote the visible organizational performance benefits, the financial gains from the project, the better business performance. Tie the results to the performance metrics or the organizational leaders and executives, e.g. higher profits because, lower services costs because, etc. Announced and share the results throughout the organization. They are needed to promote for the next round of improvements, to reinforce practices, and to inform others that were not part of the group.

## Make it stick

John Kotter, in his seminal 1995 article critiquing change efforts, notes that failure is a prevalent outcome of change efforts, whether measured in degrees (failure to reach the highest potential) if not a total failure. He takes a pragmatic position that change only succeeds when the change itself becomes the status quo — "until new behaviors are rooted in social norms and shared values, they are subject to degradation as soon as the pressure for change is removed" (Kotter, 1995, p. 8).

His best practice recommendation for implementing change is to make a " . . . a conscious attempt to show people how the new approaches, behaviors, and attitudes have helped improve performance., and . . . taking sufficient time to make sure that the next generation of top management really does personify the new approach." (Kotter, 1995, pp. 8-9).

Thus, the agile practices and behaviors need to be transferred to other departments and functions outside of the development team, including human resources, facility management, marketing, finance, procurement, and management.

- **Human resources** will have to consider changes to performance evaluations, specifically recognizing team rather than individual-based performance, recruiting for new skills set, and adopting new roles, training, and development plans.

- **Facility Management** will have to consider new models for team spaces as well as collaboration methods for distributed teams.

- **Marketing** will have to change release plans. For example, the release plans may need to be adapted to include high-level product themes and broad time ranges, instead of feature-specific, date-specific releases.

- **Finance** will have to consider how to evaluate and capitalize projects with incremental delivery. According to the accounting rules capitalization can start based on technological feasibility. Without a big design upfront, a new understanding will have to be established when the product is technically feasible.

- **Procurement** and related lawyers will have to modify contracting methods and practices. (See the Procurement chapter)

- **Senior Management** will have to consider to what extent the whole organization can benefit from adopting agile practices. The agile practices also offer an opportunity to simplify (in many cases) performance planning and monitoring.

- **Middle management** will have to develop an understanding of the agile methodologies and their benefits. They can help to educate senior management and influence the rest of the organization. They can model and support the expected behaviors. They can reinforce the expectations that individuals should be good team players, and that being technically competent, but not sharing knowledge or refusing to work outside of one's role are not acceptable behavior.

- **Communities of Practice** may be created to help groups of individuals from different parts of the organization share information and experiences on agile practices.

- **Project Management Office** will have to adjust the project reports, measures, and metrics to those that can be provided by agile projects.

## Personal Experience: My top recommendations for going agile based on my enterprise transition experience

**—Irene Michlin, certified scrum master & technical lead**

1. Agile is a big world. Know what you want to get out of it, which pains — business or technical — you're addressing.

2. Have your agile transition done in an agile way—describe acceptance criteria. How will you know that you have made your situation better, that you have addressed these pains?

3. If you want a successful transition, not one of these initiatives that die a couple of months later, be prepared to fight inertia. It is not one fight you need to win; it's a long campaign. Find allies, build up enthusiasm with a long-term vision, and plan your short-term steps (with acceptance criteria for each one). Win the first fight. Review and adjust your tactics, plan the next one. Repeat forever. The second you say, "we're agile now, we can stop the transition," — you're no longer agile.

## The challenges of going agile

VersionOne identified the following findings for organizations that have gone agile:

- The reasons for agile failure are due to lack of experience with agile methods, company philosophy or culture at odds with core agile values, lack of management support, and external pressure to follow traditional waterfall processes.
- Organizations that do have active agile projects still find barriers to future agile adoptions. The top reasons are due to cultural misalignment between agile and the company, availability of skilled people, or general resistance to change.

The surveys from 2011 through 2018 reported similar reasons for failure and barriers. The 2011 survey reported a small number (8%) of companies did not plan to continue with agile methodologies. The later surveys included tips for how to succeed in scaling agile.

In summary, going agile is difficult. The following are some of the factors that make it difficult.

## Challenges basic beliefs

Agile approaches require people to be open to examining their current beliefs and values. People need to be open to new experiences and to reflect and change their underlying beliefs (assumptions) and values. For example, if you believe software projects are predictable, then you value the process of planning. However, if you believe software projects are complex and unpredictable, then you value more adaptive, responsive approaches like agile development. Thus, basic belief systems about software development have to be challenged. They have to move from a planning focus to an adaptive focus.

## No Management Buy-in

Executives and management are involved in formulating new business strategies and running the business. They know they have software delivery needs, but they rarely look into the details of how software delivery is accomplished.

Going agile requires executive and management awareness and buy-in that something in software development radically different will happen. They need to understand the benefits to the change, but also the details of how the change will affect the operational aspects of the business.

One way to judge and measure the management understanding is based on the amount of time they invest in understanding agile: reading books, going to seminars, visiting other organizations that have gone agile, attending training sessions with the team. In addition, to review the investments they are willing to make in redeploying resources, including organizational space, required automation resources, and in changing organizational structures.

## Top-down and bottom-up

Changes require a top-down management push and bottom-up grassroots effort. From the top there needs to be a leader with the vision of the future and the benefits that can be gained by going in a new direction. From the bottom, the teams and team members need to work through the processes and address the issues to drive the change.

## Unpredictability

The agile practices as documented don't translate one-to-one into every organization. By definition, projects are unique undertakings. The people in the organization are not the same as those from other organizations. The organization practices, processes, and standards make certain demands on the project. The content and subject of the project are different from other projects. The timing is different. Therefore, there will be a degree of unpredictability to how the method or the combination of methods will really work.

## Pervasive

Going agile has an impact on not just one aspect of work but changes many aspects of work. It changes the collaboration between business and development. It changes the contract terms and types. It changes the team-working model to collaborative decision making and self-organizing work assignments. It changes the frequency and expectations of the delivery cycles.

The change is widespread throughout the organization and the way of working within the organization.

### Dramatically different

Many of the practices for software development are different from planning, estimating, and all the way through testing. Thus, old practices have to be changed to move forward with using agile practices.

### Too much change

It is already very difficult for people to keep up with changes in the business and economic environment. Going agile adds a further level of change to already changing environments.

### Adaptive practices

Many companies have gone agile, and there are many documented practices and guidelines. Nevertheless, there is no one best practice on the way to go agile. Each implementation will be different. The agile processes will have to be adapted to the company, project, and team.

---

## Personal Experience: Recommendations for going agile

### —Winson Choo, PMP CMQ/OE CSM CSP

> Have a strong sponsor (preferably the Chief Executive Officer) to ensure strong support from the entire organization. Scrum is good but many of the staff will resist changes. Office politics and a follow-the-rules culture are very hard to navigate if they don't have strong backing.
>
> Take care of the team and each of the team members. Genuinely care for them and the results will come.
>
> Even if at first it doesn't smoothly, hang in there! Have a very good sprint retrospective session. Make it the MOST important aspect. This is where it gets decided whether the next sprint is better than the current one — not.

# Getting started

There are several decisions that have to be made on how to best implement agile.

## Define the business case

The business case for going agile should be defined and agreed with the management. The desire to change has to be demonstrated with a clear business justification for going through the actions. Financial business cases that demonstrate the return on investment, net present value, or payback period are useful in gaining the necessary executive buy-in and commitment.

Johannes Ritter and Christine Marburger (2012) in their German article *Only a Business Case convinces the Top Management* describe that it's necessary to go from vision statements like "we want to be agile" to clear business propositions like "we want to improve testing to reduce bugs in the system in order to reduce the time it takes to deliver new software releases" to financial business cases "with an 80% probability that we will achieve benefits between 12.14 and 13.86 million Euro" (Ritter & Marburger, 2012).

Along with the financial business case, executive management should also be informed about the organizational implications of going agile. For example, agile requires a mindset of flexibility and adaptability, just-in-time planning, participatory decision-making, self-directed teams. Consequently, going agile can also introduce organizational risks especially in plan-driven organizations with a command-and-control culture.

## One or two agile methods?

The structure, support, advantages, and disadvantages of the different agile methodologies need to be weighed against one another to select the best option for the organization. In addition, given the requirements and diversity of the organization, it may be necessary to select a primary and optional methodology. This provides flexibility to the team to select the best methodology for the type of projects they are executing.

**Single agile method.** Choosing a single agile methodology has the benefits of being easier to support training, compare results, and share practices. However, depending upon the diversity of software projects in the organization; one method may not fit all use cases.

**Multiple agile methods.** Choosing to implement multiple methodologies (and a maximum of two would be suggested) gives the organization a choice of methodologies to use for different use cases. Conversely, the overhead and management associated with the rollout will increase.

## Starting small or big bang?

One decision is to select the breath of the initial implementation. The options are to start small or to transition all at once (i.e. big bang).

- Starting small is selecting a pilot project, learning from it, and then spreading agile practices throughout the organization.
- Start big is moving all teams and projects to agile at once.
- A hybrid approach is to use a combination of the start-small and big bang where one or more projects are selected and the rollout to all teams is paced.

Both methods require experienced coaches for each of the agile teams. Big bang should be used when there are enough coaches available as well as the management commitment to see it through. The salesforce.com case study is a good example of considerations and justifications for starting big.

**Starting small:**

- Less expensive
- Early success is a given
- Avoids risks (increased resistance, mistakes, resolving new issues)
- Less stressful
- Can be done without reorganization

**Big bang:**

- Reduce resistance (shows commitment)
- Avoid cross methodology issues
- Will be over quickly

## Publicize the transition or not?

The approach of publicly announcing to the organization that you are going agile sends a strong message of your intentions. It is a form of commitment to going agile. It makes taking a set of actions necessary.

The silent approach of not making a public announcement allows for experiments with no external pressures or visibility on the progress that is made.

In practice, a public announcement has a higher chance of success and is the preferred approach. The announcement within itself will draw cynics, but it puts a spotlight on the activities and that motivates with management and the team to go for success.

**Public display:**

- Once announced people are likely to see it through
- The goal is public and people can openly discuss it
- Firm statement of commitment
- Ask for help
- Success will be a powerful message

**Silent approach:**

- Progress can be made without resistance
- Less stress (or pressure)
- You can stop when you like
- Announcing success is in you control

## Training

Going from traditional project methodologies to agile will require some explanation of the methodologies and introduction to the new practices. Identify how many teams and people will be involved in agile projects and will be trained. The training should take place days before the project starts.

## Spreading agile

Agile teams should be staffed with people that are experienced with agile projects. The following are some of the options for growing and spreading the agile throughout the organization.

**Split teams**. One agile team is split to make a second team. The point is to have experienced members participate in each agile team. Justification for this approach:

- You add teams more quickly than the other approaches
- Each team has experienced team members
- This approach is useful when you are in a hurry.

**Increase team size and split**. Increase team sizes of an agile team with team members until it's large enough to split. Justification for this approach:

- You don't have to destroy existing teams
- Team members feel more continuity from iteration to iteration
- Use this approach for organic transitions and when you are not in a hurry.

**Internal Coaching.** Use experienced team members from one team or a central group in another team to coach them. The coaches should have responsibilities such as attending iteration planning sessions, reviews and retrospectives, attending some daily stand-ups each week, and being available for a certain number of hours for assistance.

The justification for using internal coaches include:

- Well running teams don't need to be split
- Coaches can be hand-picked
- Coaches can be moved for team to team

This approach may be used with the other two approaches or on its own. Use it:

- In large groups to spread practices
- When you have enough coaches
- When splitting a team is not practical.

**External coaching**. Hire an external agile coach; they bring in practical experience from other organizations. They can advise on potential pitfalls and recommend tips and techniques for coaching people and implementing agile practices.

## Implementing new engineering practices

The agile methodologies such as extreme programming introduce several new technical practices:

- Continuous integration
- Coding standards
- Automated testing
- Pair programming

A decision has to be made if technical practices are implemented at the same time as the project management practice (start early) or if there should be a delay in implementing the technical practices (delay).

**Start early.** The following are some of the reasons to justify implementing the new technical practices early:

- Very rapid improvements are possible as they offer quick wins
- If not tried early, they may never be tried
- Pressing issues can be addressed
- Some practices are necessary to be able to deliver in short time cycles (e.g. test automation)

**Delay.** The following are some of the reasons to justify delaying the implementation of new technical practices early:

- Strong resistance
- Already too much change
- Acquisition timeframe for new equipment.

## Listen to the team

Implementing agile methodologies to a new team can be very taxing for the team members. For example, an iteration cycle of two to three weeks with all the work that needed to go from a concept to a fully tested solution can seem hectic for the first few iterations. While there are many ideas and proven techniques listed as a reference, keep in mind that the strongest message will be sent out from the team (this is true for traditional or agile projects). Send the message that the management team cares, that they are open-minded and that would really appreciate a two-way communication. Managing two-way communications with the team members not only reduces resistant, it definitely increases participation and buy-in from the team.

## Personal experience: Recommendations to management when introducing agile practices

### —Nicky Hewgill, Marketing Manager & Agile Team Member

**Do:** Assume that some people will be skeptical. People will interpret a new way of doing things as a criticism of the old way of doing things. Address this positively. Prepare the groundwork; give people time to research agile and form some opinions. Discuss expectations in an informal meeting, well before launching into formal training or implementation.

**Don't:** Allow bullies, micromanagers or yes-men to exploit agile to continue their poor behavior. If there's tension in your team you should address this before, during and after implementation. Agile helps with task management; people management is still the manager's job.

**Do:** Make sure you understand agile as well as anyone else in the team, and take responsibility for making it work. Acknowledge that you also need to change. If you make a list of tasks, get the most junior person to write them up, assign the most (or least) aggressive person in the group to be scrum master, and — then just wander off — don't expect to come back a few weeks later and find everything ticking over nicely!

---

## Selecting a pilot

The following are the considerations for selecting the pilot project.

### Type of project

Agile methodologies are very effective in an environment where there are constant changes in the requirements. Experimental projects with no definitive specification and projects where the product is affected by a technologically changing environment will show clear benefits from using agile approaches. The stakeholders and the project team will see visible results from these projects. This will generate confidence.

### Duration

A pilot project should be selected that is not too short and not too long. The duration is important as it should be long enough to be convincing that agile will work for significant projects. However, it should not be so long that it delays the roll out to other projects and teams. Ideally, the project should be between three to four months.

## Size

The pilot should be composed of one team and eventually grow to multiple teams to start. Multiple teams allow for gaining a cross-section of experiences with the use of the tools. Ideally, at least one of the initial teams is already located in a single place (that is, co-located).

## Importance

Pick an important project. An important project will motivate the team to succeed. Furthermore, it will ensure that the project gets the necessary resources to succeed. Consequently, an important project will also be highly visible and have interest from many stakeholders.

## Business sponsor

The pilot project should have a business sponsor that has the time and motivation to be engaged. As the first project, the cooperation between the business and development team will be new.

## Start timing

The pilot project should be based on finding a project that's previously failed or one that's already running and is about to fail. A project in this state will already have a backlog of requirements or features that need to be implemented. This will allow for gaining quick momentum toward delivering a working product.

## Pilot team

The pilot team should be composed of members who are willing to try something new. It should include at least one agile lobbyist, a few people new to agile projects, and an agile skeptic. This combination will be helpful in spreading the outcome of the pilot to cynics as well as agile enthusiasts.

# Case study: Agile adoption & transformation

The following section summarizes information on two different aspects of Yahoo!'s transformation to agile. The first aspect covers the main steps and challenges that Yahoo! faced in their agile adoption from 2004 to 2009. The second case provides an example of how Yahoo! Engineering implemented agile into its project management office practices.

**Agile adoption**

In 2009, Mun-Wia Chung and Brian Drummond presented a paper called "Agile @ Yahoo! From the Trenches." It was a retrospective review of Yahoo! agile adoption. The following section provides a summary of their journey.

Yahoo!'s transition to agile was initiated by an engineering manager who valued the concept of localized decision-making over a centrally controlled process. They started using scrum as it was formally designed, i.e. "by the book." There was resistance and issues while implementing scrum as it was not adapted to Yahoo!.

They brought in a full-time, on-site agile specialist who embodied the principles of agile to work with people that were interested in trying scrum. An opt-in (optional participation) pilot program was created and four teams volunteered. They were trained by certified scrum masters who provided practical real-world examples and an adaptable approach for Yahoo!.

One pilot team developed a web-based image sharing application. The team executed their first sprint with the help of outside coaching staff. The trial exposed that the interactions between the user experience folks and the visual designers was way higher than with the other team members. There wasn't enough development capacity to keep up. From the pilot they benefited by breaking down separate work silos and having direct peer-to-peer communication as opposed to communication through the management chain. They were favorable to the new process.

Another pilot team was working on a legacy product with an intertwined code base. The product was highly visible, with a worldwide launch and tight deadlines. The team members were mixed about the decision to go agile. The product manager liked the idea of quicker releases, the engineering staff was neutral, the user experience designers were skeptical, and program management was concerned. In the end, they decided not to risk it and opted-out.

After two years, agile started to become a common practice with 150 development teams reporting that they were using scrum. There were company-wide presentations on the topic, interest groups and special events. Local spearheads were introduced into the business units to spread leaned knowledge and techniques. A centralized coaching staff was hired. Scrum practices were integrated into organizational stage gates and checklists. Challenges remained with the perception that agile would solve many different organizational issues, including delivering faster. There were not enough coaches. Alternative agile methods such as kanban were tested, causing some friction.

Due to the positive results of the pilot program, agile was mandated by some engineering management for their product teams. Reports of productivity improvements, and the resolution of organizational and communications issues due to scrum adoption, changed the mindset of many skeptical people. Steps were taken to resolve some of the challenges presented by scrum. Multi-level planning was used to solve gaps in long-term planning. Focus group lunches were used to share knowledge and experience. The shortage of agile coaches was addressed by introducing a train the trainer program. Nevertheless, finding people in the business units to carry forward the practices had mixed results.

After an economic downturn, the central agile coaches were disbanded. The first generations of agile-ist were left to drive forward the agile practices. The results were mixed: Some teams continued to drive the command-and-control management style under the banner of agile, other teams failed to apply all the elements of scrum, and yet others were extremely successful. For example:

- One team was trained on scrum but declined coaching. The product backlog was a task funnel, the user stories were difficult to trace, delivery dates were dictated to the team, daily stand-ups were status meetings, sprints were of fixed scope and fixed dates, and estimates were challenged by the manager.
- In another example, a new development team was formed from a previous scrum team. The members included high profile individuals who had entitlements — and were allowed to skip elements of scrum. Management would get involved in the planning process. Tasks would be directed to individuals. The team started out following scrum but evolved into a command-and-control model.
- Another product team started with scrum as of its initial rollout. The team enjoyed strong agile leadership. and was able to collaborate on release planning and negotiate with management when release dates were mandated. They were able to successfully deliver product and gain additional responsibility for new projects.

In conclusion, Yahoo!s evolution to agile was a multi-year journey with many successes and challenges along the way. However, "Once an individual participates in a successful implementation of Agile and understands the true benefits, that person becomes a strong devotee and locks on to the agile 'DNA' (Chung & Drummond, 2009, p. 118).

### Integrating Scum in the Process Framework

In 2008, Karl Scotland and Alexandre Boutin (2008) presented a case on how Yahoo! international engineering evolve its project management office (PMO) practices and scrum process to be compatible with the agile values and principles, their european PMO standards, and International Process Framework. They were able to integrate organizational-based checkpoints into the scrum process. Table 18-1 describes how the scrum process was adapted to fit their organizational requirements.

| Process Framework Requirements | Scrum Roles and Events | Adaption to Scrum Process |
|---|---|---|
| Roles: product manager, engineering program manager (EPM), service program manager (SPM). architect | Roles: product owner, scrum master, team | |
| A kick-off checkpoint to determine what is going to be done. Attendees. product manager, EPM, and SPM. | | Chartering session |
| An architecture checkpoint to determine how the project will be delivered. This checkpoint can be iterated multiple times. Attendees: architect, developers and SPM. | No direct concept in scrum | Added a "Start of Sprint Report" and checklist for the project office to gain transparency on how the team was working |
| The release checkpoint is used to demonstrate that the team has been delivered the right thing. This checkpoint reviews the quality of what will be delivered to production from a business and a technical point of view. | Review and retrospectives | Review and retrospective meeting were used as a "release gate " with a "Release checklist"<br>Product backlog and burndown chart are included in reviews and reports. |

Table 18-1 Scrum adaption

References:

Chung, Mun-Wai, and Brian Drummond. "Agile @ Yahoo! From the Trenches." 2009 Agile Conference, 2009: 113-118.

Drummond, Brian, and John Francis JF Unson. "Yahoo! Distributed Agile: notes from the world over." Agile 2008, 2008: 315-321.

## Summary

- Introducing agile software development projects is an organizational change. To start it requires finding an incentive to drive the change. Once the first projects have shown success, it requires changes in every administrative function in the organization. It also requires support from senior and middle management.
- Pilot projects should be important to the organization to ensure they get the resources required to succeed. Their staffing should include everyone needed to make the project a success, including someone who has experience with agile projects.
- There will be challenges in implementing agile practices. The key is to plan a long-term journey for the agile implementation, consider all of the subsidiary impacts and stakeholders, and get started with the right pilot project or set of activities.

## Recommended reading

- In *Succeeding with Agile,* Mike Cohn offers a selection of guidance on the consideration and steps for taking an organization through the agile transition. Mike has a focus on the Scrum methodology.
- In *Practices for Scaling Lean & Agile Development,* Craig Larman and Voode Bas offer guidance on going agile with large and distributed practices. They also focus on scrum.
- In *Kanban Successful Evolutionary Change for Your Technology Business,* David J. Anderson focuses on implementing Kanban practices.

# Chapter 19 Scaling Agile

One of the key areas of concern for organizations considering going agile is whether it scales to large projects. This chapter summarizes practices for setting up large agile projects, including organizing the people, the product, the project and the processes. In the context of this chapter, a 'large agile project' refers to more than one project team working on the same product.

The agile methodologies have different ways of scaling, but agile methods have been successfully used in large projects, with distributed teams, and in large organizations. Chris Fry and Steve Greene reported rolling out agile practices to more than 200 people in three months, and Craig Larman and Bas Vodde describe in detail how to run agile projects for large and distributed teams based on their experience. Yahoo! has also described their experiences in getting more than 150 teams to use agile. Like any large project (with any type of methodology), large agile projects are challenging. Nevertheless, it's possible to use agile practices in large projects and with distributed teams.

There are several agile scaling methodologies. The scaling methodologies are mostly built on the scrum methodology with varying roles, planning events, synchronization practices, and review and retrospective practices. Nevertheless, there are four themes that need to be managed when setting up large agile projects: people, product, project, and process (Figure 19-1). The following section summarizes a collection of practices and information on these four themes.

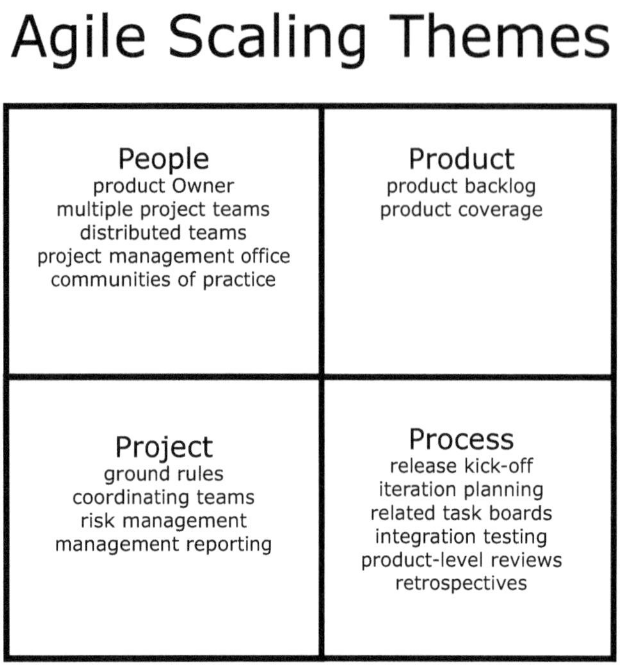


Figure 19-1 Themes in managing large agile projects

## Organizing people

The following section gives some information on organizing and cross-coordinating multiple teams that are working on the same product.

### Product owner

The product owner has responsibilities that require a high level of internal coordination with the team and external coordination with customers and users. The product owner is actively engaged in grooming the backlog and participating in planning and review meetings. After doing these activities, there is little time left for engagement with several teams. Thus, a product owner should work on a maximum of two teams. Furthermore, when engaged in more than two teams, the product owner is likely to lose sight of the product backlog or it will become too large.

To scale the product owner's involvement beyond two teams, a hierarchy of product owners should be created. For example, there may be a chief product owner who oversees all product owners, product line owners for major product themes, and product owners for individual teams.

In the scaling, there should be one overall product owner who manages the vision for the product. The product owner hierarchy should report to this person. In the hierarchy, this person would be described as the 'chief product owner.' The size and scope of the hierarchy under the chief product owner will vary depending on the project. Nevertheless, if the product owners are created for different themes, the themes should be created from the customer's point of view (e.g. the online shoe shop) and not a technical point-of-view (web-interface-team).

The individual product owners up and down the hierarchy should have the complete product owner authority and responsibilities — and not be delegates from the chief product owner with no authority to reach decisions or drive their product area forward.

## Multiple project teams

Large projects will contain multiple teams. However, the dependencies between the teams should be proactively managed and reduced as much as possible. Some examples of how dependencies may be reduced are performing rolling look ahead planning, sharing team members, having dedicated integration teams, or establishing a project management office. Rolling look ahead planning is discussed in the process section of this chapter. The assignment of user stories to project teams is discussed in the product section of this chapter.

### Share team members

A shared team member is on two teams concurrently working on both sides of a known or likely dependency.

### Integration team

An integration team works in the gaps between the two teams. Gaps occur in the interface between teams as there are usually unidentified interfaces and unattended interfaces:

- An unidentified interface is one that exists but has not yet been uncovered.
- An unattended interface is one is known about but is not being acted upon.

The integration team identifies such problems and their causes, and then the team agrees that it will resolve them. In an environment with continuous integration, they would possibly check the previous night's build, identify problems, and determine what teams are involved — and then work with those teams to resolve the issues.

The integration team can be virtual, a single person, a single team or multiple teams depending on the size of the project. Integration teams are seen when there are more than ten teams.

## Distributed teams

Osmotic communication for distributed teams is achieved when project communications are established such that remote and co-located team members can be part of on-going routine project conversations and jump in when needed.

For distributed teams, various communications media facilitate osmotic communications. The following should be considered:

- Live video conferencing and speakerphone meetings allow everyone to hear and jump into the conversation as needed.

- Webcams allow for face-to-face communications on an ad hoc basis
- Email communications sent to the direct recipients and copying (cc) the remaining team members allows for the involvement of remote and co-located team members.
- Chat tools and instant messaging allow for direct, interactive communications between team members.
- Photographs of information radiators allow the teams to see the shape of the task board and the movement of stickers.
- Common web pages.
- Easily updateable wiki pages.
- Electronic tasks boards and systems.

## Project management office

A project management office can include a dedicated team to facilitate the training, coaching, transition support, and coordination between specific teams. The project management office should include cross-functional team members; they should coordinate the cross-team activities. For example, it may include a project leader, architect, test coordinator, and systems analyst. By name, the project management office may be considered a core team or a center of excellence.

In the oversight and governance of large projects, the project management office should provide support with planning and scheduling activities. Project reporting can also be coordinated by the project management office.

## Communities of practice

The community of practice can be established for groups of individuals with similar interests to share experiences and knowledge around a specific theme with members of a community. For example, all the testers may belong to a testing community, and the architects may belong to an architecture community. Participation in CoPs is normally optional.

In his book *Mastering Organizational Knowledge Flow: How to Make Knowledge Sharing Work*, Frank Leistner refers to CoPs as "an organizational structure that sometimes can be invisible but nevertheless plays an important role in letting knowledge flow around the organization." (Leistner, 2010, p. 119) While CoPs may not be mandated by the project, they do need a leader (with a passion) to get started, as well as support from the project (available time, wikis) to survive for the long term.

The CoPs may extend to groups outside the project or even the organization.

## Project management

When working in a large project, the project will need the following basic elements to ensure that all the project teams are working towards delivering a single product:

- Ground rules for cooperation
- Coordination across teams
- Management reporting

### Ground rules

Large projects, especially if they're scattered across geographies, will have people working from different locations, at different times, and potentially in different countries. In addition to the ground rules that should be established for every project, the following additional topics should be added to the team's list of ground rules:

- Project language
- Working times
- Scheduling remote meetings
- Planning horizon

**Project language:** A common language should be agreed on for project documents and meetings. In general, when teams are co-located and everyone is a native of the country, it's normal for people to speak their native language. While this can be tolerated in the absence of foreigners, a common project language for documents — including email exchanges, chats, and wikis — should be enforced. This rule applies even when natives of the same country are communicating. Informal emails can quickly turn into important project documents that need to be forwarded or where non-natives need to be included in the communication.

**Working times:** There should be ground rules established for the core time windows when team members can reasonably be expected to be available for coordination activities. Depending on where the team members are located, the overlap in the working day may be only a few hours (or none at all). Since no one team should be required to consistently adjust their normal working day, there needs to be a project-wide understanding and agreement on acceptable contact times. This rule may be applicable for projects even if only one country is involved. (e.g. Russia covers 11 time zones.)

**Scheduling meetings:** There should be a ground-rule established on when it's acceptable to schedule remote meetings and how. All-day planning sessions via video or phone conference are difficult. Moreover, they're impossible when one team has to come in early or stay late to participate in such meetings.

- Teams or team members may be required to travel for specific meetings or for whole iterations. For example, when a team is split between California and Bangalore, there's a 12.5 hour time difference. Joint full-day meetings may require travel by one team to the other site.

- Team members may be required to adjust their working hours to have an overlap with other team members. For example, when a team is split between California and Norway, there's a 9-hour time difference. Joint meetings may require the California team members to come in an hour earlier in the morning and the Norway team to stay an hour later in the afternoon.

Whether adjusting working times or requiring travel, there should be a balance so that no one team has to make all of the adjustments. Each team should be required to either travel or adjust working times equally to avoid disfunction.

**Planning horizon:** There may be interdependencies between the teams' deliverables. Therefore, each team has to plan some degree of forward planning, which is usually accomplished through a 'rolling look-ahead planning' technique. The technique uses the iteration planning session to map out the next iteration in detail and look-ahead a few iterations, planning them just enough to understand the dependencies to other teams. There should be some ground rules about whether rolling look-ahead planning is required, and if so, how many iterations forward are expected.

## Coordinating across teams

Project management plays a role in cross-team coordination in large projects. The coordination of teams is necessary to manage dependencies and issues between teams. 'Scrum of scrums' and synchronized iterations are two methods for coordinating the agile teams.

### Scrum of scrums

The scrum of scrums is a routine meeting to cross coordinates between agile teams. One person from each team attends the scrum of scums. The event can occur two to three times a week, and it should be timeboxed from 30 to 60 minutes. The scrum of scrums is focused on problem solving. Open and un-addressed issues are placed in the issues backlog.

### Synchronized iterations

Iterations should be synchronized to start and end within a day or two of one another. Not all the iterations have to end on the same day, but they should be aligned to end within a few days of each other. Nor do all iterations have to have the same timebox duration. For example, one team could have a timebox of four weeks while the remaining teams have a timebox of two. The synchronization is important to be able to address the dependencies that may exist between iterations.

## Common estimation scale

Having a common baseline for estimates allows for common release burndown charts and evaluating the velocity across the product. This is important in release management and monitoring. The teams should decide whether they'll estimate in story points or ideal days. Then they need to establish a common baseline for estimating.

To create a common story point measure, all teams have to be brought together to define a common definition for what a story point is.

- If the teams have previously worked together, they should select a group of previous stories of various sizes and agree on the estimates for those stories.
- If the teams haven't worked together previously, they should select a set of new stories and agree on the estimates for those stories.
- For estimating, they should use the agreed stories as references for sizing future stories.

This approach of coming together to agree on estimate sizes should be repeated periodically, as estimates would otherwise drift apart.

There are some cautions that go with having a common estimation framework:

- Well-intentioned managers and team members may begin to compare team performance by comparing story points.
- If story points are used, someone will try to equate story points to a specific number of effort days for comparison.

These should both be avoided!

# Risk management

Risk management in large agile projects becomes critical due to the interdependencies between teams and their impact on the overall delivery of the entire product. Therefore:

- Consider adding some rigor to the estimation of the release end date.
- Build methods for monitoring the team's actual velocity.
- Monitor the release burndown with or without common story point estimates.
- Consider the best, worst, and most probable end date. Probabilistic models such as Monte Carlo simulations can help in this respect. (See chapter 14.)

## Management reporting

The management reporting for a large agile project is needed to assess the extent to which the product will meet the business goals, to assess the remaining risks and issues to put the product into operations, and to gain insights into the product quality.

The reporting should include the actual status and trend analysis information gained in the burnup charts, velocity charts, and risk flow diagrams. Common project-wide methods for estimating are required if the reporting is to be summarized project-wide.

If it isn't possible to establish a common estimation baseline, other methods need to be considered for monitoring performance. One alternative to a joint release burndown chart is to estimate a percentage of progress based on story points that the group has completed. Different weighting or classifications (best, worst, likely) can be added to provide a realistic view. An additional project-wide report may be needed to evaluate the system's test coverage and defect trends. Table 19-1 is an example of a multi-project performance report. In this example, the color-coding of red, yellow, and green provides performance indicators for when a topic requires attention, is within tolerance, or is on-track, respectively.

| | Project 1 | Project 2 | Project 3 |
|---|---|---|---|
| Scope Completed | 10% | 75% | 50% |
| Delivery Frequency | 1 month | 3 months | 2 months |
| Sponsor Satisfaction | 63% | 74% | 94% |
| ROI Index | 91% | 42% | 106% |
| Schedule (SPI) | 8% | -3% | 2% |
| Budget (CPI) | 4% | -4% | 15% |
| Quality | 82% | 95% | 97% |

Table 19-1 Example of a multi-project performance report

- Scope completed is the number of story points planned divided by story points implemented.
- Delivery frequency is the iteration length.
- Sponsor satisfaction is a rating based on feedback from review meetings.

- ROI index is the percent of ROI from the business case that has been realized through the project based on story value.
- Schedule (SPI) is the earned value metric for schedule performance.
- Budget (CPI) is the earned value metric for cost.
- Quality is a performance rating based on the number of escaped defects.

## Product backlog

**One product, one backlog:** For any given product, there should only be one backlog.

**Reasonable size:** The product backlog should have no more than 100 to 150 visible elements. A large product backlog should make use of epics (larger stories) or themes (grouping small stories). If the product backlog is large, it should create views so that subsets of the backlog viewed should no more than 100 to 150 items.

Maintaining a single product backlog is also necessary for the chief product owner to maintain oversight of the product backlog and the dependencies between teams.

## Product coverage

There are multiple methods for distributing the work from the product backlog across multiple teams:

- Multiple teams (or sites) work on the common user stories
- Each team (or site) works on a subset of user stories
- Work is separated based on activities (one team tests, the other develops)
- A combination of these models

Considerations should include:

- It should be as easy as possible for the team to coordinate with the product owner
- Teams working on common user stories should have at least a few hours of overlapping working time (consider time zone differences)
- Testing should be part of the development; thus, when it's possible, the work between teams should be integrated during the iterations
- The work should be interesting and motivating for the team (one team shouldn't be assigned all of the 'grunt work').

## Adapting the process

In large projects, the chartering, planning, review, and retrospective activities are interdependent across multiple teams. Since the project has a single product focus, the agile practices need to be adapted to support multiple project teams.

### Release kick-off

A release kick-off meeting can be used at the start of a release for the product owners to share what their teams are working on for the coming months (usually three). Preparation for the meeting means the product owners, together with their teams, have created a rough plan for what can be delivered in the foreseeable future.

### Iteration planning

Iteration planning sessions may share team members or product owners. If so, consider staggering the iteration planning events or use a shared room so that shared team members can attend all the relevant planning sessions.

- **Stagger by a day**. Iteration planning sessions can be conducted within a day or two of one another. By staggering the meetings, team members on multiple teams can attend the requisite planning sessions. Starting all iterations within a day or two works for up to nine teams (three teams planning per day).

- **Use a big room.** Holding multiple planning sessions in one big room is an alternative when key people need to attend multiple sessions. In this scenario, all planning sessions can be conducted in one day. This is a good solution when projects share people. The event may be loud and very active.

During the iteration planning, rolling look ahead planning is suggested to identify dependencies to other teams and to perform preparation work that should be done in the next iteration. Rolling look ahead planning requires the historical velocity and the product owner's prioritized product backlog. The stories aren't broken down into tasks and story points aren't estimated. There's also no commitment to deliver the features. The product owner can still change the priority of items in the backlog.

Depending on the interdependencies, it could be necessary to include a time contingency in the plan. For example, if Team A needs a widget on Day X from Team B, Team A could include a contingency so that they request and expect the widget from Team B on Day X minus five. This protects that Team A should Team B have a delay in providing the widget. In his book *Agile Estimating and Planning*, Mike Cohn calls this contingency a 'feeding buffer.' To include a feeding buffer, the team providing the capability, Team B, would get a lower velocity in the release plan.

## Related task boards

When a team is split between sites or there are relationships between the workflows of different teams, relating the multiple task boards may be an option. In this case, the following options exist for multi-site or multi-team task boards.

- Use electronic systems for the task board
- Keep multiple copies of the task board at each site and update them when possible
- Take pictures of the task board and distribute them electronically (while it may not be possible to see the contents of the cards, it's possible to see how the cards progress through the task board)
- Indicate through arrows that the physical task boards are connected
- Use color coding or other indicators to show that multiple teams or externals are represented in the task board

## Integration testing

A 'release train' is a strategy that predefines a future iteration as a hardening iteration for systems-level integration testing. For example, with a project of four teams the iteration timeboxes would be aligned between teams. The cadence would be agreed that every third iteration is a hardening iteration. The teams would then work independently for the first two iterations. The third iteration would be used to integration testing the complete solution from all four teams.

## Product-level reviews

In large projects, there should be joint multi-team reviews that focus on the overall product. This is justified, as it keeps the individual teams focused on delivering a single product that delivers value. Individual product reviews can promote an individual team's focus instead of focusing on the big picture.

The review may be split into parts, as some features are of interest across the entire project while others may only be of interest to a single product area.

**Product-level reviews:** Demonstrate the product in conference rooms joined by video conferencing. Representatives from the various teams present a subset of the product's topic areas that are of interest to the group.

Alternatively, hold an exhibition-style event with a demonstration area and tables staffed by team members who demonstrate specific product topics. The product owner or team members visit the individual tables to review the product features.

**Team-level reviews:** align team reviews with the product owner. When a product owner is responsible for one team, just have a normal review. When a product owner is responsible for multiple-teams, then have a multi-team joint review.

## Retrospectives

Retrospectives should continue to be conducted per project team. However, an additional multi-team retrospective should be considered to increase learning across teams and define actions that may make the project more productive.

A multi-team retrospective would consist of one to two members from each team and be held after the team retrospective. Care should be taken to make the joint retrospective not just about problems, but also what worked well.

# Scaling methodologies

Table 19-2 provides an overview of six scaling methodologies. The roles, planning events, and synchronization activities are drivers in determining the maximum team size to which the methodology can scale.

| | Team Size |
|---|---|
| Scaled Agile Framework® (SAFE) | Hundreds or even thousands of people |
| Large Scale Scrum (LESS) | Basic - 2-8 teams; huge 8+ teams |
| Nexus | 3 - 9 teams; no more than 100 people |
| Spotify - Agile at Scale | Multiple teams |
| Disciplined Agile Delivery (DAD) | Multiple teams; 1000s of people |
| Scrum of Scrum | Multiple teams |

Table 19-2 Selected agile scaling methodologies

The VersionOne *13th Annual State of Agile Report* identified the Scaled Agile Framework® as the most popular scaling framework and offered the following tips for successful scaling:

- Internal agile coaches
- Executive sponsorship
- Company-provided training programs
- Consistent practices and processes across teams
- Implementation of a common tool across teams

## Summary

- A product owner should work on a maximum of two teams and, when needed, have a hierarchy of product owners based on customer-oriented themes.
- For any given product, there should be just one backlog. The backlog should include views if it contains more than 100 - 150 items. Each team should be able to view its subset of the product hierarchy.
- Large projects should contain multiple teams, and use rolling look ahead planning, shared team members, or dedicated integration teams to manage dependencies.
- Kick-off or chartering sessions should be used to align teams to the project objectives. Time contingencies (also called feeder buffers) should be used to ensure that team interdependencies are delivered on-time. Scrum of scrums and synchronized iterations are two methods for coordinating the agile teams.
- Iteration planning sessions should respect that people may be in multiple teams and could be required to attend multiple sessions. Staggering the iteration planning events by a day or two or holding them in a big room are two options that allow people to attend more than one meeting.
- Establish ground rules and coordination forums to facilitate cross-team work. Establish a framework for a common estimation scale to facilitate common burndown charts and evaluating overall project velocity. Use rigorous risk management practices especially for planning release dates.
- Product-level reviews can be conducted as demonstrations as well as exhibition style. The focus should be on creating one product; thus, care should be taken not to perform team-level product reviews. Similarly, multi-team retrospectives should be conducted to maintain a focus on project-wide performance improvements.

## Recommended reading

- Craig Larman and Voode Bas offer guidance in *Practices for Scaling Lean & Agile Development* on going agile with large and distributed practices. They focus on the scrum methodology.

# Chapter 20 Experience from the Field

This chapter provides information on how some project managers and agile coaches have implemented agile practices in their projects.

## Business case on agile implementation at Betfair

## Quantifying the costs, benefits, and risks of implementing agile — beforehand

### —Johannes Ritter, Management Consultant, January 2013

Founded in 2000, Betfair is the largest internet betting exchange focused mainly on sports. By constantly introducing new products in 2011, Betfair had grown to 2,300 employees with worldwide annual revenue of Ł393.3 million. A system that started with a simple Microsoft Access database published to a web server, now handles more transactions a day than all European stock exchanges combined. The high number of transactions puts enormous demands on the scalability of the software system. This is especially true because of frequent innovation and software upgrades. There is tremendous time pressure, as launching a dedicated football world cup product after the event does nobody any good. Also, numerous regulatory requirements have to be implemented rapidly. After each software upgrade, customers expect the software to operate flawlessly, bug-free, and in real-time. Furthermore, since lots of personal and financial customer data is stored, tremendous effort goes into IT security.

Against this background, Betfair faced the challenge of how to further decrease its time-to-market, introducing even more products, while still increasing quality. The board of directors were enchanted with the agile approach, but wanted to see proof before committing the whole organization. The chief financial officer (CFO) and chief information officer (CIO) commissioned a business case analysis to evaluate the costs, benefits and risks of switching the product development methodology from waterfall to agile. As a steering committee, they provided guidance to the business case project team, who over a period of three weeks — collected the data and calculated the results.

Three concerns were paramount:

1) As with every new methodology, there's a risk that, initially, things might slow down and development would take longer than before.

2) In their environment, agile called for continuous integration and automated testing every night. Given that customers could be using different browsers and hardware (e.g. Windows XP, and 7; Apple OS; Firefox, Internet Explorer, Chrome, and Safari), at least 16 different hardware combinations were needed. That multiplied by the number of products and projects meant a staggering amount of hardware had to be purchased and maintained.

3) Due to the integrated nature of the business, it would not suffice to start the agile implementation in one department, e.g. software development, and let the other departments continue with the waterfall methodology. Doing so would just increase the backlog in software deployment and rollout.

In a typical year, Betfair runs about 75 projects. The agile project team picked one representative project to build a business case. As a baseline, the project duration, cost and quality using the waterfall approach were compared to an agile approach using a two-week sprint in which the software would be developed, quality-tested and deployed. Continuous integration, automated testing, and deployment tools would be used.

Representative project

- Total labor cost: Ł 248,500
- Project duration in calendar days: 129 (1/2 year)
- Labor cost per calendar day: Ł 1,926
- Potential improvement through continuous integration: 15 calendar days reduction in labor cost Ł28,895 = 11,6%

Assuming a duration of one year, the reduction in labor cost per project would be Ł57,790. Taking a representative project and assuming a total of 75 active projects per year over three years the total reduction in labor costs would be Ł13 million.

The calculated results were validated with risk and sensitivity analysis. But the most reliable proof was the comparison of these projections with the actual results of the representative project once completed. Thus, improvements were validated and the board of directors unanimously decided to implement agile across the enterprise.

"It has been really informative to work with Johannes and his team over the past few days while we've been building the business case for agile. He has a clear way of communicating and would recommend him as a specialist in this area."

Mark Wood, Betfair, Operational Director

References:

Business Case for Agile published in Projektmagazin on 14 July 2012. http://www.solutionmatrix.de/presse/projektmagazin_agile_entwicklung.pdf

Johannes Ritter will gladly provide you with the ROI calculator so you can do your own calculations on how your company would profit from agile practices. Simply send an email to agile@solutionmatrix.com

## Company transition to agile

### —Winson Choo, May 2015

This global organization is a leading market research company listed on the New York Stock Exchange (NYSE). A household name in almost every country, it focuses on the fast-moving consumer goods (FMCG) sector.

The downside of its worldwide presence was a fragmented, decentralized approach to software development. A strategy was therefore developed for standardizing software development and making use of a common practice and platform.

### Legacy challenge: overcoming inertia

The organization had long practiced the waterfall model: every level had its own set of sign-off criteria. Having spent years developing and using a proprietary system for decision-making, administration and governance, the company was disinclined to make a change. In short, they thought: it may be slow, but it works, and almost everyone understands it!

In large organizations, radical changes require engagement at all levels of the enterprise, from the executive all the way down to specific project teams. Much time and effort must be invested to ensure that the teams get aligned, that they understand and actually use the new processes.

## FUD an obstacle to progress

It's always difficult for a group representing an organization to pick a methodology and jump right in using it. Not only do fear, uncertainty and doubt (FUD) beset the team that advocates the big change, there's also the sheer volume of questions wanting answers and the hydra-like tangle of executives requiring progress reports and metrics. The resource demand is high, stemming both from the new practices themselves and from preparing the information needed to ensure buy-in and continued funding of agile pilot programs.

Likewise, tracking progress and satisfying organizational auditing standards are generally hard to do. Even when agile practices are accepted, the way agile is measured may not necessarily be. For example, since this organization was accustomed to using Gantt charts and metrics, it had trouble accepting just a burndown chart and product/sprint backlogs.

Furthermore, in global organizations, meeting up can be difficult for team members, as people with different skills are often located in different time zones. This may call for slightly adjusting agile practices: when should a 'morning meeting' take place? The morning may be at a different time for every team member!

## The final motivating factor for this organization: system creakiness

When the company's software development units were no longer able to respond quickly to changes or provide timely turnaround on requests from the commercial and business teams, things began to heat up. Put simply, if the software is one of the main enablers of output that can be sold to clients, then an inability to effect change requests promptly can cause the loss of new business. As response times from the software development team continually slowed, the one differentiator that they could see as important was the practice of agile concepts. Championed by the CTO, the technology team kicked off an initiative to halt the downward trend.

Before management could really buy into the concept, they had to understand agile, its potential benefits and how it works; so, they were the first to be exposed to high-level training. Then, consultants studied the organizational structure to identify key leaders of the various software development teams before drawing up an overall plan for a new agile center of excellence (CoE); this CoE team was sponsored by the CTO. Next, a comprehensive train-the-trainer program was developed to carry the initiative forward to diverse software development teams.

Agile encompasses a set of best practices that can be applied generally. Surprisingly, it met with even more positive resonance from outside the software development teams.

## A peek inside the engine: the nuts and bolts

The CoE was made responsible for spreading and sharing the practices, syllabus and training throughout the individual software development teams, who elected a representative to be trained as their trainer. The CoE also came up with documentation and processes to facilitate the Agile practice and align them via teams for auditing, project management and governance.

In the beginning, coaches trained and educated the product owners, the agile leaders and the scrum masters. Both during and after training, the scrum masters and product owners played an important role in ensuring that the agile practices took place, although the product owners really held the keys to success because of their role in ensuring that the application's final specifications are delivered. One key observation was that, in areas for which no single product owner could be determined (whether none or multiple), agile practices were harder to follow and produced lesser results.

A kick-off meeting and webinars created awareness, followed by regular communications from the agile CoE to maintain momentum within both the software development teams and executive management. Frequent coaching sessions in the beginning were tapered off as the product owners and agile teams grew competent to resolve issues on their own — and as uncertainty and conflict subsided. The documents in constant use included the burndown chart, the product backlog, the user story and the sprint tasks board list.

## Some surprising results

Despite costs for hiring consulting firms, training at all levels of the organization, time investments and process change, the belief is that, in the long run, the agility gained will help the business take advantage of more opportunities and, respond more quickly to clients' needs; hence, there's a financial gain for the organization.

While the overall development time was not changed by much, the ability to react to requests for customizations and enhancements was improved, and overall, there were fewer defects.

The teams also seem to work together better now, although this wasn't true in the beginning. Some team members weren't able to 'fit in' at first, but as time passed, and through more frequent meetings these outliers have adapted to the system and are now aligned with the product owners and leadership team.

## Communication and buy-in absolutely critical success factors

Because there were several teams in this case, we had a unique chance to watch them roll out agile simultaneously – but differently. We observed that team that 'bought in best' got the most out of it; coincidentally, that team also had product owners who were highly committed to the agile process. Other issues stemming from buy-in included:

- Senior team members who weren't open to the idea could cause a lot of internal confusion within the team, slowing down adoption
- Conflicts between multiple product owners will hinder the agile team in its ability to deliver the created value to the client, because the delivery wasn't aligned with the product owners in the first place

When challenges arise, especially larger ones that involve financial losses, the sponsor must step in to resolve them. This has proven an important point; it shows the organization's commitment to agile and the all-out approach to ensuring that agile works. And when team members observe this kind of commitment, they automatically gravitate towards it and start to learn, adapt and practice agile in their daily work.

It's essential that the CoE is made up of people who genuinely want to make improvements and who will listen to the issues. Moving from a traditional waterfall model to agile is a big process, requiring a change of mindset and different ways of working, and it was crucial that the members of this CoE were truly interested, always willing to go the extra mile and explain it again when necessary.

### Recommendations

Get a reputable consultant to come in and create a comprehensive plan that suits the organization. When an organization has no previous agile experience, openness is important: Only then can consultants who've seen the success of agile open up the hearts and minds of executives. This also helps create the required buy-in and commitment at the management level.

In coming up with a strategy, get the teams to participate from the very beginning, starting with the decision to engage a consultant. Ask for feedback and support up-front, as some team members may already be excited by the prospect of moving to agile practice or agile development. Use the organization's social platforms to start a discussion and encourage information sharing to build momentum.

While the consultant's suggestions are important, during implementation it is crucial to consider recommendations from team members who are working on coding and software development. They'll surely have valuable insights that can help further increase the benefit of agile practice. Great care must be taken to incorporate this type of feedback and ensure that it isn't lost.

## How to kill Taylorism using bottom-up intelligence

#### —Ralf Tauscher, July 2015

**Agile transitions are all the same but different every time.**

### An approach for agilization

At my current company, I started using scrum in 2008. After working together with several teams over seven years a pattern emerges. It's often the case that I'm tasked with improving agility within a certain project team. This task can be given by managers who have 'a bad feeling,' by a team in need of help, or by someone else. My first approach was to find out what methodology is being used, mainly scrum or kanban. But I don't do this anymore. Nowadays I have a more abstract and repeatable approach and its executable in any type of team, even those far removed from software development.

## How to foster the agility of an already existing team

If you ask someone what agile means or in which state agile is in a team, the answers are often widespread. So, the meaning of agile or scrum can differ. For one, 'it may be about moving task cards from left to right.' For another, it may be something that can work, but not at our company! What to do?

## Cynefin and selecting the habitat

When that happens, I show them the Cynefin Framework by Dave Snowden[1]. It has four quadrants and another segment that describes ways to approach managing projects[2].

- The first quadrant is simple; it belongs to the world of to-do lists for best practice.

- The second quadrant is complicated. This belongs to the world of project plans. That is, the answer isn't obvious, so you have to analyze and plan, but a working result is possible. It's called good practice.

- The third is complex, where you can do experiments and analyze afterward if the experiment helped. If so, keeping the good stuff leads to an emergent practice.

- The fourth is chaotic: Things are always new and even practices that were good in the past are not sure to help in the future.

What I really like about the framework is that there's another segment in between the four quadrants called 'disorder.' It means you don't know which quadrant you're in operating at the moment.

In the case of software development in today's world, the best guess is that it's in the complex quadrant. There are several reasons for that: shorter life cycles, more frequent updates to customers, more complex products built by lots of people who have to collaborate.

If you assume it's complicated and you build a waterfall plan and the project fails, it was all waste. Eventually you have to implement an agile approach because you assumed the wrong habitat. It can also be the other way around: That is, if you bet on an emergent practice and it was only complicated, a well-done plan can still emerge.

As a coach I let the team decide what's the right practice.

The team places itself into the main quadrant. If they decide it's mainly complex, we know why agile is really a good approach for tasks. As a side note, we can address the complexity of the work inside the value stream separately from the complexity to improve the process and collaboration. So, once we decide that agile is a valid approach, we go deeper into understanding agile.

## What are the reasons to be more agile? What are the goals to achieve?

By now I'm sure everybody has heard about the Agile Manifesto[3]. But on the same website, there's more: Scroll to the bottom of the page and there's a link to the 12 underlying principles. Having led many workshops with really different teams, I value these principles over strictly following the scrum guide[4]. For some people, the scrum guide seems too dogmatic. In my view, it's not meant that way. Nevertheless, first we need to read some sense into the 12 agile principles.

During my workshop that I use to start working with the team, we go through the principles one at a time. We discuss what each particular principle means for the team: what they see and interpret into it. That forms our common view for how agile is defined for that team.

At the end we make a dot voting and decide which principle has to be improved first, so we're thinking about possible experiments that could have a possible effect. This way, a practice can emerge. To make sure we are on the right track, we need a feedback loop so we can decide to let certain practices disappear again and to keep the good stuff. The result will be a continuous improvement process of small changes (Kaizen).

The ideas can come from anywhere but the implementation is made inside the team itself. This way, they make it their own. They self-organize to improve the remaining 11 principles with that emerged practice. Maybe they'll give it a name at some point. Every team should find its own agile way. That is: Just because a practice helped one team doesn't mean it will help another. In the complex quadrant we know that it's more than possible it won't be valid for another team because of the different situations. But it may provide input to others to foster their emergent practices.

Gaining track and speeding up

Together with on-site coaching, the team can get the support it needs to achieve its first major goals. The result is motivating the team to gain their first achievements through their own actions.

Used practices

- Because the situation is always different in a complex world, I want to give you my favorite practices. You can try them out during an experiment and see if they help.

- Natural workflow task board. To make any existing workflow visible I like, according to the complex quadrant of the Cynefin framework, to use a kanban board. But in contrast to using only open, in progress, done workflow steps, I like to focus on the real status like this is my next, nearly ready but you can't see it yet. It is fun to hear during daily meetings the real status and to just add it to their task board. That allows discussions that were not possible before and we can find new points that need improvements.

- Magic estimation. The first time I heard about that was from Boris Gloger. The idea is, if you want to introduce story points, it's hard to get into people's minds. After years of being conditioned with estimating times that were never true, people are still converting the story points into hours. I call them 'time points.' We made up a scale like this: 1,2,3,5,8,13,20. The five is in the middle, so it means average; the twenty is maximum, meaning: huh? So, we know it's not clear enough to work on it. To this day, a maximum of 20 has always been enough.

- Instead of the flow of planning poker, we have the numbers in a big spread on a table. The backlog (not the stuff of the current sprint) is printed and divided between the team members. They can then put their cards under the number. For example, this is an average ticket, I put it onto the five. Or, I don't know exactly what to do, but it's worse than the other so one place to the right onto the eight. After a maximum of one hour, we stop. We are able to estimate approximately up to 80 user stories that way. All the twenties can be discussed with the product owner again. We make a strong difference not to estimate bugs, only user stories to have a clean velocity regarding the implementation of stories only.

- Release burnup chart. Because in agile projects only the scope remains flexible, a big visible chart should show the reached story points to deliver. We have projects were the product management doesn't want to release that often to the customers. So, we need a way to see where we're heading. For that I like to make a burnup chart on paper and make trend lines, I use crochet yarn going through the first and last point and we like using trello.com for remote teams or Jira with simplified workflow put fishing lead to the end, so it's fixed into the right position.

- Remote daily scrum using two displays, one for seeing the people and one for the shared screen.

- Long table release planning. For planning a long-term release (again half a year, lots of sprints) or critical time during summer, I like this workshop: Putting the whole printed backlog of user stories in a long row on a long table. Then, getting the team on the top on both sides of the table, so they can walk along. Someone can for example push cards apart because: I'll be on vacation. So, everyone else can do it accordingly. On the long table I also put the name of the months for example. At the end we see, what remains inside the scope for a specific release.

- Story mapping. This practice comes from Jeff Patton. The idea of how to introduce it is also from him. Having a lot of post-its, asking the people how they wake up in the morning. You get everything from putting on clothes, waking kids, grinding special coffee beans. Once you have the whole story, you ask: What if you overslept 30 minutes? Then the story gets shorter and maybe it's just throwing on clothes and chewing some gum. This way everyone can learn how to slice complex stories into more agile pieces.

## Agile practices in traditional project management

**—Gloria J. Miller, July 2015**

### Background

The project was to implement and integrate several software solutions to create a high-performance analytical computing platform. The platform was for a central IT-group of a multinational organization. The IT group was creating a shared-service environment that would allow for the resale of an analytical platform to other parts of the organization.

The scope of the project was:

- Implement and integrate the platform to test its feasibility
- If feasible, determine the price for which the platform could be resold to other business units
- Implement the IT capabilities to manage the platform

The project followed a traditional waterfall methodology, but used several agile practices.

### Project organization

The project was a subproject in a bigger program. The program had a project management office (PMO) that required monthly status reports and time tracking. The project methodology was not dictated by the PMO.

The project was staffed with eight team members from a joint team with the client and multiple consulting companies. There were two consulting team members that were engaged in the project every week; other consulting team members were engaged based on the activities at the time and the availability of client resources (people, servers, etc.).

There was an office move during the project. Before the move, the team members were co-located in one room; after the move, they were in two rooms in close proximity.

In addition to the eight team members, 16 other people were involved in the project from six different organizations.

- The client's central IT group
- The client's data center
- The client's PMO
- A vendor for the hardware platform
- Two different vendors for the software platform
- Team members from three different consulting companies

The project was approximately 41 weeks.

## Backlog

The backlog was created using a business-driven development approach. The product owner, called a component manager, outlined and drove the scope of the features based on what he needed to sell the service.

First, the team created a list of items needed to implement and integrate the platform and to provide the service. Then they identified different levels of quality that could be implemented. For example, some features could be implemented as manual tasks with a checklist rather than automating them. Other items were only needed if the service was proven as valuable. Further items were needed to meet certain business objectives. For example, one business requirement was to manage the platform using only two people. In this case, additional automation features were required. Another example was that customers who wanted to buy the business services could benefit from a quick installation and set-up (called onboarding) process. This also required specific automation tasks, which are described in more detail later.

The backlog with the items was aggregated into a high-level release plan.

## Estimation

The initial project estimates were created based on a feature list of items to deliver, estimating the effort using wideband estimates, and prioritizing the items by quality (level of automation). The estimation was presented for approval and revised by phasing the activities or removing items from the scope.

The wide-band estimation technique popularized by Planning Poker® was the primary estimation technique. The estimation participants included all core team members along with the cards that represent the items to deliver. We used Planning Poker® cards and followed the rules of the process.

The first benefit was the discussion about the scope and approach for each card. The team members came to a common understanding of what is in and what is outside the scope. Since the team was mixed with junior and senior experienced team members and functional and technical experience, there was always a good discussion about what each feature meant. It was also useful to me as the project manager to understand what they believed was in and out of scope as well as how they would approach implementing the feature.

The second benefit of the approach was to move the team away from thinking they actually knew precisely how long it would take to implement something. Before starting with this estimation technique, each person considered only his or her part of the task. In addition, each person also thought they knew exactly how many hours or days it will take them to implement something. For example, someone would indicate "it'll take me two hours to implement that feature." However, after the discussion they realized they first did not consider everything and second, they understood they would need more or less than they thought. The aspect of only using wideband numbers helped them not to worry about being precise.

The client and consulting team members were involved in applying the technique. At first, there was literally fear from the consultants that their numbers would be rejected by the client as being too big. However, early-on they realized through the discussion that the client wanted the right number and the discussion of the scope and the approach was the method to manage the size of the overall estimate.

Finally, the team became comfortable with breaking features into smaller increments to estimate them or using the big numbers, e.g. 40 days, as a placeholder when they could not estimate the task.

When reviewing the task board, the estimates were reviewed and updated with the work remaining. Re-estimation occurred after each delivery.

## Risk management

A visual risk matrix was created or updated during the estimation process. A card was created anytime a risk was identified and placed in a quadrant based on low to high probability and low to high impact on the project. Strategies for avoiding or mitigating the risks were discussed, and cards created and placed in the task board or the risk matrix.

## Task boards

Task boards were used extensively and tended to become the central tool in keeping the focus on each deliverable and its role within the big picture of the project. The cards were deliverable items rather than user stories and they were grouped by whatever style was most relevant to the team at that time, for example, by work package, by work-week, or by release.

Grouped by capability, the task boards were also used to present the project scope and budget to executive management for approval. Specifically, for capability "X" feature "Y" has implementation effort of "Z", and if included it has the impact "A" on the project budget, "B" on the operational cost for the platform, and "C" on our ability to sell the service. The same board was used with the project team to keep the focus on the agreed scope.

For example, each customer to whom we wanted to sell the service needed to migrate his or her projects to the platform. We could manually migrate each project with an operational effort of 15 days per customer project. Alternatively, we could automate the onboarding process at 40-days of development effort and the operational effort to the client of one hour per client project.

A customer to whom we wished to sell the service had requested 100 projects be migrated. They indicated the cost of 1500-days for the set-up was too expensive and they would not buy the service. This feedback made the decision to automate the onboarding or not easy since the development effort of 40-days was negligible when considering the potential revenue gains.

For a different feature of automatically adding servers to increase capacity, management prioritized its implementation for the following year, i.e. not-to-implement until customer demand required it.

The daily stand-ups were a process of walking the board to review the status of each card, the next steps, and to discuss any open issues. Open issues were given their own card so they could be followed-up as well.

## Customer feedback

Given that the project was a technical feasibility study, there were several risks such as focusing exclusively on the technology and getting bogged down in details. In addition, there was the risk that the service would be developed and would be too expensive for business units to afford. Alternatively, the service would not include the features that were useful for the business units.

To mitigate these risks the project team worked with a business unit that wanted to use the service in its development. There were weekly reviews with the business unit, discussing the features, the pricing, and their use of the service. The business unit was also implemented as a pilot site.

## Retrospectives

There were two formal retrospective sessions. One at the end of the first project milestone and a second at the end of the project. Each session focused on what worked, what did not work and should be adjusted, and what actions should be taken in the next stage. Additional team process reviews were conducted at the start of each estimation session per iteration. The process reviews weren't a formal retrospective but addressed what worked and what would be executed differently in the next iteration. This strategy was chosen to consolidate and leverage the availability of team members and still improve project operations.

## Results

At the end of the project, the organization decided it was feasible to offer the service to business units, and there was already one client live on the platform. Thus, from a business point-of-view, it was considered successful. The components of the service were validated and in some cases were productive.

The project was also efficient since the project was delivered within the agreed schedule and budget (1% under the effort estimate).

There was positive feedback from the project team on cooperation, collaboration, teamwork, and short communication cycles.

## Endnotes

[1] Mr. Snowden explains it himself.https://www.youtube.com/watch?v=N7oz366X0-8 Talking about the different habitats

[2] https://upload.wikimedia.org/wikipedia/commons/4/45/Cynefin˙frameworkFeb˙2011.jpeg

[3] http://agilemanifesto.org/principles.html

[4] http://www.scrumguides.org/scrum-guide.html

# 'Afterwords'

The book has been an extensive review of the literature on agile methodologies and practices. It provides processes, recommendations, and rules of thumb for moving to an agile project methodology. I hope you found some useful materials for getting started on your agile journey and later as a reference.

Here's one additional thought before closing. Agility is a way of looking at how to achieve the goal in the given timeframe. It is not a question of if. It is a question of how. If you keep your mind open to that one thought, then you start to look at every situation in a completely different way. If you believe — I mean really believe — in something, it makes it easier to convince others. All project work is done by the team. Therefore, most of the hard work in going agile (within the scope of a single project) is getting the team to think with an open mind and getting others outside the team to be flexible.

Get the team not to do things the same old way they have always done them. Get them to put on their 'green thinking hat': Be innovative and take risks. They too need to ask how to achieve the goal, not whether they can achieve the goal. The structure provided behind the agile practices should really help on the agility journey.

Agile methodologies are mature. They've been around since the 1990s. There are thousands of organizations using them. They provide numerous benefits including a high ROI. If a specific agile methodology isn't outright adopted, the individual agile practice should be adopted until the desired level of agility is reached.

The agile coach is a new role that requires a selection of soft skills to be successful. A good agile coach will be able to build the team and coach them in decision-making, problem solving and conflict resolution. The agile coach should also facilitate that the team learns from their experience, that project impediments are quickly removed, and that the stakeholders' expectations are managed.

The project management practices from the *PMBOK ® Guide* are applicable to agile projects. However, agile projects use a set of skills, tools and techniques that promote collaboration and visibility.

## Going agile

There's more to choosing an agile method than just deciding to adopt a methodology that you've heard about in a recent article. You should consider carefully why you need to be agile, how agile do you really need to be, and what kind of projects need to be agile. After answering these questions, you can start the discussion and plan to decide the right agile methodology. The following are my personal recommendations for going agile.

1 **Select a methodology.** Agile methodologies run the gamut from highly flexible to rigid process and from low to high ceremonies. The decision on the methodology depends upon organizational culture, the types of people in your organization, and the types of projects that you are executing. Decide on one to two methodologies to apply within the organization. Customize them, but stay as close to the formal definition of the methodology for the first two to three projects before making big adjustments. There are several new practices to learn and old practices to change. If you adjust the methodology too quickly, you may not realize the benefits.

2 **Educate the leadership team.** Project management, project leadership, and functional leadership roles change significantly with the implementation of agile practices. Educate the leadership team members to understand the new dynamics expected, the responsibility changes, and how to apply collaborative and coaching techniques in leading the projects.

3 **Define success.** Agile iterations should focus each iteration on providing a 'potentially shippable product.' What does that mean? Does it mean an 'actually usable product'? Each agile team has to decide for their project the definition of done. However, there are also expectations that have to be managed between the business and the technical team and the project team and the stakeholders. Therefore, it's important to define a standard as to what's expected from the agile teams. This definition of success should then become a clause within the project charter that is used to authorize the project.

4 **Set-up infrastructure.** Define the project infrastructure for agile projects, including test automation, configuration management, team space, etc. For agile software development, new technical techniques are suggested, including continuous integration, refactoring, pair programming, etc. For these techniques to work, the technical infrastructure must support them. For example, continuous integration requires highly automated testing. Otherwise, it isn't possible to integrate and adapt to changes in short iterations.

5 **Adapt management reporting.** Adapt the expected management reports from projects. Agile projects are managed using performance metrics that focus on scope progress. Projects need to be evaluated more on their functional scope coverage than they do on their on-time performance. Update project management dashboards to capture the new metrics and eliminate items that are not available in agile projects.

6 **Implement the practices.** Select the best method for implementing the practices based on the organizational situation. The options include moving all projects to agile practices at once, starting with a few pilot projects, or a hybrid of the two approaches. The different use cases prove that all options work as long as there is a strong driving collation behind them. Organizations have gone agile in as little as three months and as long as three years. The durations and speed will depend upon the definition of success and the strategy chosen for going agile.

7 **Hold a retrospective and tune the processes.** Review what's working well and worth repeating, what could use optimizing, and what should never be repeated. There's no cookbook for going agile. Options have to be tried and then adapted as you go.

The following are the three most important things to avoid when getting started.

- **Avoid software-driven approaches.** Avoid new project management software solutions until after the first two or three projects. Agile projects can be managed in a low technology way provided you are not working with distributed teams at the start. Work without introducing new project management technologies until you learn about being agile. Introducing technology too early makes the transition about technology and not about the practices.

- **Avoid confusion.** Avoid trying to keep old practices while adapting to the new ones. It's tempting to try to keep old practices in place and not make the radical changes required. For example, going from a command-and-control project structure, where there's a project manager in charge, to a self-directed team means that the distributed authority can cause some uncertainty on who is in charge. Avoid trying to make the agile coach the project manager to avoid this discomfort. The practices do work, but they have to be given a chance.

- **Avoid thinking the agile coach is the project manager.** The project management tasks typically carried out by a project manager continue to be practiced, and should be practiced by a project manager. The agile coach has responsibility areas for developing the team and supporting all stakeholders to understand and apply the methods. Making an agile coach responsible for project management tasks or making a project manager the agile coach will lead to conflict. The domain for the agile coach is governance over the team, and the domain for the project manager is governance over the project.

Any organization or project that can apply the agile practices will reap great benefits personally and for the organization. Go agile, but proceed with care.

# Quiz

# Questions

This quiz asks questions about the topics covered in the book on a chapter by chapter basis. The answer guide is provided in the next chapter.

More than one answer can be correct.

## Chapter 1 Agile is an Innovation

1 What is the primary focus of agile methodologies?

- a People
- b Requirements
- c Process
- d Control

2 For which of these reasons are agile methodology perfectly suite instead of a waterfall methodology?

- a When the product details cannot be agreed in advance
- b When you can select a complete set of requirements upfront
- c When the project team is organized as a virtual team
- d When the project team is organized as onsite team

3 What advantages have been reported for projects that followed agile practices?

- a Reduces risk
- b Improved design
- c Improved productivity
- d Reduces change management

4 For which of the following reasons have projects that follow agile practices been reported to fail?

- a Scope creep
- b Lack of management support
- c Deliverable testing
- d Continuous delivery

## Chapter 2 The Rational for Agility

5 Which of the following statements reflect(s) the principles of the agile manifesto?

- a Ensure on time project delivery through top-down flow control
- b Trust project team members to motivate individuals
- c Deliver working software in short time intervals
- d Promote good team work by placing all team members in one room

6 Which of the following statements reflect(s) the principles of the agile manifesto?

- a Business People and developers meet once a quarter or even less
- b Change jeopardizes project success
- c Customer satisfaction through valuable software is an important goal
- d Technical excellence facilitates agility

7 What are major consequences of the publication of the agile manifesto?

- a First deployment of incremental software development methods
- b Acknowledgement that it may not be possible to define all requirements at the beginning of projects
- c Widespread use of virtual software development teams
- d Increased usage of rapid application development (RAD) techniques

8 What changes in projects when agile methods are used?

- a Scope
- b Estimation
- c Cost
- d Resources

9 Which dimensions are plotted in a Stacey matrix?

- a Certainty
- b Agreement
- c Complexity
- d Time

10 Which zone of a standard Stacey matrix is best suited for agile methods?

- a Complexity
- b Rational
- c Chaos
- d Political

11 In a standard Stacey matrix which combination of dimensional positions that is listed on the left matches the zones that are listed on the right?

- a Close to certainty/Close to agreement -> Rational
- b Far from certainty/Far from agreement -> Chaos
- c Close to certainty/Medium agreement -> Political
- d Medium certainty/close to agreement -> Judgmental

12 How could an analysis using the Stacey matrix help decide for or against the use of agile methods?

- a By defining cause and effect linkages
- b By embracing chaos and ignoring cause and effect linkages
- c By knowing when a collaborative environment between users and developers is required
- d By eliciting the complete set of requirements and design decisions

13 According to Stacey, what differentiates "mathematical chaos" from the ordinary language definition of "chaos"?

- a Unusual patterns
- b Mixture of stability and instability
- c Lack of organization
- d Mixture of incompetence and power

14 In a standard Stacey matrix, which of the following characterizes the complexity zone best?

a Agreement about details

b Accuracy of prediction

c Conflict needed

d High creativity

15 What are the levels of results of projects according to Turner and Zolin?

a Outputs

b Outcomes

c Impacts

d Operations

16 According to Turner and Zolin, what are typical metrics to measure project outputs?

a Cost

b Quality

c Learnings

d Productivity

17 According to Turner and Zolin, what can typically be affected by project outcomes?

a Operations

b Employee productivity

c Return on investment

d Reduced payback periods

18 According to Turner and Zolin, what are typical metrics to measure project impacts?

a Return on investment

b Payback period

c Product sales

d Client satisfaction

19 Comparing to traditional project management practices, what could jeopardize the success of projects executed using agile practices?

- a Team size
- b Meeting frequency
- c Productivity metrics
- d Stakeholder satisfaction

20 Which of the following were critical success factors listed in the Salesforce case study?

- a Training
- b Executive commitment
- c Automation
- d Release frequency

## Chapter 3 Methodology Comparison

21 What are characteristics of the waterfall methodology?

- a Complete set of requirements
- b Fixed development phases
- c Iterative development
- d Self-organizing teams

22 What is the main communication tool in the waterfall methodology?

- a Documents
- b Sign-offs
- c Team meetings
- d Prototypes

23 What are characteristics of agile methodologies?

- a Incremental development
- b Self-organizing teams
- c Adaptive scope
- d Frequent prototypes

24 With regards to the scope change characteristic, which approach to scope change that is listed on the left matches the agile methodology that is listed on the right?

- a 10% change can be absorbed without schedule slippage. -> FDD
- b Mix of formal controls and informal decisions -> DSDM Atern
- c Encourage changes during reviews and locked out changes during the sprint -> Scrum
- d Resist change during a workflow state -> Lean Kanban

25 With regards to the emphasis characteristics, which emphasis that is listed on the left matches the agile methodology that is listed on the right?

- a Model the business and deliver by feature -> FDD
- b Deliver business value and manage stakeholders -> DSDM Atern
- c Prioritize and deliver value through empowered teams -> Scrum
- d Eliminate waste and visualize, monitor, and improve workflow -> Lean Kanban

26 With regards to the delivery frequency characteristic, which approach to delivery frequency that is listed on the left matches the agile methodology that is listed on the right?

- a By feature in 2 week increments -> FDD
- b Incremental -> DSDM Atern
- c 2-4 week cycles -> Scrum
- d At regular intervals -> Lean Kanban

27 With regards to the business and IT collaboration characteristic, which approach that is listed on the left matches the agile methodology that is listed on the right?

- a Frequent progress reporting -> FDD
- b Daily meetings -> DSDM Atern
- c Daily meetings and review meetings -> Scrum
- d Review meetings -> Lean Kanban

## Chapter 4 Agile Practices

28 Which of the following describes time characteristics of agile practices?

- a Fixed length time boxes
- b Short iterations
- c Variable length time boxes
- d Long iterations

29 Which methods of interactions between team members are typically used in agile practices?

- a Daily stand-ups
- b Physical team colocation
- c Weekly web conferences
- d Functional team meetings

30 What are possible advantages of limiting the amount of intermediate documentation in agile projects?

- a Reduced costs
- b Increased development time
- c Better information flow
- d Better usability of the software product

31 Which of the following practices are used to improve outputs of agile projects?

- a Retrospectives
- b Refactoring
- c Restructuring
- d Retention

32 What is a typical focus of the Definition of Done?

- a Production-ready product
- b Complete set of documentation
- c Task complete definition
- d Scope contract

33 What are typical responsibilities of an agile coach?

a Build project team cohesion

b Engage the project team in decision making

c Shield the project team from conflicts

d Control the information flow in the project team

34 What are characteristics of the organization of a typical agile project?

a Small team size

b Team members with a broad set of skills

c Large team size

d Team members with selective set of skills

35 Which planning practice that is listed on the left matches the description that is listed on the right?

a Roadmap planning->Long range product planning

b Release planning->Detailed product scope across iterations

c Daily stand-up->Task planning

d Project charter->Project vision

36 Using a cumulative flow diagram, what changes over time would you typically track?

a Impact

b Probability

c Severity

d Costs

37 Which dimension is typically plotted on the horizontal axis of a burnup chart

a Story point

b Time

c Iteration

d Severity

38 Which dimension is typically plotted on the horizontal axis of a burndown chart?

- a Story point
- b Time
- c Iteration
- d Severity

39 Which engineering practice that is listed on the left matches the description that is listed on the right?

- a Acceptance test driven development (ATDD)->Unambiguous test cases that contain inputs and outputs produced
- b Test driven development->Minimum coding, refactoring
- c Behavior driven development->Identify the software features that deliver the business outcome
- d Configuration management->State of and dependencies between software deliverables

40 What information is typically shown on a parking lot chart?

- a Feature set status
- b Percentage complete
- c Target completion date
- d Project workflow

41 What is the recommended leadership style of an agile coach?

- a Authoritarian
- b Bureaucratic
- c Servant
- d Charismatic

42 What are typical practices of gathering requirements in agile projects?

- a User story
- b Prioritization
- c Daily stand-up
- d Release planning

43 Which of the following components organizes the priority of user stories and the relationship among user stories?

a Story map

b Backlog

c Task board

d Parking lot chart

44 Which of the agile practices listed on the left are used together with the agile practices listed on the right?

a Release planning -> iteration reviews, prioritized product backlog, daily standup

b Stand up -> prioritized product backlog, release planning, short iterations

c TDD -> automated testing, coding standards, refactoring

d Prioritized backlog -> iteration reviews, release planning, short iterations

## Chapter 5 The Agile Coach

45 What are core responsibilities of an agile coach?

a To build the team

b To facilitate collaboration

c To resolve conflicts

d To organize the team

46 According to Katzenbach and Smith, which of the following attributes characterize teams compared to working groups?

a Individual work products

b Collective work products

c Discuss, decide, work together

d Discuss, decide, delegate

47 According to the team building model of Tuckman, at which phase does the team develop common goals?

- a Forming
- b Storming
- c Norming
- d Performing

48 According to Yaffee and Wondolleck, what are benefits of collaboration in teamwork?

- a Production of better decisions
- b Promotion of information sharing
- c Support of complex decision making
- d Support of faster consensus building

49 In Fletcher's fist-of-five technique, what do the number of fingers represent?

- a Zero->Consensus is blocked
- b One->Discussion needed
- c Two->Minor issues
- d Three->Reluctant agreement

50 In participatory decision making, what are characteristics of the full participation principle?

- a Raise difficult issues
- b Share views
- c Share partial ideas
- d Integrate ideas

51 Which thinking hat color that is listed on the left matches the description that is listed on the right?

- a White->Objective information
- b Black->Obstacles to success
- c Green->New ideas
- d Red->Emotion

52 Which thinking hat color that is listed on the left matches the description that is listed on the right?

- a White->Objective information
- b Yellow->Make it work
- c Green->New ideas
- d Blue->Think it through

53 What are characteristics of the Six Thinking Hats method?

- a Role play
- b Brainstorming
- c Relative ranking
- d Active listening

54 What are typical applications of the Six Thinking Hats method?

- a Foster critical thinking
- b Generate new perspectives
- c Delegation of responsibility
- d Unleash energy of team members

55 When your focus is on gathering information, of which color is the thinking hat you are wearing?

- a White
- b Green
- c Yellow
- d Blue

56 When your focus is on finding reasons why things may not work, of which color is the thinking hat you are wearing?

- a Black
- b Red
- c Green
- d Blue

57 When your focus is on generating new ideas, of which color is the thinking hat you are wearing?

a Green

b White

c Yellow

d Black

58 When your focus is on likes and dislikes, of which color is the thinking hat you are wearing?

a Red

b Black

c Green

d Blue

59 When your focus is on making things work, of which color is the thinking hat you are wearing?

a Yellow

b Green

c Blue

d White

60 When you focus is on thinking things through, of which color is the thinking hat you are wearing?

a Blue

b Red

c Yellow

d White

61 Which problem solving method would you typically use to identify activities that interrupt a team's work?

a Pain snake

b BART system

c Product critique

d Health check

62 Which problem solving method would you typically use to identify deliverable issues?

- a Pain snake
- b BART system
- c Product critique
- d Health check

63 Which problem solving method would you typically use to identify process problems?

- a Pain snake
- b BART system
- c Product critique
- d Health check

64 Which problem solving method would you typically use to identify problems of team dynamics?

- a Pain snake
- b BART system
- c Product critique
- d Health check

65 To identify a problem that is listed on the left, which problem solving method that is listed on the right is typically used?

- a Activities that interrupt a team's work->Pain snake
- b Team dynamics->BART system
- c Deliverable issues->Product critique
- d Process problems->Health check

66 Given the following list of conflict attributes, what is the likely conflict level?
Emotions: short lived
Sharing information: openly
Language: clear and specific
Objective: problem solving

- a Level 1
- b Level 2
- c Level 3
- d Level 4

67 Given the following list of conflict attributes, what is the likely conflict level?
Emotions: distrust
Sharing information: selectively
Language: vague and general
Objective: self-protection

a Level 1

b Level 2

c Level 3

d Level 4

68 Given the following list of conflict attributes, what is the likely conflict level?
Emotions: antagonistic
Sharing information: compartmentalized, distorted
Language: broad generalizations
Objective: winning

a Level 1

b Level 2

c Level 3

d Level 4

69 Given the following list of conflict attributes, what is the likely conflict level?
Emotions: self-righteousness
Sharing information: limited, autistic
Language: principles, not issues
Objective: hurting

a Level 1

b Level 2

c Level 3

d Level 4

70 Given the following list of conflict attributes, what is the likely conflict level?
Emotions: out of control
Sharing information: skewed
Language: destructive
Objective: destruction

a Level 1

b Level 2

c Level 3

d Level 5

71 Given the following list of conflict attributes, what conflict resolution method would you choose?
Emotions: distrust
Sharing information: selectively
Language: vague and general
Objective: self-protection

a Collaboration

b Accommodate and negotiate

c Negotiate

d Terminate

72 Given the following list of conflict attributes, what conflict resolution method would you choose?
Emotions: antagonistic
Sharing information: compartmentalized, distorted
Language: broad generalizations
Objective: winning

a Collaboration

b Accommodate and negotiate

c Negotiate

d Terminate

73 Given the following list of conflict attributes, what conflict resolution method would you choose?
Emotions: self-righteousness
Sharing information: limited, autistic
Language: principles, not issues
Objective: hurting

a Collaboration

b Accommodate and negotiate

c Negotiate

d Terminate

74 Given the following list of conflict attributes, what conflict resolution method would you choose?
Emotions: out of control
Sharing information: skewed
Language: destructive
Objective: destruction

a Collaboration

b Accommodate and negotiate

c Negotiate

d Terminate

75 A project is stuck. One faction favors the idea of registration and authentication before users can search for information on the web site. Another faction favors the idea of letting everyone search for information without registration and authentication. During a team meeting most time is spent on the latest Super bowl games. According to the Thomas-Kilmann model of conflict responses, which conflict style do the factions use?

a Avoiding

b Competing

c Accommodating

d Compromising

76 A project is stuck. One faction favors the idea of registration and authentication before users can search for information on the web site. Another faction favors the idea of letting everyone search for information without registration and authentication. During a team meeting the two factions engage most of the time in a shouting match. According to the Thomas-Kilmann model of conflict responses, which conflict style do the factions use?

a Avoiding

b Competing

c Accommodating

d Compromising

77 A project is stuck. One faction favors the idea of registration and authentication before users can search for information on the web site. Another faction favors the idea of letting everyone search for information without registration and authentication. During a team meeting, faction 1 abandons their idea. According to the Thomas-Kilmann model of conflict responses, which conflict style do the factions use?

- a Avoiding
- b Competing
- c Accommodating
- d Compromising

78 A project is stuck. One faction favors the idea of registration and authentication before users can search for information on the web site. Another faction favors the idea of letting everyone search for information without registration and authentication. During a team meeting both factions can agree on registration first and leave authentication for a later stage of the purchase process. According to the Thomas-Kilmann model of conflict responses, which conflict style do the factions use?

- a Avoiding
- b Competing
- c Accommodating
- d Compromising

79 A project is stuck. One faction favors the idea of registration and authentication before users can search for information on the web site. Another faction favors the idea of letting everyone search for information without registration and authentication. During a team meeting both factions agree to skip registration and authentication until the user requests pricing information. Before prices are displayed, a captcha approach will be used to filter out web crawlers. Registration and authentication will be required only for any activities around ordering. According to the Thomas-Kilmann model of conflict responses, which conflict style do the factions use?

- a Competing
- b Accommodating
- c Compromising
- d Collaborating

80 What are negotiating principles according to Fisher, Ury, and Patton?

a Separate people from the problem

b Focus on interests, NOT positions

c Insist on using objective criteria

d Set targets and openings

81 How does the agile coach support the team and the product owner?

a By integrating agile practices

b By facilitating collaboration

c By resolving conflicts

d By estimating costs

e By performing quality control

82 What are practices of an agile coach?

a Listening

b Guiding

c Controlling

d Indulge

83 What are the central characteristics of Hersey and Blanchard's Situational Leadership Model?

a Task behavior

b Relationship behavior

c Coping behavior

d Learning behavior

84 According to Hersey and Blanchard's Situational Leadership Model, which leadership style (listed below on the left) is recommended for what maturity level (listed below on the right)?

a Tell->Low maturity, unable and insecure

b Sell->Moderate maturity, unable and confident

c Participate->Moderate, able and insecure

d Delegate->High, able and confident

85 According to Hersey and Blanchard's Situational Leadership Model, which categories of support and task guidance behavior that are listed on the left match the leadership behavior and team maturity that are listed below on the right?

a Low support, low guidance->Delegate, high competence

b High support, low guidance->Participate, competent but unwilling

c Low support, high guidance->Tell, Unable and unwilling

d High support, High guidance->Explain, unable but willing

86 After a team meeting an agile coach remembers and writes down a note of the meeting: "Finally the team understands the difference between authentication and authorization." Which listening style does this note represent?

a Selective listening

b Detailed listening

c Global listening

d Critical listening

87 After a team meeting an agile coach remembers and writes down a note of the meeting: "The team has a good grasp of the domain. John and Jane still need more background in JavaScript but everybody seems content with the state of affairs." Which listening style does this note represent?

a Selective listening

b Detailed listening

c Global listening

d Informational listening

88 After a team meeting an agile coach remembers and writes down a note of the meeting: "The team is focused. It looks like John and Joe are getting into a competition, need to watch. They barely need advice anymore. The team banter shows that all of them are getting along well." Which listening style does this note represent?

a Selective listening

b Detailed listening

c Global listening

d Therapeutic listening

89 What are methods of providing feedback to others?

a Repeat

b Restate

c Reflect

d Remember

90 Which of the following sequences describes the methods of providing feedback in ascending complexity?

a Repeat, restate, reflect

b Repeat, reflect, restate

c Restate, reflect, repeat

d Reflect, restate, repeat

91 According to Adkins, what are behaviors that are part of failure mode?

a Express opinions often

b Assume the role of central hub of communication

c Get involved in details

d Hear everything

92 Which tool can you used to analyze dilemma situations?

a Conflict resolution diagram

b Transition tree

c Negative branch reservations

d Core conflict cloud

93 What are typical characteristics of coaching?

a Provide insight

b Improve performance

c Transfer knowledge

d Develop skills

94 Which model helps an agile coach to select the appropriate coaching style?

- a Situational Leadership model
- b Failure and success mode model
- c Thomas-Kilman model
- d Six Thinking Hats model

## Chapter 6 The Role of the Project Manager

95 In agile projects, which of the following tasks are typically performed by the project manager?

- a Control schedule
- b Develop budget
- c Integrate agile practices
- d Develop the team

96 Which of the following roles of agile projects is closest to the role of a project manager?

- a Product owner
- b Agile coach
- c Scrum master
- d Project sponsor

## Chapter 7 Integration

97 What are elements of a project charter?

- a Vision
- b Mission
- c Success criteria
- d Earned value metrics

98 According to Moore's elevator pitch framework, what are valid sequences?

a 1. For/2. Who/3. Our product/4. Is a/5. That

b 1. Our product/2. That/3. Is a/4. Unlike

c 1. Our Product/2. That/3. Unlike/4. Who/5. For

d 1. For/2. Who/3. That/4. Unlike

99 What is a project business case?

a A financial justification for a planned project

b A feasibility study for a planned project

c A definition of the purpose of a planned project

d A management report for a planned compliance project

100 What is the typical formula for Return on Investment (ROI)?

a (Gain from investment - Cost of investment)/Cost of investment

b (Cost of investment - Gain from investment)/Gain of investment

c (Cost of investment - Gain from investment)/Cost of investment

d (Gain from investment - Cost of investment)/Gain of investment

101 For a planned project that is NOT a compliance project, financial indicators were calculated. Which analysis results could make a business case for the planned project?

a Present value exceeds net present value

b Net present value is greater than 0

c Return on investment of 2%.

d Internal rate of return of 1.5%

102 Which planning approaches are part of progressive planning?

a Roadmap planning

b Release planning

c Iteration planning

d Business case planning

103 What are central ideas of progressive planning?

- a Use the latest agile methodology only
- b Spend more time on detailed planning at the start of the project
- c Create high level plans at project start
- d Focus on the work that will be done

104 What planning phase that is listed on the left matches best the description that is listed on the right?

- a Roadmap planning->Long range product planning
- b Release planning->Quarterly time horizon
- c Iteration planning->Monthly time horizon
- d Task planning->Daily time horizon

105 Which sequence of planning steps represents the correct order from longest to shortest time horizon?

- a 1. Roadmap planning, 2. Release planning, 3. Iteration planning, 4. Task planning
- b 1. Release planning, 2. Roadmap planning, 3. Task planning, 4. Iteration planning
- c 1. Iteration planning, 2. Release planning, 3. Roadmap planning, 4. Task planning
- d 1. Task planning, 2. Iteration planning, 3. Release planning, 4. Roadmap planning

106 What are elements of release planning?

- a Success factors
- b User stories
- c Expected velocity
- d Priorities

107 In which planning phase is typically the number of iterations determined?

- a Roadmap
- b Release
- c Iteration
- d Task

108 What can you use to determine the number of iterations?

- a Expected velocity
- b Number of story points
- c Iteration length
- d Number of features

109 For a feature-driven project, how do you calculate the number of iterations?

- a Sum of story points/Expected velocity
- b Number of iterations*Expected velocity
- c Sum of story points*Expected velocity
- d Number of iterations/Expected velocity

110 What are typical goals of an initial release planning workshop?

- a Select requirements
- b Prioritize user stories
- c Fill product backlog
- d Select risk actions

111 Who should typically attend an iteration planning session?

- a Project team
- b Product owner
- c Product purchaser
- d Project sponsor

112 Who assigns stories to the first iteration?

- a Product owner
- b Product purchaser
- c Project team
- d Project manager

113 What are typical goals of an iteration planning workshop?

- a Determine target velocity
- b Adjust priorities
- c Select stories
- d Definition of done

114 What elements are typically displayed in a velocity cycle time diagram?

- a Story points
- b Target velocity
- c Actual velocity
- d Plan completion

115 For what can you use a cumulative flow diagram?

- a Determine work in progress
- b Identify bottlenecks
- c Determine cycle time
- d Determine progress of feature sets

116 Which metrics are typically calculated as part of earned value management?

- a Planned value (PV)
- b Actual cost (AC)
- c Direct cost (DC)
- d Schedule performance index (SPI)

117 You are managing a project characterized by the following values:
Budget: 500,000 USD
Iterations total: 5
Story points total: 100
Story points completed at 3 iterations: 40

Regarding earned value metrics, what are valid statements?

- a Expected percentage complete: 80%
- b Actual percent complete: 60%
- c Schedule Performance Index (SPI): 0.75
- d Expected percentage complete: 60%

118 What are typical goals of retrospective meetings?

a Plan timeline for improvements

b Agree improvements

c Prioritize features

d Change business rules

119 What are goals of a project charter session?

a Define the scope of engagement with suppliers

b Ensure that the team understands the goals of the project

c Secure funding from the project sponsor

d Outline the details of roadmap planning

120 Who can stop an iteration an any time?

a Agile coach

b Product owner

c Product purchaser

d Project team

121 Who does typically attend an iteration retrospective?

a Agile coach

b Project team

c Product owner

d Project sponsor

122 What are steps in a retrospective meeting?

a Gather data

b Generate insights

c Decide what to do

d Change business rules

## Chapter 8 Scope

123 What does a scope management plan identify?

- a Format and collection of user stories
- b Prioritization method of product backlog
- c Format of the product backlog
- d Prioritization of requirements

124 What is the role of user stories in agile scope management?

- a Describes capability needed by a role
- b Captures the conversation between developers and customer
- c Contains just the detail needed to trigger discussions
- d Describes all of the requirements of the product

125 What are elements of user stories?

- a Features needed by a role
- b Creation before the analysis stage
- c Description of a process and user interactions with it
- d Creation after analysis

126 What do story cards typically contain?

- a Short feature description
- b Test descriptions
- c Quality metrics
- d Implementation costs

127 What are examples of innovation games?

- a The Apprentice
- b Prune the product tree
- c 20/20 vision
- d Cut the current reality tree

128 What are techniques used to elicit user stories?

- a Brainstorming
- b Root cause analysis
- c Force field analysis
- d Day-to-day conflict

129 Along which dimensions are stories in a story map typically displayed?

- a Horizontal: Time/Vertical: Criticality (Ascending)
- b Horizontal: Criticality (Ascending)/Vertical: Time
- c Horizontal: Time/Vertical: Criticality (Descending)
- d Horizontal: Criticality (Descending)/Vertical: Time

130 What are elements of story maps?

- a Backbone
- b Walking skeleton
- c Fishbone
- d Walking dead

131 A new high-end smartphone is designed. Which Kano model category that is listed on the left matches the description that is listed on the right?

- a Must-be quality->Make and receive phone calls
- b One-dimensional quality->Mobile payment
- c Attractive quality->Sapphire glass
- d Indifferent quality->Headphone plug at the bottom

132 Which scope management model uses the following step?
Estimate the relative benefit on a scale from 1 to 9

- a Requirements prioritization model
- b Economic prioritization
- c Kano model
- d MoSCoW approach

133 What are typical categories in the economic prioritization model?

a Revenue potential

b Operational efficiency

c Development costs

d Customer satisfaction

134 Which of the following elements of a user story should always be provided?

a Role

b Function

c Business value

d Title

135 Which of the following elements of a user story should always be provided?

a Role

b Test

c Business value

d Title

136 Which of the following are essential elements of a test description?

a Context

b Event

c Outcome

d Function

137 Which scope validation method that is listed on the left matches the description that is listed on the right?

a Simulation->Miniature version of the product

b Wireframe->Mock-up of functionality

c Prototype->Subset of product

d Demonstration->Preview the product

138 During which sessions is the scope typically agreed and validated with the product owner?

a Release planning

b Iteration planning

c Task planning

d Roadmap planning

139 What is the purpose of functional contingency?

a To manage stakeholder expectations

b To ensure "must have" features are implemented

c To prepare the project team for unforeseen events

d To ensure implementation of at least 75% of features

140 According to the DSDM and Pareto approach respectively, which percentage of product features are must have?

a 60%

b 40%

c 20%

d 25%

141 Which element in the Kano model represents a minimum marketable feature?

a Must be quality

b One-dimensional quality

c Attractive quality

d Reverse quality

142 Which element in the MoSCoW model represents a minimum marketable feature?

a Must have

b Should have

c Could have

d Won't have

143 Which of the following groups are NOT typically linked through minimally marketable features?

a Software vendor

b Software users

c Project team

d Project stakeholders

144 When controlling scope, what are examples of the Change business rule approach?

a Set work in progress limits

b Exchange commensurate features

c Apply functional contingency

d Change the delivery baseline

## Chapter 9 Schedule

145 What are characteristics of Kanban boards?

a Cards are user stories that move through workflow

b Cards are work that progresses through states

c Work in progress is limited per process step

d Only stories and tasks that can be completed are scheduled

146 What are characteristics of task boards?

a Team members work on previously agreed work

b Team members pull work based on their own availability

c Daily stand-ups discuss today and yesterday progress only

d Daily stand-ups discuss completed and upcoming work

147 Which of the following are essential categories of a task board?

a Not started

b In progress

c Planned

d In testing

148 Using Kanban boards, what are WIP limits supposed to optimize?

- a Throughput
- b Resource utilization
- c Contingency usage
- d Lead time

149 Which of the following factors should you consider when you are trying to estimate the length of time boxes?

- a Clarity of requirements
- b Stakeholder availability
- c Number of planning sessions
- d Available budget

150 What are typical estimation unit in agile projects?

- a Story points
- b Ideal time
- c Elapsed time
- d Maximum time

151 What are characteristics of story points?

- a Less prone to intentional estimate distortion
- b Unclear relationship with work days
- c Team dependent estimates
- d Useful to predict velocity

152 Which estimation technique derives from PERT?

- a Three-point estimate
- b Relative sizing
- c Planning poker
- d Affinity estimating

153 Who does typically estimate size during a planning poker session?

- a Project team members
- b Product owners
- c Project sponsors
- d Agile coaches

154 You are an agile coach. The project team has just finished the first round of planning poker. All team members uncover different numbers. Before you continue to the next round, what do you do?

- a Let the members with the lowest and highest number explain their choices
- b Exclude the members with the highest and the lowest number from this story
- c Calculate the three-point estimate and ask the team to use it as anchor
- d Ignore the differences if they do NOT exceed twice the minimum rating

155 According to the *PMBOK Guide®*, what is the range for a rough order of estimate (ROM)?

- a -30%/+50%
- b -15%/+30%
- c -5%/+15%
- d -10%/+50%

156 For a meeting type that is listed on the left, what is the recommended meeting duration that is listed on the right?

- a Iteration planning->5% of iteration length
- b Daily stand-up->15 minutes
- c Review meeting->4 hours per month
- d Retrospective->3 hours

## Chapter 10 Cost

157 The weekly costs in your project are $50,000.
The iteration length is 2 weeks.
The number of story points per iteration is 50.
Which of the following conclusions about burnrates are valid?

a The burnrate for the iteration is $100,000

b The burnrate per story point is $2,000

c The burnrate per story point is $500

d The burnrate for the iteration is $6,250

158 For which of the following should you calculate contingency?

a Schedule

b Budget

c Scope

d People

159 What could you use for project cost controlling?

a Release burndown chart

b Release burnup chart

c Earned value management

d Review meetings

## Chapter 11 Quality

160 What should typically be considered to include in a test plan?

a Continuous integration

b Testing automation

c Agile tester

d Iteration planning

161 Why should you use quality metrics?

- a To drive the whole team's behavior
- b To encourage collaboration
- c To distribute blame uniformly across the team
- d To reduce the number of escaped defects

162 What are typical quality metrics that are used in agile projects?

- a Defect rate
- b Code coverage
- c Error feedback ratio
- d Cost savings

163 What is the main goal of the agile testing quadrant?

- a Coverage of all tests
- b Prioritization of all tests
- c Rationale for testing distributed systems
- d Automation of testing

164 What could be advantages of Extreme Programming?

- a Shorter development time
- b Higher code quality
- c Shorter unit tests
- d Higher customer satisfaction

165 Which test aspects are business facing aspects?

- a Functional tests
- b Beta tests
- c Usability tests
- d Reliability tests

166 During which category of testing that is listed on the left is the test that is listed on the right executed?

a Business testing for code quality->Prototype

b Business testing for features->Exploratory testing

c Business testing for behavior->Usability testing

d Business testing of the End-to-End system->Beta testing

167 In Extreme Programming, what is the minimum frequency for team members to integrate their work?

a Daily

b Weekly

c Bi weekly

d Monthly

168 When should the Definition of Done be clarified?

a During planning

b After testing

c Before testing

d During testing

169 In quality management, what are characteristics of verification?

a Building the right feature

b Building a feature the right way

c Ensuring the code is correct

d Ensuring the requirements are met

## Chapter 12 Resources

170 What are common team characteristics favored in agile projects?

a Colocation

b Self-organization

c Cross-functionality

d Specialization

171 According to Boehm and Turner's adaptation of the Cockburn levels, which level that is listed on the left matches the description that is listed on the right?

- a Level -1->People that are unable to collaborate
- b Level 1B->People that can be trained to perform procedural method steps
- c Level 1A->People that can be trained to perform discretionary method steps
- d Level 2->People that can tailor methods to new situations

172 What are possible consequences of "small sharp teams" of <= 10 members?

- a Better communication
- b Higher team productivity
- c Better at building large systems
- d Shorter development time

173 What are new roles in agile projects?

- a Agile coach
- b Product owner
- c Analyst
- d Data Professionals

174 With whom must an architect work closely in agile teams?

- a Product owner
- b Project sponsor
- c Agile coach
- d Users

175 How does the role of a programmer typically differ in agile projects from traditional, non-agile projects?

- a Discusses all product features with the product owner
- b Takes responsibility for all code aspects
- c Works from a written specification
- d Takes responsibility for his or her code only

176 Which behaviors are expected from members of an agile team?

- a Foresee problems
- b Deliver working solutions
- c Invent new rules daily
- d Indirect (osmotic) communication

177 Which aspects of the setup of team locations are preferred in agile projects?

- a One room, one building
- b Open workspaces
- c Multiple rooms, multiple buildings
- d Room dividers

178 What are common challenges with new agile teams regarding information radiators (IR)?

- a Keeping the IR up to date
- b Identifying the right format and content
- c Finding an appropriate room for the IR
- d Preventing the cleaners from destroying an IR

179 What is typically achieved through a big visible chart (information radiator)?

- a Reducing the need for daily stand-ups
- b Providing feedback on team progress
- c Providing a blackboard for the agile coach
- d Managing team performance

180 According to Cockburn, besides overt communication on which other type of communication do agile teams rely?

- a Osmotic
- b Deontic
- c Chaotic
- d Orthotic

## Chapter 13 Communications

181 Who determines the kind of documentation used in an agile project?

- a Product owner
- b Project team
- c Agile coach
- d Product purchaser

182 Which of the following document types is required during agile projects?

- a Product backlog
- b Requirements
- c Design specifications
- d Version control

183 Which of the artifacts, events, and information radiators that is listed on the left matches *best* the interested party that is listed on the right?

- a Task board->Project team
- b Release burnup chart->Product owner
- c Story writing workshop->Users
- d Roadmap->Stakeholders

## Chapter 14 Risk

184 How can agile projects reduce project risks?

- a Smaller scope segments
- b Better alignment with budget constraints
- c Higher resilience to late changes
- d Frequent code refactoring

185 What are methods to identify risks?

- a Champion-Challenger
- b Brainstorming
- c Sensitivity analysis
- d Monte Carlo simulation

186 Which vertical and horizontal dimensions respectively are typically used in a risk matrix?

- a Probability
- b Consequence
- c Sensitivity
- d Difference

187 What are typical methods of quantitative risk analysis?

- a Expected monetary value
- b Sensitivity analysis
- c Monte Carlo simulation
- d Risk matrix

188 In which risk analysis approach, would you typically use a tornado diagram?

- a Expected monetary value
- b Sensitivity analysis
- c Monte Carlo simulation
- d Risk matrix

189 Which negative risk responses that are listed on the left correspond to the positive risk responses that are listed on the right?

- a Avoid->Exploit
- b Transfer->Share
- c Mitigate->Enhance
- d Accept->Accept

190 To schedule risks for action, where would you typically put the risks?

a Risk adjusted backlog

b Risk report card

c Risk burndown chart

d Risk retrospective

## Chapter 15 Procurement

191 Which contract types should NOT be used with agile projects?

a Fixed price

b Capped time and materials

c Time and materials

d Optional scope

192 Compared to a traditional, non-agile project, which contract terms always change for the agile project?

a Scope

b Termination

c Pricing

d Indemnification

193 A contract has been agreed that sets a price per iteration. What is the contract type?

a Capped time and materials

b Fixed price per unit of work

c Graduated fixed price

d Time and materials

194 Before constructing a project contract, who must be instructed on the agile methodology used?

a Lawyers

b Team members

c Human resources personnel

d IT help desk

## Chapter 16 Stakeholders

195 Which stakeholder group that is listed on the left corresponds best to the project interest that is listed on the right?

- a Project sponsor->Performance efficiency
- b Product users->Product performance
- c Product purchaser->Useful prototype is provided
- d Project manager->Satisfying work environment

196 During which of the following activities is stakeholder feedback more required than during others?

- a Story writing workshops
- b Backlog grooming
- c Daily stand-ups
- d Security testing

197 In agile, what are ways of providing feedback about project progress to stakeholders?

- a Information radiators
- b Retrospectives
- c Monte Carlo simulations
- d Risk report cards

198 Due to the different nature of agile projects compared to traditional projects, for which of the following aspects must stakeholder expectations be managed differently?

- a Project progress
- b Involvement
- c Reliability
- d Working hours

## Chapter 17 Selecting an Agile Project Approach

199 Which of the following criteria would make you choose an agile project management approach?

- a Project criticality: low
- b Subject matter expertise of team: low
- c Flexibility of requirements: high
- d Customer availability: high

200 With regards to the agile Technical Excellence principle, which level that is listed on the left corresponds to the description that is listed on the right?

- a Level1->Coding standards
- b Level 2->Software configuration management
- c Level 3->Continuous integration
- d Level 4->Daily progress tracking

201 For which purposes would you primarily use a value stream map?

- a To support team decision making
- b To create a common language
- c To identify waste
- d To identify coordination costs

202 Which of the following represent waste?

- a Transaction costs
- b Coordination costs
- c Failure load
- d Workload

## Chapter 18 Going Agile

203 What are common obstacles against running a project using an agile methodology?

- a Lack of understanding of agile principles
- b Cultural misalignment between the agile approach and the company
- c Availability of too many agile methodologies
- d Lack of support by regulatory bodies

204 Which criteria would you choose to select a pilot for an agile project?

- a Collocated team would be available
- b Business sponsor involved in many other projects
- c Planned duration of 3 weeks
- d Planned duration of 12 weeks

## Chapter 19 Scaling Agile

205 Which ground rules need to be specifically defined with large and geographically dispersed agile teams?

- a Project language
- b Working times
- c Planning horizon
- d Status report templates

206 What are typical ways to manage large agile projects?

- a Create a hierarchy of product owners
- b Set up integration teams
- c Set up a project management office
- d Create virtual information radiators

207 With large agile teams, what can you do to establish a common estimation scale?

a Create a common story point measure

b Set up one release burndown chart

c Set up a scrum of scrums

d Organize iterations to have the same length

208 What would you use to integrate members of a remote team into the agile project?

a Live video conferencing

b Chat rooms

c Project wikis

d One to one e-mail

209 What are interdependent team meetings in large agile projects?

a Project chartering

b Iteration planning

c Review

d Lunch

# Answers

## Chapter 1

| | |
|---|---|
| 1 | A |
| 2 | A |
| 3 | AC |
| 4 | A |

## Chapter 2

| | |
|---|---|
| 5 | BC |
| 6 | CD |
| 7 | B |
| 8 | AB |
| 9 | AB |
| 10 | A |
| 11 | ABCD |
| 12 | C |
| 13 | AB |
| 14 | CD |
| 15 | ABC |
| 16 | ABC |
| 17 | AB |
| 18 | ABC |
| 19 | ABC |
| 20 | ABC |

## Chapter 3

| | |
|---|---|
| 21 | AB |
| 22 | AB |
| 23 | ABC |
| 24 | ABCD |
| 25 | ABCD |
| 26 | ABCD |
| 27 | ABCD |

## Chapter 4

| | |
|---|---|
| 28 | AB |
| 29 | AB |
| 30 | AB |
| 31 | AB |
| 32 | A |
| 33 | AB |
| 34 | AB |
| 35 | ABCD |
| 36 | ABC |
| 37 | C |
| 38 | B |
| 39 | ABCD |
| 40 | ABC |
| 41 | C |
| 42 | AB |
| 43 | A |
| 44 | ABCD |

## Chapter 5

| | |
|---|---|
| 45 | AB |
| 46 | AD |
| 47 | C |
| 48 | ABC |
| 49 | ABCD |
| 50 | ABC |
| 51 | ABCD |
| 52 | ABCD |
| 53 | AB |
| 54 | AB |
| 55 | A |
| 56 | A |
| 57 | A |
| 58 | A |
| 59 | A |
| 60 | A |
| 61 | A |
| 62 | C |
| 63 | D |
| 64 | B |
| 65 | ABCD |
| 66 | A |
| 67 | B |
| 68 | C |
| 69 | D |
| 70 | D |
| 71 | A |
| 72 | B |
| 73 | C |
| 74 | D |
| 75 | A |
| 76 | B |
| 77 | C |
| 78 | D |
| 79 | D |
| 80 | ABC |
| 81 | ABC |
| 82 | AB |
| 83 | AB |
| 84 | ABCD |
| 85 | ABCD |
| 86 | A |
| 87 | B |
| 88 | C |
| 89 | ABC |
| 90 | A |
| 91 | BC |
| 92 | A |
| 93 | AB |
| 94 | A |

## Chapter 6

| | |
|---|---|
| 95 | AB |
| 96 | A |

## Chapter 7

| | |
|---|---|
| 97 | ABC |
| 98 | AD |
| 99 | A |
| 100 | A |
| 101 | BCD |
| 102 | ABC |
| 103 | CD |
| 104 | ABCD |
| 105 | A |
| 106 | ABC |
| 107 | B |
| 108 | ABC |
| 109 | A |
| 110 | ABC |
| 111 | AB |
| 112 | A |
| 113 | ABC |
| 114 | ABC |
| 115 | ABC |
| 116 | ABD |
| 117 | ABC |
| 118 | AB |
| 119 | AB |
| 120 | B |
| 121 | AB |
| 122 | ABC |

### Chapter 8

123 ABC
124 ABC
125 AB
126 AB
127 ABC
128 ABC
129 C
130 AB
131 ABCD
132 A
133 ABC
134 ABC
135 ABC
136 ABC
137 ABCD
138 AB
139 AB
140 AC
141 A
142 A
143 AB
144 ABC

### Chapter 9

145 AC
146 AC
147 AB
148 A
149 ABC
150 AB
151 ABC
152 A
153 A
154 A
155 A
156 ABCD

### Chapter 10

157 AB
158 ABC
159 BCD

### Chapter 11

160 ABC
161 AB
162 ABC
163 A
164 AB
165 ABC
166 ABCD
167 A
168 A
169 AC

### Chapter 12

170 ABC
171 ABCD
172 AB
173 AB
174 AD
175 AB
176 AB
177 AB
178 AB
179 B
180 A

### Chapter 13

181 A
182 A
183 ABCD

### Chapter 14

184 ABC
185 AB
186 AB
187 ABC
188 B
189 ABCD
190 A

### Chapter 15

191 AB
192 ABC
193 A
194 A

### Chapter 16

195 ABCD
196 AB
197 AB
198 ABC

### Chapter 17

199 ACD
200 ABCD
201 ABC
202 ABC

### Chapter 18

203 AB
204 AD

### Chapter 19

205 ABC
206 ABC
207 AB
208 ABC
209 ABC

# Appendices

# Selected Software Development Methodologies

The following section provides an overview of the waterfall, spiral, and some agile software development methodologies. The purpose of this section is to give insight into the features, practices, and characteristics of the methodologies.

## Waterfall

The Waterfall model is a sequential design process that progresses through a series of phases from the conception through to the maintenance of the solution.

In its initial definition, the Waterfall model consists of six development phases, five documents, and five risk mitigation strategies.

### Origin

Based on his experiences, Dr. Winston developed a specific view on how to deliver large software projects to an operational state on time and within cost. In 1970, he presented his views in a paper that formed the basis for the Waterfall method. He advocated a structured phase approach to software development and five risk mitigation strategies.

### Phases

Dr Winston advocated the phases for software development from collecting the requirements through to operations. The phases were presented sequentially with the closure of one phase occurring before the next phase started. He did note that there would be design iterations where the design would need to be revisited and would lead to changes in the previous phases.

### Documents and artifacts

Quite a lot of documentation is needed. This is especially the case early in the design process as it acts as the guide for the activities and people throughout the project. Dr Winston recommends the following documents.

- Software Requirements
- Preliminary Design (Specification)
- Interface Design (Specification)
- Final Design (Specification) (As Built)

- Test Plan (Specification) and Test Results
- Operations Manual.

These documents go through version updates and, as they progress through the different phases, they are updated with the new findings and information.

### Practices

Having quite a lot of documentation was one of Dr Winston's risk mitigation strategies to assure project success. In addition, he suggested four more ways of reducing the risks of project failure:

Perform a preliminary design of the solution before detailed programing and analysis begin. This additional step ensures that the system does not fail due to technical constraints such as storage or data flows.

For unique and innovative solutions, build a simulation first by going through all the phases of the waterfall methodology. The simulation should build the competency of the team and provide insights to better manage and estimate the remaining project activities. He estimated that the simulation would be about 25% of the total project efforts.

Plan, monitor, and control testing. Projects should include test specialists for visual inspection and thorough logical tests.

Involve the customer for his insight, judgment, and commitment at the end of the design, coding and testing phases.

## Spiral

The Spiral methodology is an iterative and incremental methodology presented by Barry Boehm (1985). This method for software development suggests progressive elaboration of the software. Each iteration begins with a definition, prototype, and risk assessment, followed by the design, coding, testing, and implementation of the software, and finalizes with creating a plan for the next phase and a review of the current phase. Thereafter, the next phase starts as a new iteration with the same activities.

## Feature-Driven Development

Feature-Driven Development (FDD) breaks a product down into features, plans and delivers the product features in an iterative and incremental method, and provides standardized progress reports. FDD consists of five processes across two phases, nine practices, and six key roles.

## Origin

In 1997, three software managers and five software developers created Feature-Driven Development as a software development approach to help save a failed project for an international bank in Singapore. Jeff de Luca of Nebulon and Peter Coad were two of the main contributors to FDD (Deluca, 2005; Goyal, 2007; Palmer & Felsing, 2002).

## Processes

FDD uses an object model-driven approach to gathering requirements. This approach is designed to help the project team to understand and speak the same language as the user. It comprises five processes that separate into two distinct project groups. The first three processes are performed once and form planning and start-up:

- develop an overall model
- build a features list
- plan by feature.

The last two processes are incremental and form the development processes:

- design by feature
- build by feature

## FDD milestones

FDD defines six sequential milestones to track to the process of each feature through the Design by Feature and Build by Feature processes. The milestones are assigned a percentage weighting that can be used for calculating the percentage complete for each feature and the sum of both percentages provides the percentage complete for the whole project.

These milestones (Table A-1) are used in the FDD reporting guidelines, and are designed for knowing the project status and reporting to the stakeholders. In FDD, the team members are not asked for the status of the project. The states of features in the milestones determine the status.

| Milestone | Domain Walk through | Design | Design Inspection | Code | Code Inspection | Promote to Build |
|---|---|---|---|---|---|---|
| Process % Weight | 1% | 40% | 3% | 45% | 10% | 1% |

Table A-1 Feature-driven development milestones

## Practices

FDD recommends nine practices for the execution of the project:

- **Domain Object Modeling**—Colorized visual models for the components and overall solution
- **Unified Modeling Language (UML) in color.** UML is an industry standard modeling language used in the object-oriented software engineering field for modeling software-intensive systems. The UML color codes quickly identify the problem domain's dynamics.
- **Developing by Feature**—develop client-valuable functions and features in two-week increments.
- **Class (Code) Ownership**—individual team members are responsible for a set of classes from a domain object-model. A class is a piece of software code that defines properties and behaviors.
- **Feature Team**—Class-owners lead small teams to develop a team and class owners may be on multiple teams.
- **Inspections**—apply validation and verification techniques to detect and resolve issues.
- **Regular Build Schedule**—have a regular schedule to include completed features; always have a demonstrable system available.
- **Configuration Management**—keep track of latest completed source code files
- **Progress Reporting**—accurate, frequent and relevant progress reporting within the team and to the stakeholders.

## Roles

FDD describes six key roles and outlines a few additional roles:

- **Project Manager**—traditional project management role of managing time, budget, scope and quality
- **Chief Architect**—responsible for the overall design
- **Development Manager**—day-to-day technical leadership
- **Chief Programmers**—experienced developers responsible for design, analysis, and leading small teams
- **Class Owners**—developers on a team responsible for designing, coding, testing, and documenting the features

- **Domain Experts**—users, sponsors, or business analysts that are the source of information for the developers.

## Lean

Lean production practice is to eliminate any activity that absorbs resources that does not create value (that is, waste). There are seven lean principles that can be applied to software development.

### Origin

Lean practices and concepts were created as part of the Toyota Production System.

Lean is a term that was first coined by John Krafcik in his 1988 article, "Triumph of the Lean Production System." The goal of the Lean production practice is to eliminate any activity that absorbs resources that does not create value (that is, waste). Mary Poppendieck applied lean practices to software developed and documented seven principles for software projects.

The lean principles underlie many of the practices and rules in extreme programming and scrum. Therefore, the lean concepts can be used independently of or jointly with the other agile methodologies.

### Principles for software development

The following are the lean principles that are applied to software development according to Mary and Tom Poppendieck (2003).

#### ELIMINATE WASTE

The software development process should eliminate meetings, documents, activities, or other items that use resources and do not create value.

The seven types of waste for software projects are in Table 17-1.

#### BUILD-IN QUALITY

The development process construction for each step of the process ensures that the system is correct. This involves ensuring that the different tests are adequate and implemented to find and fix issues as early in the process as possible. The goal of the final step of verification and validation is to find zero defects.

The systems design and architecture allows for adding new features at any time without breaking the whole or other parts of the system.

### CREATE KNOWLEDGE

Learning is a key part of delivering a quality system that meets a customer's needs. The team uses early and frequent feedback so as not to have to guess the customer's needs or the expected value.

The system is designed and implemented to make the system able to accept changes.

### DELAY DECISIONS

Decisions that bind the team to architectural or irreversible courses of action have a long-term effect on the project. Decisions should be delayed to the last possible moment or when it is almost too late to decide. If possible, all decisions should be reversible. This keeps options open and supports the team's ability to respond to change.

### DELIVER FAST

The team should understand the value expected from the system by the customer and stakeholders. They should create a work process that delivers results at a steady, rapid pace.

They should focus on managing the workflow and reducing cycle times to maximize performance.

### RESPECT AND EMPOWER THE TEAM

The team is empowered to make decisions and the team is accountable for the decisions that it makes.

The team's work should be connected to the value it is expected to deliver so the team members understand their contributions to the big picture.

### OPTIMIZE THE WHOLE

The team should understand the entire product value stream. That is, all aspects of the product being developed from how it will be marketed and sold, how it will be used, and how it will be serviced and supported.

Customers want systems that address their problems and they want them to look and feel like one system; not like parts of different systems that have been cobbled together.

All parts of the development process should be optimized. If not, performance will suffer over time from the sub-optimal parts.

# Kanban

Kanban is a scheduling system concept related to lean and just-in-time (JIT) production that helps determine what to produce, when to produce it, and how much to produce. Five kanban processes create Lean behaviors in software development activities.

## Origin

Kanban practices and concepts were created as part of the Toyota Production System.

Kanban is Japanese meaning "sign board" or "billboard." It is a scheduling system that is used as part of a Just-in-Time (JIT) production process. In kanban, a card follows a product along the production process. This card gives a visual sign or signal to produce the product or carry out the next step in the process. The card is pulled along the process. A pull system reduces or eliminates over or underproduction by producing no more or no less than what is needed.

In software development, Kanban is used to maximize the throughput or performance of the development process. David Anderson (2010) recommends five properties for using a Kanban system in software development. When used, these five properties create Lean behaviors in software development activities.

## Properties for software development

The following section defines the properties for applying the Kanban scheduling process for software development.

### DEFINE AND VISUALIZE THE WORKFLOW

A Kanban board displays the work processes. It is visible for the entire project team, and contains cards for the work that needs to be completed.

The team members should be cross-trained to be knowledgeable about the various work processes so they can perform different tasks as needed. When an employee is free to perform the work, he or she adds an ID against a card and starts to work on the task. Once the task is completed, it is moved to the appropriate space on the Kanban board.

### LIMIT WORK-IN-PROGRESS

Work-in-progress (WIP) limits are based upon the available capacity. The WIP limits are established for each process step. The focus of WIP limits is to maximize the throughput of work processes; it is not to maximize resource utilization.

### MEASURE AND MANAGE FLOW

Kanban is a continuous flow system where cards flow into and out of the system. Therefore, management reporting is not focused on measuring time-to-plan delivery. Management reporting is more focused on measuring the predictability and the performance of the flow. That is, indicators are tracked over time to support the optimization and continuous improvement of the system. The following are some of the indicators that are interesting.

- Performance against WIP Limits
- Predictability of lead times (for the class of service)
- Due date performance
- Throughput
- Issue and blocked work items
- Flow efficiency
- Initial quality (defect cost and time reporting)
- Failure load (work items due to poor quality).

### MAKE PROCESS POLICIES EXPLICIT

The team must define in an explicit way the workings and rules around the Kanban. The process policies that must be defined are similar to those for other agile methodologies and include such topics as:

- **Delivery cadence**—the pattern for delivering software at regular intervals
- **Input cadence**—the prioritization cadence for adding items to the system
- **Work-in-progress limits**—choosing limits for work tasks
- **Service level agreements**—defining classes of services, prioritization rules, and service delivery targets.

The rules must be explicit within the team and to the stakeholders.

### USE MODELS TO SUGGEST IMPROVEMENT

Use quantitative and scientific methods to evaluate and improve the process. Specifically, applicable to Kanban is to identify constraints or bottlenecks in the process and take action to remove the bottlenecks. This practice use is based on the Theory of Constraints.

# Scrum

Scrum is an interactive, incremental methodology that has a highly flexible development phase that empowers the team to act as needed to meet the customer requirement and be productive. Scrum has five events (called ceremonies), three deliverables (called artifacts), three roles, and a set of rules that govern the relationship and interaction between the different components.

## Origin

In 1993, Jeff Sutherland at Easel created "scrum" by defining as "a loose set of activities that combines known, workable tools and techniques with the best that a development team can devise to build systems" (Schwaber, 1996, p. 1).

## Principles

Scrum advocates transparency, inspection, and adaptation as three pillars to control the development process.

- **Transparency**—use common languages and definitions amongst the team and with those responsible for the outcome and make significant aspects of the process visible to all

- **Inspection**—perform frequent, diligent, non-intrusive inspections of the process and the product

- **Adaptation**—make adjustments as soon as possible to remedy product or process issues.

The Scrum events, team language, and working practices are designed to realize the principle behind these pillars. Additionally, the following principles are built in the Scrum rules:

- Changes can be requested at any time and they are prioritized for implementation

- Planning is broken into stages and conducted when it is most likely to be accurate

- Outside influence into the team is managed.

## Roles

A Scrum team should be cross-functional and work together in a co-located area on a daily basis. The Scrum team consists of three roles:

**Product Owner**—a single person, who is accountable for setting priorities for the product features to deliver the maximum business value

**Team**—a self-organizing development team that has all the members needed to deliver the product. The team size should be kept to a reasonable size (7 ± 2 people) to avoid complexity.

**Scrum Master**—a single person that coaches the Team, Product Owner, and organization in the application of the Scrum practices, services the team to remove obstacles, and supports the organizational change needed to benefit from Scrum

## Events

Scrum has five events for planning, executing, and learning from the project experiences. These events include:

- **Sprint (the development)**—a timeboxed project iteration where a usable product should be created

- **Sprint Planning Meeting**—within a Sprint, a meeting to agree what will be delivered in the next sprint and how it will be delivered

- **Daily Scrum (the daily stand-up)**—within a Sprint, a daily meeting (for a maximum of 15-minutes) with the development team to synchronize activities and create a plan for the next 24 hours

- **Sprint Review**—at the end of a Sprint, a meeting to inspect the product with the stakeholders and adjust the product backlog

- **Sprint Retrospective**—before the next Sprint, a meeting for the team to reflect on the product and process from the previous Sprint and plan improvements

## Artifacts

Scrum has three key deliverables (called artifacts). The artifacts are:

**Product Backlog**—a prioritized list of items (for example, features, requirements, or bugs) that should be implemented into the product

The Product Backlog is maintained by the product owner with the help of the team. The product backlog is very dynamic and priorities may shift routinely as well as the content of the backlog.

**Sprint Backlog**—a subset of the product backlog that is realized in the sprint

The Sprint backlog is maintained by the team, and represents a commitment from the team on what they will deliver during the Sprint. Only the team can change the Sprint backlog.

**Product Increment**—the product features that are implemented into the product and are considered done. The team agrees on the definition of done. However, the expectation is that each Sprint delivers a potentially shippable and usable product with all features tested and ready to be used.

### Definition of done

The scrum team together with the Product Owner must reach an agreement on what defines that work is complete. This is the "definition of done," and is used to determine when work is complete in an increment.

## Extreme programming

Extreme programming (XP) is an iterative, incremental development methodology with values that emphasize simplicity, communication, testing, and aggressiveness.

XP has four values that are realized through the execution of 13 practices. There are five key roles required for executing XP.

### Origin

In 1997, 20 software managers working for the Chrysler Corporation stated in an article that they used Kent Beck's Extreme Programming or XP to turn around a failing software project (C3 Team, 1998).

### Practices

The Extreme Programming practices are designed so that their execution enforces the values of Communications, Simplicity, Feedback, and Courage. These values are meant for individuals to sacrifice their individual goals and work towards the shared goals of the project. They are:

- Communications between the team and all stakeholder,
- Simplicity in design and coding,
- Feedback at different time intervals—hours, days, weeks, months, and
- Courage to make difficult decisions.

XP practices consist of 13 practices (Figure A-1):

- **Whole team**—co-located team that includes a real user
- **Planning game**—scope, prioritize, and estimate quickly and change as needed
- **Small releases**—release to production in short cycle
- **Metaphor**—guide development with shared stories
- **Simple design**—remove complexity and go for simple designs
- **Customer tests**—customers write tests
- **Test-driven development**—write test first, code to test, unit test until no errors

- **Refactoring**—improve and restructure programs without changing their behavior
- **Pair programming**—two programmers write production code
- **Continuous integration**—build and integrate multiple times a day
- **Collective ownership**—anyone can change code anytime
- **Sustainable pace**—40-hour work week—no continuous overtime
- **Coding standards**—write code according to standards

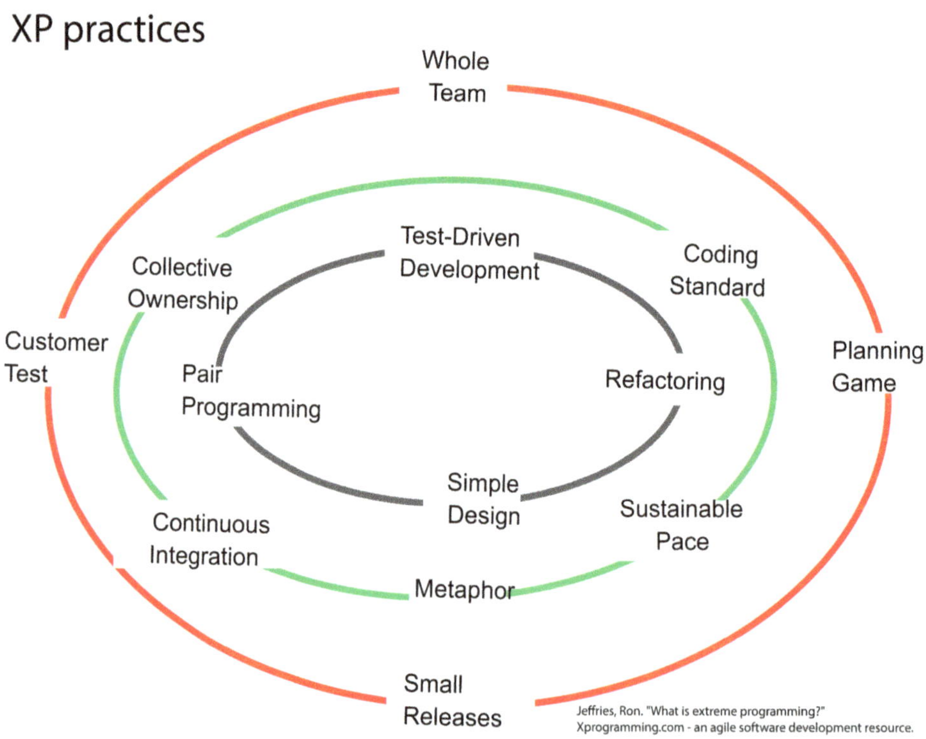


Figure A-1 Extreme programming practices

## Roles

XP defines the five project roles as follows:

- **Programmer**—writes code in a simple fashion, and refactors and unit tests code
- **Customer**—writes user stories and tests, makes decisions on the solution
- **Tester**—helps the customer chose and write functional tests; may also run functional tests and post the results

- **Tracker**—keeps track of the big picture, tracks estimates and different results (for example, tests, defects)
- **Coach**—supports, coaches, and directs the team in the application of the XP practices

## Crystal methodologies

The Crystal methodology was developed by Alistair Cockburn (2001) as a family of methodologies that include different levels of methodology components depending upon the project characteristics such as criticality and team size. The methodologies map on to the Cockburn matrix of team size and system criticality. The more critical the system the more control elements are needed to prevent error and defects. The larger the team the more complex the communications and the more written intermediate documents are needed.

Each Crystal method contains a set of practices, roles, work products, techniques, and notations. The Crystal methodologies allow the teams to choose the amount of ceremony and discipline that is required for the project (that is, high tolerance) and the methods provide the processes needed to support the people and their communications and collaboration (that is, the human component). Crystal clear and Crystal orange methodologies are described in the following section.

### Crystal clear

The Crystal clear methodology is designed for small teams working on systems that do not result in the loss of life or essential money. It contains the following elements:

**Team space:** the team sits together in one room.

**Roles:** sponsors, senior designer programmer, designer, and real user (at least part-time).

**Process:** incremental delivery every two to three months; some automated regression testing, at least two users viewing per release, the team decides on kinds of documentation needed, policy standards are required.

**Work products:** release, scheduled user viewings, annotated use cases or feature descriptions, design sketches, mock-ups, common object models, running code, migration code, test cases, and user manual.

**Reporting:** progress tracking of software delivery and decision milestones.

## Crystal orange

The Crystal orange methodology is for project team with up to 40 people that are working on systems that do not result in a loss of life. It has the following elements.

- **Team space:** the team sits in one building.
- **Roles:** sponsor, business expert, usage expert, technical facilitator, business analyst/designer, project manager, architect, design mentor, lead designer-programmer, other designer-programmers, UI designer, reuse point, writer, tester. The people are divided into sub-teams or functional teams.
- **Process:** incremental delivery every three to four months; some automated regression testing, at least two users viewing per release, the team decides on what kinds of documentation is needed, and what policy standards are required.
- **Work products:** requirements document, release sequence, schedule, user interface design document, common object model, inter-team specifications, user manual, source code, test cases, migration code
- **Reporting:** status reports are part of the progress tracking.

# Other agile methodologies

The following is a list of several other agile methodologies not discussed in this book.

- Agile unified process (AUP)
- Disciplined agile delivery (DAD)
- Essential unified process (EssUp)
- Graphical system design (GSD)
- Open unified process (OpenUp)
- Rational unified process (RUP)

# Roles & Tasks

This section identifies the responsibilities for the scrum roles and an agile tester.

The boundary of work for the product owner is the product features; his or her work starts before the project and continues well after the project is completed. The agile coach's boundary is the team; his or her work is during the project. The team's boundary is the work during the project iterations and is authorized by the product owner. Agile testing is important for quality assurance. The tasks per role are as follows.

## Product Owner

- Agree on the definition of done with team and stakeholders
- Coordinate requirements with users and stakeholders
- Document requirements as user stories/features
- Develop the product roadmap
- Develop the release plan
- Create and maintain the product backlog
- Define the user story acceptance criteria
- Prioritize items in the product backlog
- Add agreed with estimates to items in the product backlog
- Explain user stories in the iteration planning
- Abnormally terminate an iteration (if necessary)
- Lead the product review session
- Accept or reject an increment during the product review meeting
- Answer team questions to complete increment

## Team

- Agree on the definition of done with the product owner
- Support the product owner to prioritize items in the product backlog
- Estimate items in the product backlog
- Clarify understanding of user stories in the iteration planning
- Agree with user stories that should be included in the iteration backlog
- Estimate tasks needed to complete items in the iteration backlog
- Participate (daily) stand-up
- Demonstrate the increment in the iteration review
- Deliver a working product increment
- Participation in the iteration retrospective
- Update burndown chart (daily)
- Update burnup chart (at iteration end)

## Agile Coach

- Coach all on the values and principles of agile
- Coach all on the rules of the agile process
- Schedule the iteration planning meeting for the product owner
- Schedule the review (demo) meeting for the product owner
- Organize and moderate the Retrospective for the Team
- Facilitate (daily) stand-up for team
- Protect the team from distractions and interference
- Identify and remove issues for the team
- Schedule the (daily) stand-up for team
- Support the product owner

## Agile Tester

- Help the product owner define feature functionality
- Help the product owner define acceptance criteria
- Gather examples and ask questions to clarify user stories
- Pair with developers to support test automation
- Conduct exploratory testing; offer timely feedback

# Bibliography

AACE. (2004). Recommended Practices, No. 17R-97, Cost Estimate Classification System, and No. Retrieved from Morgantown:

Adkins, L. (2010). Coaching Agile Teams. Boston, MA: Addison-Wesley.

Ambler, S. W. (2011a). Agile Teams Mini-Survey Results: April/May 2011. Retrieved from http://www.ambysoft.com/surveys/agileTeams2011.html

Ambler, S. W. (2011b). Dr. Dodd's How Successful Are IT Projects, Really? Retrieved from http://www.drdobbs.com/architecture-and-design/how-successful-are-it-projects-really/232300110

Anderson, D. J. (2010). Kanban: Successful Evolutionary Change for Your Technology Business. Sequim, WA: Blue Hole Press.

APM. (2012). APM Body of Knowledge 6th Edition. Buckinghamshire, United Kingdom: Association for Project Management.

Atern The Handbook. (2008). Atern E-Book. Retrieved from http://www.dsdm.org/dsdm-atern/atern

Bakker, R. M. (2010). Taking Stock of Temporary Organizational Forms: A Systematic Review and Research Agenda. International Journal of Management Reviews, 12(4), 466-486. doi:https://doi.org/10.1111/j.1468-2370.2010.00281.x

Beck, K. (1999). Extreme Programming Explained (First Edition). Retrieved from http://www.ittelkom.ac.id/staf/apk/ngajar/RPL%20OOT/papers/RUP%20dll/extreme%20programming%20explained.pdf

Beck, K., Beedle, M., Bennekum, A. v., Cockburn, A., Cunningham, W., Fowler, M., . . . Thomas, D. (2001, Dec). Manifesto for Agile Software Development. Retrieved from http://agilemanifesto.org/

Beck, K., & Cleal, D. (2009). Optional scope contracts. Extreme Programming. Retrieved from http://xprogramming.com/ftp/Optional+scope+contracts.pdf

Begel, A., & Nagappan, N. (2006). Usage and Perceptions of Agile Software Development in an Industrial Context: An Exploratory Study. Retrieved from Redmond, WA:

Bellani, F. (2013). Adoption and evolution of agile method practice.

Boehm, B. (1985, Mar). A Spiral Model of Software Development and Enhancement. Paper presented at the International Workshop on Software Process and Software -- March 27-29, Coto de Caza, Trabuco Canyon, California.

Boehm, B., & Turner, R. (2003). Observations on Balancing Discipline and Agility. Paper presented at the Agile Development Conference, Los Angeles, CA.

Booch, G., & Brown, A. W. (2003). Collaborative Development Environments. Advances in Computers, 59.

Brooks, F. P. (1995). The Mythical Man-Month Essays on Software Engineering Anniversary Edition. Boston: Addison Wesley Longman, Inc.

Buwalda, H. (2004). Soap Opera Testing. Retrieved from http://www.logigear.com/logi_media_dir/Documents/Soap_Opera_Testing.pdf

Carr, M. J., Konda, S. L., Monarch, I., & Ulrich, F. C. (1993). Taxonomy-Based Risk Identification. Retrieved from Pittsburgh, Pennsylvania:

CHAOS Report 2015. (2015). Retrieved from https://www.standishgroup.com/sample_research_files/CHAOSReport2015-Final.pdf

Chung, M.-W., & Drummond, B. (2009). Agile @ Yahoo! From the Trenches. 2009 Agile Conference, 113-118.

Cockburn, A. (2001). Agile Software Development.

Cohn, M. (2004). User Stories Applied: For Agile Software Development. Boston, MA: Addison-Wesley.

Cohn, M. (2006). Agile Estimating and Planning. Upper Saddle River, NJ, USA: Pearson Education Inc.

Cohn, M. (2010). Succeeding with Agile. Boston, MA: Addition-Wesley.

Crispin, L., & Gregory, J. (2009). Agile Testing: A Practical Guide for Testers and Agile Teams. Boston, MA: Addison-Wesley.

Cunningham, W. (Producer). (1992, Mar). The WyCash Portfolio Management System. Retrieved from http://c2.com/doc/oopsla92.html

de Bono, E. (1985). Six Thinking Hats. Boston: Little, Brown and Company.

Deluca, J. (2005). Feature Driven Development (FDD) Overview Presentation. Retrieved from http://www.nebulon.com/articles/fdd/download/fddoverview.pdf

DeMarco, T., & Lister, T. (2004). Riskology. Retrieved from http://www.systemsguild.com/riskology/

Drummond, B., & Unson, J. F. J. (2008). Yahoo! Distributed Agile: Notes from the World Over. Agile 2008, 315-321.

Fink, L., & Pinchovski, B. (2020). It is about time: Bias and its mitigation in time-saving decisions in software development projects. International Journal of Project Management, 38(2), 99-111.

Fisher, R., Ury, W., & Patton, B. (1991). Getting to Yes: Negotiating Agreement Without Giving In (Second Edition). Boston: Houghton Mufflin Company.

Fletcher, A. (Producer). (2002). FireStarter Youth Power Curriculum Participant Guidebook. Retrieved from http://www.freechild.org/Firestarter/Fist2Five.htm

Fry, C., & Greene, S. (2007). Large Scale Agile Transformation in an On-Demand World. Paper presented at the AGILE 2007, Washington, DC.

Goyal, S. (2007). Major Seminar on Feature Driven Development. Retrieved from http://csis.pace.edu/~marchese/CS616/Agile/FDD/fdd.pdf

Greenleaf, R. K. (1991). The Servant as Leader. Retrieved from http://www.leadershiparlington.org/pdf/TheServantasLeader.pdf

Grenning, J. (Producer). (2002). Planning Poker or How to avoid analysis paralysis while release planning. Retrieved from http://renaissancesoftware.net/files/articles/PlanningPoker-v1.1.pdf

Griffiths, M. (Producer). (2012, Jun). Collaborative Games for Risk Management. Retrieved from http://leadinganswers.typepad.com/leading_answers/2012/06/collaborative-games-for-risk-management.html

Hersey, P., & Blanchard, K. H. (2008). Management of organizational behavior (5th Ed.). Englewood Cliffs, NJ: Prentice Hall.

Hohmann, L. (2007). Innovation Games: Creating Breakthrough Products Through Collaborative Play. Boston: Pearson Education, Inc.

Jackobsen, C. R., & Johnson, K. A. (2008). Mature Agile with a twist of CMMI®. Paper presented at the Agile 2008 Conference.

Jeffries, R. (2001). What is extreme programming? Xprogramming.com - an agile software development resource. Retrieved from http://xprogramming.com/xpmag/whatisxp

Johnson, J. (2002). It's a New World! And it's Called ROI! Paper presented at the XP2002, Alghero, Sardinia, Italy.

Kaner, S. (2014). Facilitator's guide to participatory decision-making: John Wiley & Sons.

Katzenbach, J. R., & Smith, D. K. (1993). The Discipline of Teams. Harvard Business Review.

Kerievsky, J. (Producer). (2003, Aug). Velocity Measurements are NUTs! Retrieved from http://comments.gmane.org/gmane.comp.programming.extreme-programming/31897

Kilmann, R. H., & Thomas, K. W. (1975). Interpersonal conflict-handling behavior as reflections of Jungian personality dimensions. Psychological reports, 37(3), 971-980.

Kotter, J. P. (1995). Leading Change: Why Transformation Efforts Fail. March-April.

Larman, C. L., & Vodde, B. (2010). Practices for Scaling Lean & Agile Development: Large, Multisite, and Offshore Product Development with Large-Scale Scrum Boston, MA 02116: Addison-Wesley.

Larman, C. L., Vodde, B., & Arbogast, T. (2010). Practices for Scaling Lean & Agile Development. Boston, MA 02116: Addison-Wesley.

Larsen, D., & Derby, E. (2006). Agile retrospectives: Making good teams great.

Leistner, F. (2010). Mastering Organizational Knowledge Flow: How to Make Knowledge Sharing Work. Hoboken, New Jersey.: John Wiley & Sons, Inc.

Levinson, M. (2012). IT Skills Shortages Inside Companies Hamper Profitability, Productivity. Retrieved from http://www.cio.com/article/702176/IT_Skills_Shortages_Inside_Companies_Hamper_Profitability_Productivity_?page=1&taxonomyId=3123

Lindvall , M., Basili, V., Boehm, B., Costa, P., Dangle, K., Shull, F., . . . Zelkowitz, M. (2002). Empirical Findings in Agile Methods. Paper presented at the Proceedings of the Second XP Universe and First Agile Universe Conference on Extreme Programming and Agile Methods - XP/Agile Universe 2002, London.

Magazinius, A., Borjesson, S., & Feldt, R. (2012). Investigating Intentional Distortions in Software Cost Estimation - An Exploratory Study. Journal of Systems and Software, 85.

Mah, M. (2008). How agile projects measure up, and what this means to you. Retrieved from

Marick, B. (Producer). (2003). Exploration Through Example. Retrieved from http://www.exampler.com/old-blog/2003/08/21/

McConnell, S. (1998). Software Project Survival Guide: How to Be Sure Your First Important Project Isn't Your Last. Redmond: Microsoft Press.

Mezick, D. (2009). Boundary, Authority, Role and Task: BART Analysis Applied. Paper presented at the Agile 2009, Chicago.

Miller, G. J. (2019). Project Management Tasks in Agile Projects: A Quantitative Study. Paper presented at the Annals of Computer Science and Information Systems.

Moore, G. A. (1991). Crossing the Chasm: Marketing and Selling High-Tech Products to Mainstream Customers. Pymble, NSW, Australia: HarperBusiness.

Palmer, S. R., & Felsing, J. M. (2002). A Practical Guide to Feature Driven Development: Prentice Hall.

Patton, J. (2005). It's All in How You Slice It. Better Software, 16 - 40. Retrieved from http://www.agileproductdesign.com/writing/how_you_slice_it.pdf

Pisculli, B. F. (Producer). (2010, January 06). The New Competency of Global Listening. Retrieved from http://bfeild.typepad.com/transcending_leadership/2010/01/the-new-competency-of-global-listening.html

PMI. (2013). A Guide to the Project Management Body of Knowledge (PMBOK Guide) -- Fifth Edition (Sixth Edition ed.). Newtown Square, Pennsylvania, United States: Project Management Institute, Inc.

PMI. (2017a). Achieving Greater Agility: The people and process drivers that accelerate results. Retrieved from

PMI. (2017b). Agile Practice Guide. Newtown Square, Pennsylvania, United States: Project Management Institute, Inc.

PMI. (2017c). A Guide to the Project Management Body of Knowledge (PMBOK Guide) -- Sixth Edition (Sixth Edition ed.). Newtown Square, Pennsylvania, United States: Project Management Institute, Inc.

PMI. (2020, Jan). PMI Fact File. PMI Today, 4.

Pons, D. (2008). Project Management for New Product Development. Project Management Journal, 39(2), 82-97. doi:10.1002/pmj.20052

Poppendieck, M., & Poppendieck, T. (2003). Lean Software Development: An Agile Toolkit. Upper Saddle River, NJ, USA: Addison Wesley.

Prechelt, L. (1999). The 28:1 Grant/Sackman legend is misleading, or: How large is interpersonal variation really? Retrieved from http://www.ipd.ira.uka.de/EIR/

Rico, D. F. (2008). What is the Return on Investment (ROI) of Agile Methods? Retrieved from http://davidfrico.com/rico08a.pdf

Ritter, J., & Marburger, C. (2012). Nur ein Business Case überzeugt das Topmanagement: Agile Methoden einführen – ist das rentabel? , Ausgabe 14/2012.

Ritter, J., & Röttgers, F. (2008). The Definitive Guide to Getting Your Budget Approved: Solution Matrix.

Sackman, H., Erikson, W. J., & Grant, E. E. (1968). Exploratory experimental studies comparing online and offline programming performance. Magazine Communications of the ACM, 11(1), 3-11.

Schlabach, K. E. (Producer). (2008, December 4). Snake on the Wall. Retrieved from http://agile-commentary.blogspot.de/2008/12/snake-on-wall.html

Schwaber, K. (1996). Scrum Development Process. Object Technology Jeff Sutherland. Retrieved from http://www.jeffsutherland.org/oopsla/schwapub.pdf

Schwaber, K., & Sutherland, J. (2017). The Scrum Guide: The Definitive Guide to Scrum: The Rules of the Game.

Scotland, K., & Boutin, A. (2008). Integrating Scrum with the Process Framework at Yahoo! Europe. Paper presented at the Agile 2008 Conference, Toronto, Canada.

Serrador, P., & Pinto, J. K. (2015). Does agile work? — A quantitative analysis of agile project success. International Journal of Project Management, 33(5), 1040-1051. doi:https://doi.org/10.1016/j.ijproman.2015.01.006

Sidky, A. (2007). A Structured Approach to Adopting Agile Practices: The Agile Adoption Framework. Retrieved from Blacksburg, Virginia:

Speed, L. (1989). How bad is the conflict? Leadership Journal, 1(Winter).

Stacey, R. D. (2011). Strategic Management and Organisational Dynamics: The Challenge of Complexity, 6th Edition: Pearson Education.

Sulaiman, T., & Smits, H. (2007). Measuring integrated progress on agile software development projects. Methods & Tools, 15(3), 2-9.

Tabaka, J. (2006). Collaboration Explained: Facilitation Skills for Software Project Leaders. Upper Saddle River, NJ, USA: Addison Wesley Professional.

Tavares, B., Silva, C., & Diniz de Souza, A. (2019). Practices to Improve Risk Management in Agile Projects. International Journal of Software Engineering and Knowledge Engineering, 29(03), 381-399. doi:https://doi.org/10.1142/S0218194019500165

Team, C. (1998). Chrysler Goes to "Extremes". www.DistributedComputing.com. Retrieved from http://www.xprogramming.com/publications/dc9810cs.pdf

Team, C. P. (2010). CMMI® for development, version 1.3 CMMI-DEV. Retrieved from

Thourp, L., & Jensen, B. (2009). Collaborative Agile Contracts. Paper presented at the IEEE 2009 Agile Conference, Chicago.

Tuckman, B. W. (1965). Developmental Sequence in Small Groups. Psychological Bulletin, 63(6), 384-399.

Turner, R., & Zolin, R. (2012). Forecasting Success on Large Projects: Developing Reliable Scale to Predict Multiple Perspectives by Multiple Stakeholders Over Multiple Time Frames. Project Management Journal, 43(5), 87-99.

Universal Credit: early progress. (2013). Retrieved from London, United Kingdom:

VersionOne. (2012). 6th Annual State of Agile Survey. Retrieved from http://www.versionone.com/state_of_agile_development_survey/11/

VersionOne. (2018). 13th Annual State of Agile Report. Retrieved from https://www.stateofagile.com/#ufh-i-521251909-13th-annual-state-of-agile-report/473508

Wake, B. (2005, Sep). Twenty Ways to Split Stories. Retrieved from https://xp123.com/articles/twenty-ways-to-split-stories/

Wiegers, K. (1999). First things first: prioritizing requirements. Software Development, 7(9), 48-53.

Winston, R. D. W. (1987). Managing the development of large software systems. Paper presented at the Proceedings, 9th International Conference on Software Engineering, Monterey, California, United States.

Yaffee, S. L., & Wondolleck, J. M. (2000). Making Collaboration Work: A comprehensive assessment of over 200 wide ranging cases of collaboration in environmental management. Conservation in Practice, 1(1), 17-24.

Zimmerman, B., & Hayday, B. (1999). A board's journey into complexity science: Lessons from (and for) staff and board members. Group decision and negotiation, 8(4), 281-303.

# Glossary

**20/20 Vision.** An innovation game where the features are placed in their relative order of importance on the white board.

**80/20 Rule.** See Pareto principle

**AACE.** American Association of Cost Engineers. They provide a Rough Order Of Magnitude model.

**Acceptance Test Driven Development (ATDD).** Acceptance tests that are defined early in the project as unambiguous test cases that describe the inputs and outputs of a function or feature.

**Active Listening.** Listening and providing feedback on what has been heard.

**Adaptation.** A Scrum practice to make adjustments as soon as possible to remedy product or process issues.

**Affinity Estimating.** A team estimation method where feature and user stories are grouped based upon their relative effort to implement them.

**Agile.** A set of values and principles that, once implemented, should result in a team or organization is able to produce quality software in the shortest possible time and adapt to changing environments.

**Agile Coach.** A Servant-Leader to an agile team responsible for mentoring and coaching the project team, supporting the product owner, and managing the stakeholders.

**Agile Manifesto.** A set of values and principles published on www.agilemanifesto.com_that, at a high-level, describes a framework for software development.

**Agile Modeling.** A collection of practices for modeling and documenting software-based systems...

**Agile Tester.** A professional tester who embraces and practices testing according to agile principles and values.

**Alpha Testing.** An evaluation of an early version of the product.

**Agile Unified Process (AUP).** An agile methodology.

**Apprentice.** An innovation game that requires a team member to navigate through the system while other team members observe.

**Artifact.** The process outputs or process deliverables from the project.

**Backlog.** A prioritized list of items (for example, features, requirements, or bugs) that should be implemented into the product.

**Behavior-Driven Development (BDD).** An approach for writing stories by identifying the expected business outcome first, and then the feature set that will deliver that outcome. Each feature becomes a user story with its acceptance criteria or tests.

**Beta Testing.** An evaluation of a stable version of the new product that may still have bugs.

**Brainstorming.** A technique for a group to generate ideas.

**BRUF.** Big requirements up front, meaning a major requirements document detailed up front. This is not an agile practice.

**Build-In Quality.** A lean principle where each step of the process ensures that the system is correct.

**Burn Rate.** The cumulative costs of all people on the project for the given time period.

**Burndown Chart.** A chart that shows planned and actual work remaining until the target end date.

**Burnup Chart.** A chart that shows how much work is included in the project and how much work is completed.

**Business Case.** The justification for performing the project.

**Buy A Feature.** An innovation game where stakeholders are given a budget, they are shown features with their estimated price, and the stakeholder has to decide which features to purchase on the fixed budget.

**Ceremony.** The amount of formality and controls imposed on the process, for example, stage gates, approvals, reviews, or sign-offs.

**Champion-Challenger.** A methodology for a new idea—the challenger—to test the current leader—the champion. The concept originated in the analytical field.

**Chaos.** An unusual pattern. See mathematical chaos.

**Chartering.** A collaborative event the team performs to understand the project, the product they will be producing, and the parameters and context of the project.

**Chasm.** A lifecycle point between a product having a few visionary customers to it having many pragmatic customers.

**Chickens.** A metaphor for people that may be involved in the project, but are not accountable for getting work done.

**Chief Architect.** A FDD role that is responsible for overall design.

**Chief Programmer.** A FDD role that is an experienced developers responsible for design, analysis, and leading small teams

**Class.** A piece of software code that defines properties and behaviors.

**Class (Code) Ownership.** A FDD practice to have individual team members responsible for a set of classes from a domain object-model.

**Class Owner.** A FDD role that are developers on a team responsible for designing, coding, testing, and documenting the features:

**Closed Story.** A user story that finishes with the achievement of a meaningful goal and that allows the user to feel that something has been accomplished.

**Coach.** An XP role for someone who supports, coaches, and directs the team in the application of the XP practices:

**Coaching.** The process of providing perspective, insight, and guidance to help an individual or team achieve improvements or changes in performance, learning, or development.

**Cockburn Levels.** A reference to explain skill levels of professionals.

**Code Coverage.** A measure that evaluates how much of the code is covered by tests.

**Coding Standards.** An XP practice to write code according to standards

**Collaboration.** Team members working together to realize shared goals.

**Collaborative Events.** Meetings where the team communicates with itself and the stakeholders.

**Collective Ownership.** An XP practice to have anyone can change code anytime

**Co-location.** The whole team in close proximity to one another.

**Command And Control.** A structure, where there is a project manager in charge and assigns tasks to the team members. This is not an agile practice.

**Community Of Practice.** A group of individuals with similar interests that share experiences and knowledge around a specific theme.

**Compatibility.** Tests of the system working with the different software and hardware versions for which the system should function.

**Complexity Zone.** An area where you can neither specify the details on the product in advance nor agree upon these details with any degree of accuracy. See Stacey Matrix.

**Compliance.** A requirement to meet the criteria established by external regulation or internal governance policies.

**Component Tests.** Tests that verify a larger part of the system than unit tests such as a group of classes that provide a service.

**Compound Epics.** User stories that are made up of several constitute stories.

**Cone Of Uncertainty.** The uncertainty ranges for cost and schedule estimates based upon the phases of a waterfall project.

**Configuration Management.** A practice to keep track of latest completed source code files. This practice is suggested by FDD and DSDM.

**Conflict.** An area of disagreement.

**Conflict Resolution Diagram (CRD).** A tool that can be used to understand conflicts between two ideas, courses of action, or situations that seem mutually exclusive (Also known as Cloud.)

**Constraints.** Restrictions that must be obeyed.

**Continuous Integration.** A software development practice where members of a team integrate their work frequently.

**Cost of Coordination.** The effort or costs related to any activity that involves communicating and scheduling team activities.

**Cost of Making a Change.** The cost impact of making software changes during the project lifecycle.

**Cost Performance Index (CPI).** An Earned Value Management index that is the earned value as compare to the actual costs.

**CRACK Customer.** Collaborative, Representative, Authorized, Committed, Knowledgeable customer.

**Create Knowledge.** A lean principle where learning is a key part of delivering a quality system that meets a customer's need.

**Criticality.** The consequence should undetected defects be used by the system.

**Crystal Methodology.** A family of agile methodologies that include different levels of methodology components depending upon the project characteristics such as criticality and team size.

**Cumulative Flow Diagram (CFD).** A chart of the status of features and stories are represented by a graph over time.

**Customer.** An XP role for someone who writes user stories and tests, makes decisions on the solution

**Customer Tests.** An XP practice to customers write tests

**Customer-Valued Prioritization.** The team engaging the customer in the process of prioritizing the features that are incorporated into the product.

**Cycle Time.** A lean measurement that represents the time it takes to complete a task once started..

**Cynefin Framework,** a Welsh noun that means "usual abode" or "habitat" or an adjective that means, "habitual, ordinary," is used by Dave Snowden to describe the evolutionary nature of complex systems and their inherent uncertainty in the "The Cynefin framework."

**Daily Scrum.** The Scrum term for a Daily Stand-up. See Daily Stand-up.

**Daily Stand-Up.** A daily team meeting where the team members share the project activities and impediments.

**D.E.E.P.** The characteristics that the users stories should have in the product backlog: Detailed appropriately, Emergent, Estimated, and Prioritized.

**Defect Rate.** The number of open bugs in the system.

**Defects.** System errors; a type of waste in software projects that results from defective documents or software that needs correction

**Defined Process Control.** A process that produces an output of acceptable quality when repeatedly executed.

**Definition Of Done (DoD).** A Scrum concept where the team must define what it means that the software is fully done for the iteration.

**Delay Decisions.** A lean principle for decisions should be delayed to the last possible moment in the project or when it is almost too late to decide.

**Deployment.** A phase in the DSDM framework.

**Design The Product Box.** An innovation game where the stakeholders design the retail box or carton that they would use to sell the product in retail stores.

**Develop By Feature.** A FDD practice to develop client-valuable functions and features in two-week increments.

**Development Manager.** A FDD role that is day-to-day technical leadership.

**Disciplined Agile Delivery (DAD).** An agile scaling framework.

**Discount Rate.** The interest payment used to calculate the present value of expected yearly benefits and costs.

**Distributed Teams.** Projects that have team members or teams at multiple sites.

**Documentation.** Documents (such as user manuals, maintenance manuals) that are prioritized into the backlog and the extent of documentation should be determined by the product owner or customer.

**Domain Experts.** A FDD role that is users, sponsors, or business analysts that are source of information for the developers

**Domain Object.** A FDD practice of colorized visual models for the components and overall solution

**Done Done.** When a user story has passed all levels of functional and technical tests.

**Doomsday Clock.** A collaborative approach for involving the team in identifying and categorizing negative risks.

**Dynamic Systems Development Method (DSDM).** An agile approach that has evolved from a rapid application development methodology.

**Early Termination.** The end of an iteration that ends abnormally. Also called Abnormal termination.

**Earned Value Management (EVM).** A practice for measuring project's cost and schedule progress against a plan; not a traditional agile practice.

**Elevator Pitch.** A framework for defining the purpose of the product (i.e., the product that should be produced during the project).

**Eliminate Waste.** A lean principle to eliminate meetings, documents, activities, or other items that use resources and do not create value.

**Emotional Intelligence (EI).** The ability to understand, identify, assess, and control the emotions of oneself and of others.

**Empirical Process Control.** A continuous cycle of inspecting the process for correct output and operations and adapting the process as needed.

**Emulators.** Recreating the functionality of the system so that it acts like the system under test.

**Epic.** A story that is too large for estimating. Epics can be compound or complex.

**Error Feedback.** A measure for the number of errors created per fix.

**Escaped Defects.** A measure for the defects reported by the customer after all software quality processes have been completed and the system delivered to the customer.

**Essential Unified Process (EssUp).** An agile methodology.

**Estimable.** One of the INVEST attributes that describe a good user story. Estimable indicates that the developer should be able to estimate the size of a user story based upon the information on the story card and the discussion with the customer.

**Evolutionary Development.** A phase in the DSDM framework.

**Expected Monetary Value (EMV).** The financial impact a risk may have on the project.

**Exploratory Testing.** A way of testing the system using small tests that are executed immediately, and then further tests are defined based upon the results of the last tests.

**External Regulation.** A regulator, such as a government organization or industry watchdogs, that require an organization to comply with a set of rules, regulations or laws.

**Extra Processes.** A type of waste in software projects that results from extra work that does not add value

**Extreme Characters.** Personas that have extraordinary characteristics of the target audience.

**Extreme Programming (XP).** An agile methodology with values that emphasize simplicity, communication, testing, and aggressiveness.

**Failure load.** The project work that could have been avoided by higher quality work earlier in the project.

**Feasibility.** A phase in the DSDM framework.

**Feature Team.** A FDD practice for class-owners lead small teams to develop a team, and class owners may be on multiple teams.

**Feature-Driven Development (FDD).** An agile methodology that breaks a product down into features, plans and delivers the product features in an iterative and incremental method, and provides standardized progress reports.

**Fist-Of-Five.** A group consensus technique where team members vote on a topic using their figures.

**Five Whys.** A method of looking at problem by asking "why?" five times to reach the root cause of a problem.

**Flexible Change.** One of the principles of the Agile Manifesto. "Welcome changing requirements, even late in development. Agile processes harness change for the customer's competitive advantage."

**Force Field.** A method to analyzes the forces for and against (or positives and negatives) when moving towards a goal.

**Foundation.** A phase in the DSDM framework.

**Functional Testing.** Business tests to analyze the way the system will work in its real application.

**Give Them A Hot Tub.** An innovation game to transform extreme or outrageous features into something the customer would use or buy.

**Graphical System Design (GSD).** An agile methodology.

**Groan Zone.** The stage of uncertainty when team members may feel as if it will not be possible to reach a decision.

**Grooming.** Preparing the backlog for the next iteration, including adding new stories, prioritizing existing stories, incorporating leanings and feedback, and breaking existing stories into smaller stories.

**Ground Rules.** Rules that define acceptable and non-acceptable behavior for the team.

**Harding Iteration.** An iteration where integration testing and other non-feature related activities occur to prepare the product for release.

**Ideal Time.** The time a person would spend working on a task if there were no interruptions and a good environment.

**Impact.** The long-term impacts expected by the sponsoring organization from the new capabilities delivered through the project.

**Incremental Development.** The development, integration, and release of parts of the system at different times.

**Independent.** One of the INVEST attributes that describe a good user story. Independent indicates that stories should avoid being dependent upon other stories.

**Information Radiator.** Any project artifact displayed in the project working area that shows project information. These are also referred to as big visible charts.

**Innovation Games.** A technique for engaging the customer and user in collecting requirements in a fun way.

**Inspection.** A practice to perform frequent, diligent, non-intrusive inspections of the process and the produce. This practice is promoted by Scrum and FDD.

**Installability.** Installation and set-up of the system

**Inter-communications.** The exchange of information between the sender and the receiver.

**Intermediate Document.** A project artifact that is produced between process steps in the software development process (e.g., requirement document, design document).

**Internal Rate-Of-Return (IRR).** The discount rate where the present value of inflows equals the present value of cash out flows.

**Internal Regulations.** Regulations or policies adopted by an organization and not imposed by an external body.

**Interoperability.** The operations of the system with other heterogeneous systems, organization, and data working together and sharing content as required.

**INVEST.** User Stories must be INVEST worthy: Independent, Negotiable, Valuable, Estimate-able, Small, and Testable.

**Iteration.** A timeboxed project iteration where a usable product should be created.

**Iteration Length.** The duration of the iteration timeboxes.

**Iteration Plan.** The plan that details the user stories or features that are included in the iteration.

**Iteration Planning.** An activity at the beginning of a project iteration to plan, prioritize, select, review agree the scope (or stories) that will be completed for the iteration and to define and estimate the work needed to deliver the agreed scope.

**Iterative Development.** When parts of the system are developed, integrated, and released and revised based upon feedback from the users or new requirements.

**Kanban.** A Japanese word meaning "sign board" or "billboard." It is scheduling system concept related to lean and just-in-time (JIT) production that helps determine what to produce, when to produce it, and how much to produce.

**Kanban Board.** A type of task board that displays the work processes. It contains cards for the work that needs to be completed, has a way to signal when the next step should be taken, and shows the limits for the work-in-progress per step.

**Kano Model.** A prioritization model that classifies a product's attributes based upon customer preferences.

**Karma Day.** A collaborative approach to involving the team in identifying and categorizing positive risks or opportunities.

**Lean.** A set of principles and practices to optimize a work process.

**Lean Production Practice.** A practice to eliminate any activity that absorbs resources that does not create value (that is, waste).

**LeSS**. An acronym for Large Scale Scrum, an agile scaling framework.

**Limit Work-In-Progress.** A kanban practice where limits are based upon the available capacity for each process step.

**Little's Law.** A principle that the cycle time is proportional to the amount of WIP.

**Live Defects.** See escaped defects.

**Load Testing.** Testing that evaluates the system response with more and more users on the system.

**Loci.** A memory technique that indicates items can be remembered by mentally associating them with their location or relative position.

**Maintainability.** The ability to change and maintain the code base overtime.

**Make Process Policies Explicit.** A Kanban practice

**Mathematical Chaos.** A dynamic where instability and stability are intertwined so that in every stability there is also instability and they cannot be separated.

**Mean Time Between Failure.** The average time between two failures.

**Mean Time To Failure.** The average time until the first failure.

**Measure And Mange Flow.** A kanban practice for measuring the predictability and the performance of the flow.

**Mentoring.** Transferring relevant knowledge and experience to an individual or team.

**Metaphor.** An XP practice to guide development with shared stories.

**Minimally Marketable Feature (MMF).** The smallest set of functionalities that must be realized for the customer to perceive value from the product.

**MoSCoW.** A prioritization model that classifies items based upon Must have, Should have, Could have, and Won't have this time.

**Motion.** A type of waste in software projects that results from communication or moving information or documents around

**Pain Snake.** A technique to visually track issues using post-its on the wall.

**Nebulous Units Of Time (NUTs).** An alternative name for story points; it indicates story points can vary from team to team and therefore do not have a clear meaning beyond the team that estimated them.

**Negotiable.** The INVEST attributes that describe a good user story. Negotiable indicates that the details about how a feature will be developed are negotiated between the customer and the developer.

**Net Present Value (NPV).** The value of the investment once all of the costs are taken into consideration.

**Nexus.** An agile scaling framework.

**Number Of Passing Test.** The number of passing test involves tracking the number of tests at each level: unit, functional, story tests, user interface, load, etc.

**Open Space Technology.** A method of gathering (for example, meeting, seminars, conferences) where the agenda remains open.

**Open Unified Process (OpenUp).** An agile methodology.

**Optimize The Whole.** A lean principle where the team should understand the entire product value stream.

**Optional Scope Contracts.** Contracts that fix the time, cost, and quality and allow the scope to evolve during the project.

**Osmotic Communication.** The information gained by hearing background discussions from other team members.

**Pair Programming.** A concept from Extreme Programming where two programmers at one computer create the production code.

**Pareto Principle.** A rule (for most events) that says a large percentage (80%) of effects are from 20% of causes. (Also known as the 80/20 rule.)

**Parking Lot Chart.** A visual, low maintenance way to report the progress of feature sets.

**Participatory Decision-Making.** Decision-making principles that produce stronger agreements within a group.

**Payback Period.** The number of years required to recapture an initial investment.

**Performance Testing.** Evaluates how the system responds from a temporal point of view.

**Persona.** An imaginary representation of a user role.

**PERT formula.** A formula to combine three-point estimates that considers that heavily weights the mostly case. The optimistic (O), most likely (M), and pessimistic (P) estimates are combined using the following formula: PERT = (O + 4M + P) /6).

**Pigs.** Project team members that are accountable for tasks.

**Plan-Driven Methods.** Software development lifecycles where the work begins with a collection of the complete requirements followed by design, development, and testing.

**Planning Game.** An XP practice to scope, prioritize, and estimate quickly and change as needed

**Planning Poker.** A wide band Delphi estimation method used to estimate the relative size of tasks in software development.

**Position.** The thing on which a person has to decide in relations to negotiation.

**Post An Ad.** A collaborative way for the team to use relative ranking to assign probabilities and impacts to risks and opportunities.

**Post-Project.** A phase in the DSDM framework.

**Power Of Three.** The process of getting three different viewpoints when a disagreement or issue arises.

**Pre-Project.** A phase in the DSDM framework.

**Present Value (PV).** The future value (FV) of a payment discounted at the discount rate (R) a number of periods (N). FV is the future value of money and R is the discount rate.

**Prioritization.** Techniques to rank the features and user stories in terms of value and risks.

**Process Analysis Techniques.** An analysis technique for understanding the users of the system are and their main requirements.

**Process Configuration.** A DSDM practice to configure the use of DSDM lifecycle based on the size and formality needed by the project

**Process Cycle Efficiency.** The value-added time in the process divided by the cycle time for the process.

**Product Backlog.** See Backlog.

**Product Increment.** The product features that are implemented into the product and are considered done.

**Product Owner.** A single person, who is accountable for setting priorities for the product features to deliver the maximum business value

**Product Roadmap.** A visual overview of future planned or proposed product releases.

**Programmer.** An XP role for someone who writes code in a simple fashion, and refactors and unit tests code

**Progress Reporting.** A practice of providing accurate, frequent, and relevant progress reporting within team and to stakeholders. FDD uses this practice.

**Progressive Planning.** Creating a high-level plan, and as more information and details are uncovered, the plans become more detailed.

**Project Charter.** A document that defines the vision for the project, why it is being undertaken, and the business outcomes and impacts that are expected.

*PMBOK® Guide*. *Project Management Institute Body Of Knowledge Guide* is a standard that describes the norms, methods, processes, and practices for the project management profession.

**Project Manager.** The person responsible for achieve the project objectives. In DSDM and FDD, the project manager is a traditional project manager role, who is responsible for cost, time, scope, and quality.

**Project Outcome.** The new capabilities that using the new product should provide to the sponsoring organization.

**Project Output.** The new capabilities that using the new product should provide to the sponsoring organization.

**Project Schedule.** The overall project schedule is based upon a series of iterations.

**Prototypes.** Demonstrations of a subset of system functionality.

**Prune the Product Tree.** An innovation game where the stakeholders place the product features on a tree drawn on the white board.

**Qualitative.** Factors that are not quantified numerically.

**Quantitative.** Factors that are numerically quantified.

**Rational Unified Process (RUP).** An agile methodology.

**Refactoring.** An XP practice to improve and restructure programs without changing their behavior.

**Regular Build Schedule.** A FDD practice to have a regular schedule to include completed features; always have a demonstrable system available.

**Relative Ranking.** Placing items in an ordered list based upon their nearness or proximity to the other items around them.

**Relative Sizing.** Estimating the size of work to be completed by comparing it to the size estimated for another piece of work.

**Release.** The cumulated product results based upon multiple iterations of product.

**Release Plan.** A plan for the details the product scope across a number of iterations.

**Release Planning.** An activity to plan the goals, timing, and wish list of a release or shippable product.

**Release Train.** A strategy for managing team dependencies that predefines a future iteration as a hardening iteration for systems-level integration testing.

**Reliability.** The system consistently works as expected under normal and abnormal circumstances.

**Risk Response.** A decision on how to address each risk.

**Requirement.** The user story (from the front of the card), a conversation that occurs between the developer and the customer to add details to the user story, and examples that exemplify what is expected from the user story, and tests (from the back of the card).

**Respect And Empower The Team.** A lean principle where the team is empowered to make decisions and the team is accountable for the decisions that it makes.

**Retrospective.** A meeting where the project team reflects and discusses a topic, including what was completed, what worked well, and what needs improvements.

**Return On Investment (ROI).** The quotient of the difference between the gain from an investment and the cost of investment.

**Review.** A meeting between the team, Product Owner, and stakeholders where the product is demonstrated and the product backlog is discussed.

**Risk Adjusted Backlog.** The risks prioritized into the backlog.

**Risk Burndown Chart.** A chart of individual risks accumulated with respect to total risk to track the changes in the impact, probability, and severity of risks over time.

**Risk Report Card.** A list of the risks, the chosen response, and the economic value normalized for secondary and residual risks.

**Risk Retrospective.** A review and lessons learned session for the risk artifact, processes, and team's capability in this area.

**Riskology.** An excel spreadsheet that estimates the duration (time window) needed to cover the uncontrollable risks in the project.

**Risks.** Unexpected events that if they occur will have an impact on the project (positive or negative).

**Roadmap Planning.** Details the long range planning for the product.

**Role.** Represents a set of responsibilities and not an individual person.

**Root Cause.** An analysis method for evaluating the source of an issue.

**Rough Order Of Magnitude (ROM).** Estimates to provide a range that becomes increasingly more accurate as the project proceeds.

**SAFE**. An acronym for Scaled Agile Framework, an agile scaling framework.

**Scalability.** The system's ability to continue to function as expected when more and more users are added to the system.

**Scenarios.** Workflows or cases that mimic end user behavior.

**Schedule Performance Index (SPI).** An Earned Value measure of the percent of completed scope as compared with the planned scope.

**Scrum.** An agile methodology that has a highly flexible development phase that empowers the team to act as needed to meet the customer requirement and be productive.

**ScrumMaster.** A person that coaches the team, product owner, and organization in the application of the Scrum practices, services the team remove obstacles, and support the organizational change needed to benefit from Scrum

**Scrum of Scrum.** A meeting to coordinate between multiple scrum teams. A method for scaling agile to multiple teams.

**Security Testing.** Technical test to analyze the confidentiality and integrity of the system and the required business rules.

**Self-Assessment.** Part of a retrospective conducted to identify development needs, understand the opinions and commitment levels of individuals in an agile team.

**Self-Organizing Teams.** The team members assign tasks amongst themselves, participate in decision-making, and resolve their own problems and conflicts.

**Servant-Leader.** A practice the agile coach uses to provide leadership to the team by servicing the needs of the team.

**Session-Based Testing.** A form of exploratory testing that is timeboxed and structured.

**Shu-Ha-Ri.** The levels of learning from Aikido. It means learn-detach-transcend.

**Sidky Agile Measurement Index (SAMI).** A five-level maturity model to measure the organization's level of agile adoption.

**Simple Design.** An XP practice to remove complexity and go for simple designs

**Simulators.** A process that creates data that mimics the key aspects of data system that will be used in production.

**Situational Leadership Model.** A tool for agile coaches to determine the team's readiness to adapt agile practices, and the coaching style they should adopt depending upon the team's readiness.

**Six Thinking Hats.** A method of separating thinking into six distinct modes; it offers a method for mapping out problems, supporting decision-making, facilitating discussions.

**Size.** An estimate for story based upon a criteria defined by the team.

**Small.** One of the INVEST attributes that describe a good user story. Small indicates that smaller or tiny stories such as bug reports or user interface changes should be combined into stories that require a half day to several days' work.

**Small Releases.** An XP practice to release to production in short cycle

**Smells.** A metaphor to indicate the presences of symptoms of a problem or something is wrong or not going in the right direction.

**Spike.** A brief investigative or experience to learn about and understand the new topic area.

**Spiral Methodology.** An iterative and incremental methodology presented by Barry Boehm.

**Sprint Planning Meeting.** A meeting within a sprint to agree what will be delivered in the next sprint and how will it be delivered. See Iteration Planning.

**Sprint.** A timeboxed project iteration where a usable product should be created. The Scrum term of an iteration.

**Sprint Backlog.** A subset of the product backlog that is realized in the sprint. See Iteration Backlog.

**Sprint Retrospective.** A meeting for the team to reflect on the product and process from the previous sprint and plan improvements. See Retrospective.

**Sprint Review.** A meeting to inspect the product with the stakeholders and adjust the product backlog. See Review.

**Spotify.** Agile at Scale, an agile scaling framework.

**Stacey Matrix.** A two dimensional model based on the degree of certainty and the level of agreement.

**Stakeholder.** Anyone with a positive or negative interest in the project.

**Story Cards.** The user stories written on cards although they may be documented in an electronic system.

**Story Map.** A two-dimensional visual view of the product backlog that organizes user stories to show the priority of stories and the relationship of stories to one another.

**Story Point.** A unit of measure for the overall size of a user story, feature, or other piece of work.

**Stress Testing.** Test that evaluate the system with a higher-than-expected user load.

**Success Factor.** The agreement between the parties on the definition of release success.

**Sustainable Pace.** An XP practice to work only 40-hour workweek; to avoid continuous overtime.

**Swarming.** The entire team focused on focused on a single user story.

**System Span.** The group of features that logically belong together, that cut through the business processes.

**Systems Development Life Cycle (SDLC).** A process for creating or altering information systems.

**Task.** A unit of work with an estimated effort to accomplish a user story.

**Task Board.** A visible project board that uses cards that represent a task, story, or feature placed on a time line that represents the project workflow.

**Task Switching.** A form for waste; a person stops activities on one project and starts activities on another project.

**Team.** A self-organizing development team that has all the members needed to deliver the product.

**Team Space.** The physical team working space, usually an open work area that encourages collaboration and osmotic communications.

**Technical Debt.** A metaphor for the efforts and costs that are built up when a development team delivers a code base that is more and more difficult to maintain over time.

**Technology Tests.** Tests that analyze the product include evaluating the non-functional requirements such as performance, security, reliability, inter-operability, scalability, etc.

**Test First Development.** See Test Driven Development

**Test Plan.** A project-specific plan for how testing will occur; it may or may not exists as a document.

**Test Strategy.** A long-term plan of action for how testing will occur.

**Testable.** One of the INVEST attributes that describe a good user story. A user story must be testable so that the developers know when they have successfully implemented the features.

**Test-Driven Development (TDD).** A concept where a test is written first and the programmer writes code that is designed to pass the test. This is a core concept in XP.

**Tester.** An XP role for someone who helps the customer choose and write functional tests; may also run functional tests and post the results

**Three-point estimate.** An estimation technique of asking experts for the best case, most likely case, and worst-case estimate. The results can be used in Monte Carlo simulations or translated into single point estimates using the PERT formula.

**Time And Materials (T&M).** Pricing per hour and day depending upon an agreed rate for the resources and materials.

**Timeboxing.** A planning technique where the duration is fixed and the project scope, deliverables and activities are adjusted to fit within that time window.

**Top Tip.** A risk identification technique from the DSDM methodology

**Tracker.** An XP role for someone who keeps track of the picture, tracks estimates and different results (for example, tests, defects)

**Transaction Costs.** Costs for the activities that are not seen or valued by the customer, but necessary to set-up or clean up the project.

**Transparency.** A Scrum practice to use common languages and definitions amongst the team and with those responsible for the outcome and make significant aspects of the process visible to all

**Trend Analysis.** The process of analyzing the projected direction of the variance.

**Triangulating.** Estimating a story based upon it relationship to one or more other stories.

**UML In Color.** An FDD practice.

**Unified Modeling Language (UML).** An industry standard modeling language used in the object-oriented software engineering field for modeling software-intensive systems.

**Unit Tests.** Tests to verify a small subset of the systems such as an object or method.

**Usability Testing.** Testing the use and usability of the system.

**Use Models To Suggest Improvement.** A kanban practice use quantitative and scientific methods to evaluate and improve the process.

**User Acceptance Testing (UAT).** A user or customer evaluation of the features in the system.

**User Story.** A requirement or a feature that should be implemented in the product.

**User Story Or Product Feature.** A requirement that should be implemented in the product.

**Validation.** Activities for determining that the product is being built in the right way.

**Value Stream.** The end-to-end delivery steps (for example, from customer request to delivery) required to complete a process.

**Value Stream Map.** A visual diagram that shows the value stream.

**Velocity.** A measure of the rate at which teams consistently deliver business value. It is the sum of the estimates of delivered (that is, accepted) features per iteration.

**Verification.** Activities for defining if the right feature is being built.

**Virtual Team.** See distributed teams.

**Visibility.** The degree that a project outsider can determine if the methodology is being followed.

**Waiting.** A type of waste in software projects that results from delays waiting for reviews or approvals

**War Room.** See team space

**Waste.** An activity that uses resources but does not create any added value.

**Waterfall.** A sequential design process that progresses through a series of phases from the conception through to the maintenance of the solution.

**Wide Band Delphi**. A consensus-based estimation method derived from the Delphi Method that was developed by the RAND Corporation.

**WIP.** Work in Progress. Work started but not completed.

**WIP Limit.** Limiting the work-in-progress. This is a core concept in Kanban.

**Wireframe.** A drawing or mock-up prototype of the user requirement.

**Work Breakdown Structures (WBS).** Breakdown of tasks or work packages; WBS is not an agile practice.

**Work Flow.** A sequence of steps or activities that the team follows in the production of the product, .e.g., design, develops, test.

**XP.** See extreme programming.

# Index

## D



## E



## F



## G

## N



## O



## P

## Q



## R

## U



## V



## W



## X

www.ingramcontent.com/pod-product-compliance
Lightning Source LLC
LaVergne TN
LVHW070906210926
848482LV00017B/1010
* 9 7 8 0 9 9 8 3 4 8 4 3 8 *